COGNITIVE APPROACHES TO CULTURE
Frederick Luis Aldama, Patrick Colm Hogan, Lalita Pandit Hogan, and Sue Kim, Series Editors

Literatures of Liberation

Non-European Universalisms
and Democratic Progress

Mukti Lakhi Mangharam

THE OHIO STATE UNIVERSITY PRESS
COLUMBUS

Copyright © 2017 by The Ohio State University.
All rights reserved.

Library of Congress Cataloging-in-Publication Data
Names: Mangharam, Mukti Lakhi, author.
Title: Literatures of liberation : non-European universalisms and democratic progress / Mukti Lakhi Mangharam.
Other titles: Cognitive approaches to culture.
Description: Columbus : The Ohio State University Press, [2017] | Series: Cognitive approaches to culture | Includes bibliographical references and index.
Identifiers: LCCN 2017018029 | ISBN 9780814213469 (cloth ; alk. paper) | ISBN 0814213464 (cloth ; alk. paper)
Subjects: LCSH: Postcolonialism in literature. | Postcolonialism. | Enlightenment. | Colonies in literature. | Literature and society.
Classification: LCC PN56.P555 M36 2017 | DDC 809/.93358—dc23
LC record available at https://lccn.loc.gov/2017018029

Cover design by: Martyn Schmoll
Cover illustration by: Kavita Ramachandran in collaboration with Mukti Lakhi Mangharam
Text design by: Juliet Williams
Type set in: Adobe Minion Pro

∞ The paper used in this publication meets the minimum requirements of the American National Standard for Information Sciences—Permanence of Paper for Printed Library Materials. ANSI Z39.48–1992.

9 8 7 6 5 4 3 2 1

When will we stop allowing ourselves to think of humanism as a form of smugness and not as an unsettling adventure in difference, in alternative traditions, in texts that need a new deciphering within a much wider context than has hitherto been given them? . . . [The proper role of humanists should not be to] consolidate and affirm one tradition over all the others. It is rather to open them all, or as many as possible, to each other, to question each of them for what it has done with the others, to show how many traditions have interacted and—more importantly—can continue to interact in peaceful ways, ways never easy to find but nonetheless discoverable also in other multicultural societies like the former Yugoslavia or Ireland or the Indian subcontinent or the Middle East. . . . [Humanism is] a democratic contention over the canon and its meaning that is open to all classes and backgrounds, that unfolds into a process of unending disclosure, discovery, self-criticism, and liberation.

—Edward Said, *Humanism and Democratic Criticism*

> We have been in the world
> and we have gained all of what there
> is and was, since the highest expression
> of the world, is its total
>
> & the universal
> is the entire collection
> of particulars
>
> —Amiri Baraka, "In the Tradition"

The sphere of . . . commodity exchange, within whose boundaries the sale and purchase of labor power goes on, [seems to be] a very Eden of the innate rights of man. It is the exclusive realm of Freedom, Equality, Property . . . Freedom because both buyer and seller of a commodity . . . are determined only by their own free will . . . Equality, because each enters into relation with the other . . . and they exchange equivalent for equivalent. Property, because each disposes only of what is his own. In fact the only force bringing [buyer and seller] together, and putting them into relation with each other, is the selfishness, the gain and the private interest of each.

—Karl Marx, *Capital*

CONTENTS

List of Illustrations　　　　　　　　　　　　　　　　　　　　　　　　viii
Acknowledgments　　　　　　　　　　　　　　　　　　　　　　　　　ix

INTRODUCTION　Democratic Universalisms of the Global South　　　　1

CHAPTER 1　Rewriting the History of Radical Rationality from
　　　　　　　Precolonial to Postcolonial Protest Poetry　　　　　　　35

CHAPTER 2　Restaging Freedom from Precolonial and Colonial
　　　　　　　Theater to Contemporary Bollywood Film　　　　　　　84

CHAPTER 3　Redefining Economic Exchange from Precolonial
　　　　　　　Proverbs to the Colonial and Postcolonial African Novel　133

CHAPTER 4　Electing the Demos from Tribal Praise Poetry to
　　　　　　　Twentieth-Century Trade Union Protest Poetry　　　　175

CODA　　　Contextual Universalisms and the Path to a New
　　　　　　　Postcolonialism　　　　　　　　　　　　　　　　　　220

Bibliography　　　　　　　　　　　　　　　　　　　　　　　　　　231
Index　　　　　　　　　　　　　　　　　　　　　　　　　　　　　243

ILLUSTRATIONS

FIGURE 1   Sheetal Sathe singing as part of the Kabir Kala Manch   8

FIGURE 2   A poster demanding the release of members of the KKM   72

FIGURE 3   Photograph of Binodini Dasi   103

FIGURE 4   Nandini worshipping Yash at a family *puja*   125

FIGURE 5   Rahul making a vow   130

FIGURE 6   Nandini rejecting *pativratadharma*   131

FIGURE 7   Logo of Ubuntu Sports Outreach   139

FIGURE 8   *Ubuntu* in Coca-Cola advertisements on buses in Johannesburg 141

FIGURE 9   Qabula performing his praise poem to FOSATU   201

FIGURE 10   Hlatshwayo performing "Black Mamba Rising" at a rally in 1985 202

FIGURE 11   Structure of FOSATU   213

FIGURE 12   Sweet Food and Allied Workers Union strike at Bakers
            Biscuits, February 1985   215

ACKNOWLEDGMENTS

THIS BOOK began with a seed of an idea that was nurtured by countless invaluable conversations with Satya Mohanty, Elizabeth Anker, and Durba Ghosh at Cornell University. I am grateful for their guidance and thankful to Elizabeth for continuing to be a support as I brought this project to fruition. I have also been lucky to find a uniquely supportive and generative environment at Rutgers. I am especially beholden to Rebecca Walkowitz for guiding me through the obstacle course that is academic publishing. Other colleagues in the department also offered invaluable advice or feedback on individual chapters. This book (and my experience writing it) would not have been the same without the careful suggestions of Lynn Festa, Carolyn Williams, Michelle Stephens, Stephane Robolin, Carter Mathes, Richard Dienst, John Kucich, David Kurnick, and the members of the Junior Faculty and AMESALL writing groups. Teaching at Rutgers has been a true pleasure not just because of my colleagues' generous contributions of brainpower but also their friendship. A special thanks to Sarah Novacich, Abigail Zitin, Abena Busia, Elin Diamond, and Anjali Nerlekar for the various lunches, weekends, and tea breaks that sustained me and my writing.

Rita Barnard, Patrick Colm Hogan, Andrew Ascherl, Liz Gunner, Sue Kim, Elizabeth Swanson Goldberg, Megan Jones, and Alexandra Schulteis Moore have continued to support my work through critical feedback, offers of hospitality, or by providing me with opportunities I otherwise may not have had. Priyamvada Gopal's radical spirit and passion for social justice continues to inspire me. I consider it one of life's serendipities to have encountered her and her work so early on in my career.

Heartfelt appreciation for the friendships that have guided and nurtured me throughout this process, especially to Virginia Kennedy, Tsitsi Jaji, Kirsten Ginckels, Anne Helness, Danielle Haque, and Parul Mehra.

I am thankful to the various academic institutions, programs, archives, and forums, including Cornell Peace Studies, the Rutgers Center for Cultural Analysis, Rutgers British Studies, the Penn Humanities Forum, Wits Historical Papers, and the Wits Institute for Social and Economic Research, that have provided archival materials, funding, or a platform for the arguments in this book.

My siblings: Nidhi, Bipin, Prabhu, Minal, Vivek, Anusha, Vipul, Roshni, Puneet, and Nitya, have provided constant emotional succor and rejuvenation when I most needed it. Nirmala aunty and Prakash uncle have given me a home away from home and my daughter a second set of maternal grandparents. I am blessed to have them in my life. I also thank Rahul's parents for helping me view setbacks as necessary hurdles toward making the book as strong as possible.

My parents, Motiram and Lajwanti Lakhi, were my first models for how to care about others, about the world, and how to effectively express myself. They were also my first available sounding boards, patiently receiving my most flawed arguments in order that I may think deeper and refine them. This book would not have been possible without your constant unconditional love, support, and encouragement through the tough process of writing and rewriting. You sustained me when I didn't think this book would ever see the light of day.

A woman writing a book who is also a new mother has more claims on her than she can handle. Jagir Kaur is the person who gave me the time to work on this manuscript and the energy to revel in the miracle that is my daughter. She deserves more than gratitude.

I owe the utmost to Rahul, Pari, Goju, and Jobi. They are my peace, my most enduring loves, my deepest friendships, and the sources of my ultimate comfort and joy. This book is dedicated to them and to Param, who is on his way.

A Note on Translation: Translation as a basis for literary analysis is bound to be a fraught endeavor, although also a necessary one for the comparatist. This book studies the literatures of many languages, including English, Hindi, Bengali, Sanskrit, Oriya, Zulu, and Afrikaans. When I quote from texts in languages other than English I rely on my own as well as established translations. Except for medieval verses of Kabir, for which I use Vinay Dharwadker's excellent work, translations of Hindi dialects are mine. Bengali quotes come from well-regarded translations of the texts that I supplement with my own when I think the translation fails to convey an important meaning. For Sanskrit, Oriya, and Zulu texts, the languages in which I am the least proficient, I rely almost wholly on translations. In the interest of thoroughness and accuracy, I often refer to different translations of the same text. Refer to footnotes for further details.

INTRODUCTION

Democratic Universalisms of the Global South

AN ORIGIN STORY: "Man was born free. And everywhere he is in chains." One of the most well-known axioms of the Enlightenment. Articulated by the Francophone philosopher Jean-Jacques Rousseau, this pithy phrase, along with countless other Enlightenment characterizations of freedom as a right due to every rational being,[1] described the world in terms of the universal characteristics that were natural to all human beings and sought to organize social, economic, and political life based on these conclusions.[2] The Enlightenment's rationalization of cultural and social life worked to guarantee human rights and political freedoms through open public debate, while its rationalization of economic life through capitalism worked to ensure general prosperity by allowing individuals to energetically pursue their own interests as long as they did not impede the like pursuits of others. Moreover, the story continues, these Enlightenment universalisms were responsible for the spread of

---

1. For instance, the French philosopher Denis Diderot argued that "every individual of the same species has the right to enjoy freedom as soon as he is in enjoyment of his reason." Diderot, "Article on Political Authority," 46.
2. This remains the dominant characterization of Enlightenment universalisms despite multiple convincing critiques. For instance, Sankar Muthu argues that Enlightenment thinkers from Kant to Diderot were actually rejecting any notion of a universal morality and that eighteenth-century political thought included multiple nonunified Enlightenments. Muthu, *Enlightenment Against Empire*, 1–10, 52–65, 172–200.

democratic progress to the colonized world through imperial expansionism, where they were syncretized with indigenous traditions to produce hegemonic but also democratic ways of being.[3]

This story about Enlightenment universalisms continues to appear at the center of many transnational histories of democratic change, a process usually defined as constituted by widespread challenges to authoritarian power from the 'demos,' or 'people,' who fought to overcome exclusionary social orders. By universalisms, I refer to discourses that are simultaneously categorical—they posit 'universal' categories such as 'humanity' or 'Man'—as well as conceptual—they elaborate universalizing notions such as 'equality' or 'freedom' on the basis of these categories. Like the above story, narratives about democratic progress usually begin with Enlightenment universalisms of just this type, identifying the eighteenth century as the locus of empathy and humanitarian feeling that eventually led to the human rights and democratic social orders of the postwar United Nations world.[4] Scholars then customarily proceed to problematize this triumphalist narrative. Some point out that Enlightenment humanisms are inherently Eurocentric and unsuited to their engagement with the rest of the world.[5] Others elaborate that Enlightenment universalisms are always already implicated in dominant ideological systems such as colonialism, capitalism, and the power relations they generate.[6] Still others argue that representative cultures and institutions arose in Europe at different historical junctures than the Enlightenment.[7] And some dismiss the very idea of uni-

---

3. Consider Dipesh Chakrabarty's argument that India's battles against caste, oppressions of women, and the struggle for democratic rights were unthinkable without Enlightenment rationalism, individualism, and "liberty, equality and fraternity." Chakrabarty, *Provincializing Europe*, 21.

4. Hunt, *Inventing Human Rights*, 15–69.

5. Paul Gilroy affirms and sums up this common critique: "Since the Enlightenment, [the humanist vision of 'Man'] combines belief in human uniqueness with an intrinsically Eurocentric understanding of what counts as the basic unit of reference for the human." Braidotti and Gilroy, *Conflicting Humanities*, 16.

6. Huggan and Tiffin argue that Eurocentric Humanism "provided both the ideological grounds and the practical basis for imperial expansion and colonial governance in many different regions of the world." Huggan and Tiffin, *Postcolonial Ecocriticism*, 3. Similarly, in just one of countless statements linking humanism, colonialism, and capitalism, Gayarti Spivak declares: "there is an affinity between the imperialist subject and the subject of humanism." Spivak, *In Other Worlds*, 202. In the same vein, Ania Loomba comments: "the central figure of Western humanist and Enlightenment discourses, the humane, knowing subject of these regimes, now stands revealed as a white, male colonialist." Loomba, *Colonialism/Postcolonialism*, 60. Lynn Festa and Daniel Carey have countered that Enlightenment thought was itself a varied, disjointed, and complex entity that is too often simplified in postcolonial critiques. Carey and Festa, *Postcolonial Enlightenment*, 2, 4–17.

7. Samuel Moyn has argued that it was not until the late 1970s that human rights became a major force in international relations through U.S. Cold War foreign policy. For a summary

versalisms, arguing that even when universalisms posit themselves as transcendent, they always vary according to the vested interests within which they are articulated.[8] Nevertheless, all these responses put the familiar Eurocentric story at their center, assuming that Enlightenment universalisms alone are responsible for modernity's inclusive as well as hegemonic manifestations of social change.

But there are universalisms that have arisen wholly outside the European Enlightenment. Take, for instance, the universalism touted by the medieval Indian poet Kabir (circa 1398–1448), who described the category "all of creation" as containing the same essence of divinity, regardless of caste or social status, and then made a claim for lower-caste equality on this basis. In the postcolonial present, Kabir's ideas are invoked by low-caste activist-poets in verses that also speak of a post-Enlightenment Marxist idea of working class liberation. Similarly, the precolonial South African universalism of *ubuntu*, or "a person is a person through other people," spoke of a universal community of 'persons' in order to support communal discourses of reciprocal exchange and the noncapitalist economies that underpinned them. And in the postcolonial present, the concept continues to sustain nonracist and noncapitalist modes of being in conjunction with a post-Enlightenment notion of the commons. What are the epistemic and ontological contours of these other universalisms? How are they similar to—and how do they differ from—the universalisms of the Enlightenment? How did these other universalisms interact with Enlightenment universalisms during the colonial encounter, and how have they also worked to reinforce various hegemonies when appropriated by colonialism or capitalism? And, most importantly, what part have disparate versions of these situated universalisms played within democratic struggles for liberation?

In asking these questions, this book revises the premises of some of the most prominent postcolonial thinkers—including Gayatri Spivak and Dipesh Chakrabarty—about democratic ideals in the colonized and postcolonial worlds. For these thinkers too often—either implicitly or explicitly—attribute the ideologies and processes of representative change—both liberating and hegemonic—predominantly to European universalisms and the colonial encounter.[9] In the process, such postcolonial narratives grant

---

see Moyn, *The Last Utopia*, 1–10.

8. See Foucault in Chomsky and Foucault, "Human Nature: Justice vs. Power, " 43–50, and Cheah, *Inhuman Conditions*, 9.

9. See footnote 3 on Chakrabarty. On Spivak, see "More on Power/Knowledge" in Landry and Maclean, *The Spivak Reader*, 174, in which she comments: "the political claims that are most urgent in decolonized space are . . . coded within the legacy of imperialism: nationhood, constitutionality, citizenship, democracy, socialism. . . . [In decolonization] what is being effectively reclaimed is a series of regulative political concepts, whose supposedly authoritative narrative

too much homogenized agency not only to what were complex, internally differentiated, and often contradictory European discourses but also to the varied imperial agendas that employed them in the global south. Take, for instance, the two most populous nations—India and South Africa—within the colonized African and Asian regions most often mentioned in these arguments. While both India and South Africa experienced early forms of Dutch colonialism as well as the more sweeping forms of British Empire, the most lasting and impactful forms of European expansionism within the two sites operated primarily in two overlapping but ultimately dissimilar modes. India experienced exploitation colonialism, involving the conquest of land for its natural resources and its native population. South Africa, meanwhile, experienced settler colonialism, which meant that colonizers sought to establish a residential branch of the metropole, as well as to exploit the land's natural resources and native population. Could this uneven and contradictory scheme really bear sole responsibility for seeding the fairly consistent universalizing project of representative governance that subsequently took hold the world over?

I suggest that arguments that attribute the origins of such change wholly to Enlightenment ideals during the colonial encounter ignore the locally grown universalisms that were used to reinforce anticolonial struggles and to translate relevant Enlightenment ideals into the comparative vocabularies of subaltern subjects. These "contextual universalisms" are translatable yet distinct cultural discourses that are articulated in precolonial popular and oral literatures and may well have been central, and not inimical, to the spread of representative cultures and institutions. While the bureaucracies of the democratic nation-state may have been constructed in the period of decolonization through the official negotiations of nationalist leaders and colonial officials, these representative institutions were fought for by, and gained traction through, Enlightenment universalisms as well as the contextual universalisms of subaltern subjects.

The term 'contextual universalisms' may at first seem oxymoronic. Bear with me. Contextual universalisms are universalisms because they posit ever-expanding relations between subjects in different social positions in order to overcome exclusionary divisions. As such, these universalisms insist on relating diverse people by gesturing toward an always-growing community of beings to which everyone can belong. Yet these universalisms are simultaneously contextual because they developed locally, relatively independently of Enlightenment universalisms even as they are put to work alongside Enlight-

---

of production was written elsewhere, in the social formations of Western Europe. They are thus being reclaimed, indeed claimed, as concept-metaphors for which no historically adequate referent may be advanced from postcolonial space."

enment universalisms toward various inclusive practices and egalitarian material arrangements, including ethical systems of exchange and political systems of self-rule. These universalisms are also contextual in another sense; the selves referenced in these universalisms are produced through mutually constitutive and evolving relationships with others and the various contexts within which both are embedded. As such, these selves are not self-contained entities who exist autonomously from others. The universal essence that these discourses offer, in other words, is always already contingently established through locally enmeshed relations between selves and others within particular contexts.

The contingency of these universalisms is also partly a result of their form. Contextual universalisms are realized and consolidated through dynamic precolonial aesthetic mediums such as oral poetry (like Kabir's), proverbs, or indigenous drama. Through innovative cognitive techniques, these performative forms interpellate readers, viewers, and participants into the inclusive ideas and subject positions of subaltern communities and their contexts. I turn to such oral texts because they were the modes of expression available to the subaltern classes to achieve liberation. They illuminated and sometimes disrupted power relations through an experimental formal thrust that was performative, critical, and participatory, sustaining radical social movements through repeated rhythms, trickster narrative voices, and the production of embodied affects in listeners. Moreover, these precolonial literatures contain some of the overlooked roots of experimental postcolonial literary devices such as multivocality and nonlinear narrative forms and continue to constitute many postcolonial literatures, including the African novel in English and Bollywood film. In reading contextual universalisms within these dynamic oratures and tracing them into postcolonial texts, I offer an alternative history of the progressive present that is also an alternative genealogy for universalism grounded in literary form.

For representative and evocative case studies of the contextual universalisms in these literary texts, we turn to India and South Africa, which together provide an optic for locally grown indigenous universalisms in other colonized locations. Both nations contained some of the largest colonized populations in the global south, were colonized for long periods of time, and have resultantly had their representative political institutions consistently described as colonial imports. Yet both regions also offer examples of a rich heritage of precolonial universalisms grounded in subaltern vernacular and oral literatures that was partly responsible for powerful critiques of colonial rule and still manifests itself in struggles for social justice. I also choose these two locations in the interest of making my argument as representative as possible because, despite their similarities, they each exemplify two very different modes of colonialism that were nevertheless followed by the setting up of democratic nation-states. India and South Africa's differing experience of exploitation and settler colonialism each yielded singular education programs and literary outputs from colonized thinkers.

In India, the British strategy from 1835 onward aimed to "form a class Indian in blood and color but English in taste, in opinions, in morals, and in intellect."[10] This produced separate spheres of artistic production, including that of the elite cosmopolitan classes writing in English and the bourgeois vernaculars and that of the subaltern masses composing in oral and performative vernacular modes. In South Africa, on the other hand, the Bantu Education Act of 1953 sought to do the opposite, differentiating colonizing settlers from the native masses by confining all blacks to vernacular education in indigenous languages. As a result, black writing did not exhibit a strong elite-subaltern split as Indian writing did, with black writing in English often working alongside vernacular universalisms and aesthetic forms as a tool of resistance rather than conformity. Both regions, then, exhibit distinctive universalizing literatures in response to different colonial modernities. My choices of postcolonial texts containing nonelite contextual universalisms—vernacular forms such as Bollywood film and urban protest poetry in the case of India and vernacularized English language novels and poetry in South Africa—reflect these historical differences. Together, these case studies rethink democratic change and its universalizing thrust as local, circumstantial, and multiple, not as produced by a singular 'rupture' in the West that was imported into colonized societies through imperialism.

The rest of this introduction lays out the theoretical premises through which my revisionist account of democratic change in the global south is developed. The next section describes how contextual universalisms produce solidarities against social hierarchies by harnessing notions of freedom and justice to create shared spaces of democratic struggle. *Literatures of Liberation* pays careful attention to these universalisms, stressing their importance toward constructing a syncretic, multivocal, nonelitist, and constantly evolving critical humanism. The second section of the introduction builds a conceptual apparatus for contextual universalisms in the global south to explore how these notions sustain emancipatory struggles. I argue that historically specific and unique contextual universalisms differ from and cohere with their Enlightenment counterparts within syncretic conceptual networks that are more expansive than has been previously recognized. These networks are transmitted into individual minds through inclusive models of cognition and

---

10. Macaulay, "Minute on Indian Education," 237.

via specific politically performative vernacular literary devices. The third section argues that these same devices and ontologies recur in some postcolonial texts, thereby rethinking theorizations of postcolonial literatures of the world. The fourth differentiates capitalism's universalizing processes from democratic contextual universalisms, for the latter often exist as countercurrents within modernity, which, through Neil Lazarus, I define as a global process marked by the spread of capitalism.[11]

I. CONTEXTUAL UNIVERSALISMS AND THE EXPANSION OF THE DEMOS

Contextual universalisms form the discursive and ideational ground to equitable material arrangements and practices. In the global south, the specific universalisms in which I am interested, involving comparative yet distinctive concepts of 'rational social organization,' 'freedom,' 'ethical exchange,' and 'rule by the people,' developed as regional phenomena tied principally to local relations of power and resistance, including caste, gender, and religious struggles that did not always intersect with colonial rule or nationalist politics. And when they did, they existed within conjoined genealogies of universalisms, whether colonialist, anticolonial, or acolonial.

I came across one such contextual universalism on a warm evening in 2007 in a suburb of Mumbai. I watched as a spirited young man and woman stood on a makeshift podium and sang a version of these electrifying words, attributed to Kabir, into the humid air:

> We're all one skin, one bone,
> One shit, one piss,
> One blood, one intestine.
> All of creation's composed
> From a single point of origin—
> Then who's a *Brahmin* (upper caste),
> Who's a *shudra* (low caste)?[12]

Kabir poems like this verse are known for espousing a rational social order that does away with caste hierarchies in favor of a universalizing notion of equality. The singers were Sheetal Sathe and Deepak Dengle, both members of the Marathi language protest poetry group, the Kabir Kala Manch (Kabir's

---

11. Lazarus, *Nationalism and Cultural Practice*, 16.
12. Kabir, *The Weaver's Songs*, 171.

FIGURE 1. Sheetal Sathe singing as part of the Kabir Kala Manch. Source: Still from Anand Patwardhan, *Jai Bhim Comrade*.

Stage of Talent, henceforth KKM). They were performing on the tenth anniversary of a police firing on a Dalit protest that killed ten low-caste (*shudra*) men and women. As was apparent that day, this verse still had the power to move noisy onlookers to silence over five hundred years after Kabir first sang it. Residents of Ramabai colony in Ghatkopar, Mumbai, listened avidly, their eyes filling with tears in memory of this brutal act of state violence. The KKM is clearly relevant and threatening to those in power. In 2013, years after I heard her sing, a pregnant Sheetal Sathe, accused of being a *Naxalite* (Communist), wasted away in jail.[13] She was arrested on the basis of a confession allegedly obtained while being tortured in police custody, after publicly giving herself up for a trial that has yet to take place.

The KKM aims to foster anticaste resistance through Kabir's verses and its own songs, one of which fervently declares:

> Hear out the torment my friend, the torment of our lands
> There is but one blood in humans
> There is but one blood
> The bones are made the same
> The bones are but one

---

13. The term 'Naxalite' is pejoratively used to refer to various guerrilla groups in India, mostly under the influence of the Communist Party of India-Maoist.

This body, natural, is the same
Then why this difference?
How come this division by caste?
Why are humans valued differently
According to the yardstick of caste?[14]

The above verses—constituted by the ever-evolving discourse that forms the Kabir oeuvre—are partly grounded in a precolonial medieval mysticism and syncretized with other cultural genealogies. They posit universalizing categories ranging from the religious "all of creation" to the more secular "human"[15] to argue for equality on the basis that all contain the same divinity within, an entity that can only be realized through virtuous thought and action in the world. Such a challenge to the caste system, then, is a prime example of a contextual universalism that is rooted in local cultures and developed in relation to ever-changing regional networks of power—not solely in relation to European, Enlightenment derived, colonial universalisms imposed from above. But KKM's contemporary message is composed through a blend of relatively unembedded universalizing discourses too; along with Kabir's precolonial diatribes against the business of organized religion and his statements on equality, the KKM also contains conjoined genealogies of a post-Enlightenment Marxist activism that speaks of organized religion as the "opium of masses" as well as the anticolonial secular Buddhism of nationalist anticaste leader, B. R. Ambedkar, with other verses in the song speaking of "reaffirming my Buddha." The Kabir Kala Manch, then, is an example of a conjoined genealogy of universalizing strands, each seeking to relate the self to the other in antihierarchical ways. Each strand is the outcome of its own philosophical contexts and seemingly incompatible with the other, yet each works with other universalisms to proclaim a common message of equality.

As this disparate intermix of universalisms shows, contextual universalisms amount to discontinuous, polemical, and situational concepts within syncretic networks that are sometimes not even explicitly named by the actors harnessing these concepts. They are fragmented and do not consistently add up to a tradition or permanent feature. So, in order to respect various articulations of these categories without imposing an overly stable framework of general concepts, *Literatures of Liberation* seeks to redefine progressive contextual universalisms not as a unified, singular position or program but an

---

14. Translation from the Marathi by Ashutosh in Mahabal, "The Best Songs and Poems of Kabir Kala Manch."

15. 'Human' is the word that Ashutosh, one of the KKM's own members, uses in his translation, referenced in the above footnote, of the verse.

ensemble of provisional, varied, and diffuse concepts, narrative strategies and tactics. These contextual universalisms exist within diverse conceptual networks that have historically been crucial to the realization of democratic ideals and infrastructures.

The word 'democratic' is vast and contested, but at its European foundation lie two Greek terms—*demos,* which simply means "the masses" or "the people," and *kratos,* which is "strength" or "to rule." Democracy, then, refers to the principle whereby the strength to rule rests in the common people. Moreover, the concept need not refer only to the democratic nation-state that arose in Europe but to any system that grants sovereignty to the people in social, political, and economic matters as well as to the aspirational principles and radical movements that support the creation and sustenance of a variety of such systems. This means that I am not only concerned with the 'people' as an aggregate of citizens but of 'people' as a radical form of agency. Such a seemingly simple definition of 'demos' belies its contestability, which has been a feature of 'rule by the people' since it became a recognized idea. Who, after all, are the people? The wealthy or the poor? The racial, religious, ethnic majority or minority? Everyone or the many? For Rancière, "democracy is not the power of the poor, but the power of those who have no qualification for exercising power."[16] These "uncounted" are the political community because they verify their supposed equality by what Rancière calls 'dissensus,'[17] which is "a struggle between those who set themselves as able to manage social interests and those who are supposed to be only able to reproduce their life." This struggle constitutes the process whereby the uncounted

> make visible the fact that they belong to a shared world the other does not see. . . . The worker who argues for the public nature of a "domestic" matter (such as a salary dispute) must indicate the world in which his argument counts as an argument and must demonstrate it as such for those who do not possess a frame of reference to conceive of it as argument. Political argument is . . . the construction of a paradoxical world that relates two separate worlds.[18]

---

16. Rancière, "Who is the Subject of the Rights of Man?," 78.

17. 'Dissensus,' Rancière writes, is constituted by the reconciliation of differences between the sensibilities of the ethnos and demos. The ethnos are "the people who have the same origin, are born on the same soil or worship the same god. It is the people as a given body opposed to other such bodies." The demos, meanwhile, are "the count of the uncounted." The differing senses of the ethnos and demos need to be reconciled within a new space in order to expand the demos to include the uncounted. Rancière, "The Thinking of Dissensus: Politics and Aesthetics," 1, 5.

18. Rancière, "Ten Theses on Politics," 12.

This is a particularly useful notion of demos because it relies on the possibilities of relating differences between selves and others to connect with those in radically dissimilar social and political positions from one's own, and even to those whose interests may be pitted against one's own. Such a notion of relating the self to the other, then, is about dissolving hierarchies, rendering demos not simply an aggregate of other surplus or sovereign selves but a subaltern politics that acts to "separate the [dominant] community from its parts, places, functions, and qualifications" so that it has to confront and accept the 'other' as part of a space that both occupy and co-constitute. Abstract universalisms such as the Rights of Man in this paradigm do not apply to any particular kind of man a priori, for they come into being through the "back and forth movement between the initial inscription of the right and the dissensual stage on which it is put to the test."[19] I am, then, interested in demos as a signifier of the universalizing agency of subaltern subjects who remain uncounted within national projects, and who seek to form new shared worlds of mutually constitutive selves and others to materialize their visions of equality.

The nineteenth-century Bengali stage actress Binodini Dasi (1863–1942), whose writings are explored in chapter 2, provides an example of a subaltern figure "without any qualifications for exercising power" who sought to overcome her marginalization through her writing and acting. Binodini was a wage-earning woman who did not fit the nationalist model of high-caste Hindu womanhood. The latter ideal occupied prime symbolic status within colonial modernity's reformist projects of emancipation. Binodini, on the other hand, represented the opposite of this symbolically pure womanhood, for she was a woman in the public sphere at a time when such a position was regarded as equivalent to being a prostitute. Binodini challenged her ostracism through the indigenous theatrical device of *rasa*, which unsettled the boundaries between selves and others by transferring the emotions of her subaltern characters to an audience of high-caste males. This *rasa-ic* method was based on the universalizing assumption that human actions are shaped by the capacity to feel the affects of others. In a bid for equality and understanding, Binodini Dasi sought to embody grief and anger at her mistreatment, using local dramatic forms to transfer these emotional states to a privileged audience of theater goers. In doing so, she sought to inscribe a place for subaltern women like herself within colonial modernity.

In apartheid South Africa, meanwhile, there was no question of inscribing the black self into a colonial modernity comprised of completely separate racial spheres, so trade union poets fought against apartheid through another

---

19. Rancière, "Who is the Subject of the Rights of Man?," 71.

kind of dissensus. As I explore in chapter 4, relating the self to the other in this case involved first uniting the differences among multiple selves, or the various black workers from different tribes and industries. Worker-poets did so through praise poetry that rallied all to a fight against apartheid. After turning these others into selves, trade union poets turned to overthrowing the racist capitalism of the apartheid state, using the precolonial contextual universalism of 'a chief is a chief through other people' to posit the trade union as the new chief whose position, power, and even personhood was constituted by the people. As one praise poet sang of the Federation of South African Trade Unions (FOSATU):

> Is FOSATU also going to hug you with those warm Hands?
> His hands that know no racism?
>
> Protect us too with those Sacred wings of yours
> That know no discrimination[20]

Within this poetry, the 'chief' or trade union "knows no color." The new community, the dissensual slate on which rights must be reformulated, is made up of a people that may be of any color or gender. The content and form of the poetry stages a shared space on which political change can be wrought, with trade union poets chanting their verses during mass worker rallies and protests open to all.

The democratic politics within the texts of both Binodini Dasi and South African worker-poets are very different from each other, but both are clearly examples of demos expansion through universalisms that are contextual in the following ways. First, the shape of these universalisms is culturally determined through local epistemes that include but are not restricted to enlightenment philosophies. And second, they combine the idea of contingency and universalism within themselves by gesturing to the category of 'everyone' or 'all beings' and then by making the realization of this category dependent on historical circumstance and situated action. This idea of a contingent universal essence suggests that the meaning of the category 'all' or 'everyone' is constantly made and remade through changing contexts. My four case studies of such contextual universalisms in the global south examine Kabir's proposition that all beings contain the same divinity within, which can be reached by embodying a rational continuity between virtuous thought and action, Sanskrit dramatic theory's postulation (harnessed by Binodini) that all actions are

---

20. Qabula, "Praise Poem to FOSATU," 12.

shaped by the capacity to feel the affects of others; and the Bantu assumptions that "a chief is a chief through other people" and "a person is a person through other people."

Let us take the latter proposition as an example of the simultaneously contextual and universalizing nature of these ideas—it is universalizing in its supposition that the individual becomes herself through her relationships with others. Within this ground of mutual becoming, one is expected to share one's food and belongings with an other who is also the self, for when giving, one is also understood as receiving. The Zulu proverb *adla ngandoda* or "they eat through other men," for instance, refers to the practice of helping a man to slaughter and skin his beast and then of sharing the meat with him, enforcing the idea that the sustenance of another directly translates into the sustenance of the self. Clearly then, this universalism is also *contextual* because "a person is a person through other people" is constituted through culturally specific ontologies regarding the production and distribution of food and is only realized through historically situated action relating to these ontologies. Moreover, this postulation invokes a contingent universal essence because it depends for its realization of a shared personhood on the shapes that one's relationships take—whether as a parent, friend, worker, sibling, chief, employer, stranger, or visitor—within a particular context. In the event of violence in 2008 against African immigrants in Johannesburg, for instance, leaders such as Archbishop Desmond Tutu sought to create a more cohesive national community by extending this notion of *ubuntu* to its immigrant members. "A person is a person through other people," in other words, occurs differently within historically contingent versions of this schema. Finally, the contingency of this ideal is also enacted and reinforced through its form, which is made up of an evolving orature of proverbs that interpellates listeners and participants differently according to the changing settings within which it is put to work. As we will discover in the chapters, in the case of each of these contextual universalisms, solidarity across caste, gender, class, and race is made through historical circumstance rather than found, achieved on the basis of an idea of a contingent universal essence.

Such a notion of contingent universal essence contests Lisa Lowe's assertion that universalisms are inherently hegemonic because any ideology that attempts to define the human also ends up dividing and excluding those who do not fit that definition. Speaking of European universalisms involved in the colonial encounter, she writes: "Even as it proposes inclusivity, liberal universalism effects principles of inclusion and exclusion; in the very claim to define humanity, as a species or as a condition, its gestures of definition divide the human and the nonhuman, to classify the normative and pathologize deviance."[21] But Lowe's stressing of the definitional content of universalisms as the primary reason for their divisive tendencies ignores the determining role of the ways that these universalisms are instrumentalized. Unlike Lowe, I stress that the universalisms examined here, whether derived from the Enlightenment or otherwise, do not inevitably lead to exclusion and division because they are determined as much by their form and practice within a particular context as they are by their content. As such, they posit a universal essence that is always contingent.

The dependence of any discourse, at least partially, on its contextualization within particular sets of social and material relations is the reason why J. S. Mill's *Considerations on Representative Government* was as much a provision for the colonial state's "necessary" use of force to educate those "unfit for liberty," as it was the argument for liberal representation in Britain. Recognizing this double nature is not to say, however, that universalizing discourses are essentially and wholly indeterminate. Rather, it is to acknowledge the complexity of their content and instrumentalization so that when these universalisms are harnessed towards exploitative ends in confirmation of their exclusionary content, they may also be contradicting their own democratic potential. Rather than dismiss universalisms wholesale, then, the task of humanists is to emphasize their democratic elements and articulations while exposing the contradictions and inconsistencies involved in exclusionary versions. As Edward Said notes, "great anti-authoritarian uprisings made their earliest advances, not by denying the humanitarian and universalist claims of the general dominant culture, but by attacking the adherents of that culture for failing to uphold their own declared standards, for failing to extend them to all, as opposed to a small fraction of humanity. Toussaint L'Ouverture is the perfect example of a downtrodden slave whose struggle to free himself and his people was informed by the ideas of Rousseau and Mirabeau."[22] Along similar lines, I show that Binodini Dasi harnessed Mill's ideas of freedom alongside a dramatic contextual universalism to critique the hypocrisies that excluded her from the right to self-determining action. Acknowledging such instrumentalizations, Edward Said bemoans the number of postcolonial scholars who so quickly dismiss the very same grand-narratives of emancipation and enlightenment that the first generation of anticolonial activists and intellectuals, including Fanon, Ambedkar, and others, were so passionately invested in.[23]

My argument here in defense of universalisms belies the oft repeated postmodern and poststructuralist idea, also challenged by other critics such as

---

21. Lowe, *The Intimacies of Four Continents*, 6.
22. Said, "The Politics of Knowledge," 31.
23. Said, *Humanism and Democratic Criticism*, 13.

Antony Appiah and Lalita Pandit,[24] that universalisms are inherently tools of hegemonic power. The emancipatory ends to which these ideas are put contest Pheng Cheah's assertion in *Inhuman Conditions* that universalizing discourses are themselves always products of global capital and cannot transcend the subjective, unequal relations between individuals and nations. Cheah thus argues that the humanities should "question" the idea of the universal human and even "give it up."[25] However, as I elaborate later in this introduction, such an assertion conflates two very different kinds of universalizing forces—of capitalism and of democratic progress—with each other. Such a collapsing means that Cheah's argument disregards the universal human's diverse iterations within real world instrumental relations. Stressing the diversity of instrumentalizations of universalisms, Antony Appiah thus clarifies that anti-universalists are not against universalism but against "Eurocentric hegemony posing as universalism."[26]

While not all the universalisms in this book are premised on the category of the 'human,' their gesturing toward universal categories akin to or even broader than the human (such as "all of creation") allows one to recuperate Said's idea of humanism as a critical practice that is grounded in the notion of a shared world of people who have much to say and learn from each other. *Literatures of Liberation* is inspired by Said's insistence that a critical humanism must involve the study of traditions and concepts of other cultures so as to open itself up to resources by which it may become self-criticism. For "the other is the source and resource for a better, more critical understanding of the self."[27] Critical humanism views human history as a complex, collective entity "not limited to the white, male, European, and American," for "there are other learned traditions in this world, there are other cultures, there are other geniuses." Said thus dismisses Saul Bellow's appallingly condescending phrase "Show me the Zulu Proust" to insist on "the humanist's proper role," which is "not to consolidate and affirm one tradition over all the others. It is rather to open them all, or as many as possible to each other, to question each of them for what it has done with the others, to show how . . . many traditions have interacted in peaceful ways."[28] This book's study of the way that contextual universalisms interact with post-Enlightenment universalisms toward democratic change works toward precisely these goals. In focusing on the collective work of inclusive cross-cultural discourses as they are harnessed

---

24. Pandit, "Caste, Race and Nation." See also Appiah, *In my Father's House*, 58
25. Cheah, *Inhuman Conditions*, 9.
26. Appiah, *In my Father's House*, 58
27. Said, *Humanism and Democratic Criticism*, xii.
28. Said, *Humanism and Democratic Criticism*, 7.

against local as well as global hierarchies, including capitalism, I also heed Neil Lazarus's invocation of Adorno's injunction to "hate tradition properly." Adorno is referring here to hating the tradition of capitalist modernity but not the "philosophical discourse of modernity," for the latter involves "an extraordinary command of and respect for the European humanist canon existing alongside an equally extraordinary knowledge and critical endorsement of other cultural works, social projects and historical experiences, the necessary consideration of which cannot be accomplished on the provincial soil of the European canon."[29] In the same vein as Said, Lazarus asks the humanist critic to dismiss hierarchical "bourgeois humanism, bourgeois culture" rather than humanism in toto, instead reworking the notion into a Saidian "adventure in difference." In this spirit, I now turn to an analysis of the variegated conceptual networks and cognitive modes through which democratic universalisms challenge colonial and capitalist social structures within individual minds and larger cultures.

II. CHANGING COGNITIVE FRAMEWORKS THROUGH CONTEXTUAL UNIVERSALISMS

The contextual universalisms that are central to demos expansion are put to work within conceptual networks that have too often been understood only through their Enlightenment counterparts. Contextual universalisms, then, are not about equating locally grown notions of 'freedom,' 'rational social organization,' 'ethical exchange,' or 'rule by the people' with their very different Enlightenment counterparts. Rather, historically specific and unique concepts differ and cohere within conceptual networks that are more expansive than has been previously recognized.

The terms 'conceptual network' and 'concept' are used here in a manner that is derived from the insights of research in cognition, which largely agrees that concepts are mental entities, or ways of thinking that are internal representations within the human mind[30]—but which are also simultaneously cultural and shared.[31] 'Freedom' as well as other notions such as 'rational social

---

29. Lazarus, *Nationalism and Cultural Practice*, 8.

30. A mental or cognitive representation in philosophy of mind is a hypothetical internal cognitive symbol that represents external reality and that which is not currently seen, sensed, or experienced. In philosophy of mind, a mental representation is one of the prevailing ways of explaining and describing the nature of concepts. See Marr, *Vision* for an application of these concepts.

31. Concepts considered in this way are said to be mental representations that have non-shareable instantiations, called tokens, which testify to how a concept is always formulated in

organization' and 'rule by the people' are simultaneously cultural and individual cognitive concepts that provide commonly "identifiable labels to particular routes for thinking such and such, and for getting from one thought to another."[32] These labels activate and support cognitive processing and enable us to sense that we have arrived at understanding. They provide maps or blueprints for enabling comprehension of large items of cognition, sitting, as Peter de Bolla notes, in the background of mental processing. Moreover, these concepts set in motion complex ways of thinking because their coherence is established by the tension that connects them in a network with other concepts. The concept 'freedom,' for example, operates in the cognitive background when we encounter other related concepts such as 'democracy' and 'equality.'[33] Thus, a concept contains both an internal structure as well as external connections to associated yet different concepts within a contextually and historically situated network. Taken together this conceptual network forms a concept's architecture.[34] Collectively, one's conceptual architectures—themselves produced through our bodily interactions in the world and enacted through various literary forms—determine one's cognitive frameworks, or the ontological and epistemological conceptual scaffolds through which we think about ourselves, others, and our environments.

Even though de Bolla's idea of a conceptual network is limited to notions of 'rights' in the Anglophone world, the categories of 'concept' and 'conceptual network' themselves allow a parallel analysis of universalizing concepts in the global south. These categories allow one to capture the cultural specificity of the concepts that make up contextual universalisms even as it relates these concepts to other associated yet different ideas within syncretic postcolonial conceptual networks. Each chapter asserts that Enlightenment conceptual networks of 'rationality,' 'freedom,' 'ethical exchange' and 'rule by the people' are only one consolidation of universalizing impulses by outlining comparable conceptual networks that differ in their specificities elsewhere in the world. So instead of designating these orienting English language terms as untranslat-

---

the mind of individuals differently. See Carr, "The Philosophy of Phonology," 404. Building on this, cognitive thinkers argue that concepts can be both individual and products of a shared culture because people can have the same type of mental representation or concept even if they possess different tokens in relation to it, thus rendering concepts mental counters and also counters in the world at large. See Laurence and Margolis, "Concepts and Cognitive Science," 7.

32. Ibid., 4.

33. This account of concepts, which I derive from Peter de Bolla has affinity with what Margolis and Laurence call the "theory-theory of concepts," which understands concepts as being like theories; they are "representations whose structure consists in their relations to other concepts as specified by a mental theory," de Bolla, *The Architecture of Concepts*, 47.

34. Ibid., 4.

able across cultural contexts and tracing them back to their Anglophone roots, I designate these terms as placeholders for conceptual networks that include associated yet unique concepts in Indian or South African epistemes.

For instance, as we will see in chapter 3, inclusive cultures in postcolonial South Africa contain a conceptual network pertaining to the notion of ethical exchange. This conceptual network is broad and in its hegemonic manifestations includes the neoliberal concept of 'free trade' (which operates through a notion of trickle-down economics). However, it also includes more inclusive Christian ideas of neighborly sharing, a post-Enlightenment concept of "the greatest happiness for the greatest number," as well as the very different contextual universalism of *ubuntu*, or "a person is a person through other people," which relies on giving and receiving through the understanding that other people are extensions of the self. And, as I show in chapter 4, the conceptual network pertaining to 'rule by the people' in antiapartheid South Africa included the Enlightenment concept of majoritarian popular sovereignty, the Marxist concept of the self-rule of the working class, as well as a Bantu idea of self-rule based on principles of "a chief is a chief through other people." And all these concepts played a role in achieving the postapartheid transition to democracy in South Africa through literary forms and structures of thought that enacted universalism in different yet related ways.

Conceptual networks that enact social change are similarly expansive in India. Chapter 1's exploration of the conceptual network pertaining to rational social organization shows how postcolonial Indians fight for democratic change through the Enlightenment concept of empirical and pragmatist rationality, a post-Enlightenment Marxist-derived socialism, as well as the Kabirian bhakti universalism of rationality as a program of ethical and equitable action that expresses the divinity within. In chapter 2, the postcolonial conceptual network pertaining to 'freedom' in India includes the hegemonic neoliberal ideal of individualism and self-development but also the post-Enlightenment notion of individual freedom and the *rasa* contextual universalism that truly free actions are shaped by the capacity to feel the affects of others. This conjoined genealogy of freedom is represented in the postcolonial Bollywood film, *Sometimes Happiness, Sometimes Sadness* (K3G), which employs *rasa* dramatics along with a post-Enlightenment concept of individual freedom to argue that "people should make their own choices about who they will marry."

The very different concepts within a conceptual network provisionally occupy the same space in the work of marginalized subjects because they are harnessed together toward the goal of constructing solidarities across class, caste, and gendered divides. Moreover, universalizing concepts within these genealogies often alter the hegemonic elements of a conceptual network, such as those tied to exploitative forms of capitalism, in order to better serve the goal of achieving progressive solidarity. Through such examples, this book illuminates how people alter and create new conceptual architectures so that they can better achieve representative goals.

Locating contextual universalisms within syncretic conceptual networks that are represented through multiple languages relies on the idea debated by many cognitive linguists and philosophers that concepts are not identical to words. Thus, concepts connected to the word 'freedom' exceed any one term used to express them; the anglophone concept of 'individual freedom' is not identical to the agency theorized within the Sanskrit-derived notion of *'rasa'* or the bhakti notion of *'mukti,'* yet all of these concepts are associated with the word 'freedom' in India. Language cannot alone provide the aperture that gives access to concepts because particular terms do not always encompass the complex mental processing that constitutes conceptual understanding. As Reinhart Koselleck argues, "the concept is fixed to the word, but at the same time it is more than the word."[35] Language here is most of all a convenient tool for expressing thought that can never quite encompass or fully express the ever-evolving mind map associated with a particular conceptual network.

The idea that concepts are not identical to words is a controversial claim in the climate of poststructuralism. Pheng Cheah notes that the terms associated with the 'universal human,' such as 'dignity,' should be abandoned precisely because of their lack of linguistic rootedness; the "arbitrariness of the universal human's signs" produces radical differences in its social use.[36] However, such a perspective disregards the fact that all language operates arbitrarily, which does not lead us to abandon language altogether. This argument also overlooks the fact that 'dignity' is not only an Anglophone term. It is also a notion that represents an entire extra-linguistic conceptual network, which encompasses various unique yet different concepts related to the semantic 'dignity,' each cohering and diverging from the other in revealing ways and expressed only partially through different languages and vocabularies in diverse locales within Europe as well as the rest of the world. Instead of having to commit to one model of 'human dignity' or 'human freedom,' the notions are themselves problems that various languages attempt to solve in different ways at various times. The humanist re-education carried out by literary texts, then, consists not so much in teaching readers, viewers, or listeners the proper terms to express 'freedom' but rather in teaching them to recognize that the relationship between 'freedom' and words has to be reenacted each time.

---

35. Koselleck in de Bolla, *The Architecture of Concepts*, 21.
36. Cheah, *Inhuman Conditions*, 9.

I am not suggesting here that the word 'freedom' or 'dignity' as the head of a syncretic conceptual network functions as descriptive evidence of 'universally true' and consistent qualities. They are not proof of a human that is necessarily realized in all contexts, or a suggestion that the human of '*cogito ergo sum*' is the same as the '*umuntu*' or 'person' of *ubuntu*. Rather, investigating geographically and historically specific manifestations of the universal human is to recognize the ways in which certain material contexts may activate comparable cognitive capacities that were previously latent. And such an exercise is also to recognize the syncretic histories that produce coexisting, interlinked yet different ideals within a single context, for instance the Anglophone notion of 'human/humane' alongside the Bantu '*ubuntu*' in the global south. Both these notions are representative of universalizing constructs of humanity that are quite different in their inflections. And yet both exist within the broad conceptual network of 'humanity' in postcolonial South Africa, often working together to combat hierarchical political forms of power. A context may produce associated yet unique concepts that work toward the same goals, even though the linguistic terms denoting these concepts may differ within a conceptual network that cannot be completely captured by the labels used to express them.

Retaining the distinction between words and concepts allows one to register the ways that there were no coherent mass movements being formed around particular terms in India or South Africa in the way that political movements were launched around post-Enlightenment phrases such as the "rights of man." The subaltern contextual universalisms I examine cannot be pinned down to particular words or phrases and are not searchable within any database of a historical period as Peter de Bolla's search terms are, for they occur largely as modes of being performed through embodied action, spiritual poetry, or through expressions, folktales, and proverbs. With the exception of one or two examples, my case studies reveal contextual universalisms that are cognitively activated and transmitted through verbal and ontological matrices rather than through a single word or phrase. And, because of their vernacular subaltern status, they are not always crystallized into repeatedly occurring expressions and rallying phrases in the whole of a culture. It should not be surprising, then, that these mixed conceptual networks are put to work not within official documents such as state papers, legal documents, or philosophical treatises but within popular literatures. It is this *literary* aspect of contextual universalisms that I explore now.

Literature is the medium through which contextual universalisms alter cognitive frameworks, thereby orchestrating dissensus and expanding boundaries of belonging. For through its form and content, literature serves as the bridge via which culturally held universalizing concepts are activated as mental representations within the human mind. I stress the findings of cognitive research in my explorations of how contextual universalisms change cultural and mental conceptual frameworks not to make a positivist claim that contextual universalisms describe cognitive characteristics that are universally realized—that all humans display everywhere—but because the literatures in question use and intensify certain latent modes of cognitive processing (which are themselves manifested, subdued, or highlighted differently within diverse contexts). In activating universalizing concepts through the harnessing of related modes of cognitive processing within individual minds, these literatures are able to activate and transmit their socially inclusive messages. For instance, chapter 2 investigates the *rasa*-based contextual universalism that all actions are shaped by the capacity to feel the affects of others, as it is directed against patriarchal oppression by the protagonists of three different dramatic texts. I show that these texts, and the *rasa* literary devices they employ, posit and harness a cognitive process whereby emotions and rationality are inextricably linked within processes of thought, decision making, and action. Moreover, this contextual universalism makes use of such an affective cognition not only to activate a universalizing conceptual network pertaining to personal freedom but also to transmit it via a Sanskritic dramatic form of what cognitive psychologists have called emotional contagion.[37] Within this situated form of dramatics, the culturally specific concept of freedom is grasped when the audience successfully receives the emotional moods that the actor embodies and transmits to them, thereby activating our expectations about what emotions mean and highlighting political ways to act on them in accordance with the conceptual networks being activated. Similarly, chapter 1 explores the contextual universalism within Kabir's poetry that all beings can realize the divinity within by modeling rational continuity between their thought and their bodily actions. This contextual universalism highlights and harnesses what researchers have called an 'embodied cognition' to fight caste discrimination, thereby activating a universalizing conceptual network pertaining to rational social organization and effectively transmitting it through the 'upside down language' of collapsed opposites and overturned logics, which trains its listeners to rethink what they consider rational ways of being in the world.

In the South African context, the literary contextual universalism of "a person is a person through other people" amplifies listeners' and readers' cognitive capacities to mentally represent the other as a way of imagining and understanding the self. Precolonial praise poems extend this process into the

---

37. Hatfield, Cacioppo, and Rapson, "Emotional Contagion," 96–97.

political sphere through oral performances related to "a chief is a chief through other people." These literatures turn a cognitive process into a political one by using metaphor and metonymy, which, as cognitive linguists George Lakoff and Mark Johnson point out, structure not just our language but our thoughts, attitudes, and actions. For instance, praise poems describe the democratic sharing of chiefly power through the metonym of shared milk, which the chief was also responsible for allocating through fairly distributed cattle. The poems use such metonyms, then, to make a concrete association between democratic government and the equitable distribution of material resources to subjects. These universalizing ideas, moreover, are transmitted through oral literatures that are explicitly structured to shape conceptual architectures in politically and ethically active ways, existing as fluid communicative processes within a society rather than simply as textual objects. Zulu praise poetry (*izibongo*) chanted in evaluation of chiefly power involves the poet-speaker inciting the audience to participate and respond. The audience, in turn, repeats after, challenges, and prompts the speaker within repeating refrains. These forms of repetition create a democratic multivocality, emphasizing the mingling of different vocal registers to transmit universalizing conceptual networks pertaining to 'rule by the people,' all while presenting a forceful unified criticism of despotic chiefs. Audience participation means that hegemonic forms of power are disrupted in favor of an innovative performance that becomes a common ground for building an expanded demos.[38] These texts make good on aspirational democratic goals by amplifying cognitive processes attuned to their inclusive messages.

III. RETHINKING POSTCOLONIAL LITERATURES OF THE WORLD

These precolonial literary contextual universalisms continue to structure political engagement in the colonial and postcolonial periods. Contemporary Indian anticaste protest poetry in cosmopolitan locations such as Mumbai, as well as tribal contestations of colonially sanctioned upper-caste privilege in nineteenth century Orissa, are poetically composed in the spirit of Kabir's 'upside down language' of overturned logics; Kalidasa's rethinking of affective theatrical form was used by the nineteenth-century Bengali actress Binodini to upset exclusionary nationalist paradigms and survives into contemporary Bollywood film to question globalized Hindu patriarchies. In South Africa,

---

38. Finnegan, *Oral Poetry*, 50.

the pre- and postapartheid novel draws on multivocal narratives based on "a person is a person through other people" to resist corporate, state, and tribal violence. These literatures suggest that what scholars recognize as postcolonial literature's disruptive, experimental thrust is at least partially constituted by indigenous aesthetic modes, folktales, vernaculars, and oralities.

These alternative literary lineages are very different from those present within the dominant strain of Global Anglophone world literatures. The latter are often recognized as a mirror and conduit to the unifying and homogenizing condition of global modernity. In this analysis, many Global Anglophone texts emerge as objects that serve a global marketplace, constituting and being constituted through capitalist forces that radiate from and for the English-speaking world. As Joseph Slaughter and Elizabeth Anker, among others, have shown, genres of Global Anglophone novels therefore simultaneously consolidate and problematize capitalism.[39] Unlike these texts, the literatures of liberation examined here, even when they are in English, do not necessarily emanate from, or respond to, colonial logic nor the logic of the global literary marketplace and cannot therefore be adequately thought through current categories of the Global Anglophone.

As a result, it becomes imperative to distinguish between Global Anglophone world literatures and, following S. Shankar, other "literatures of the world," which stem from "a pluralized and historicized world of human imagination and achievement."[40] Building on this idea, I define these 'literatures of the world' as those texts, both in English and in local vernaculars, that take local contexts and concerns as their starting point to illuminate a shared condition of being human in the world. Through the alternative narrative devices of these "literatures of the world," forms such as the novel are driven by, and appropriated in the service of, local plots, literary devices, and realities. This is very different from how canonic 'world literatures' work, including, for instance, *Midnight's Children,* which can, to different extents, justifiably be interpreted as doing the opposite. As Amit Chaudhuri puts it, a novel like *Midnight's Children* "with its features of hybridity, national narrative, parody and pastiche—is connected to the movements and changes in the history of the West itself, and to the possible notion that, in the Indian English novel, the West had found a large trope for its own historical preoccupations at least as much as it has discovered in itself a genuine engagement with Indian history and writing."[41] Chaudhuri notes that the dominant Global Anglophone Indian novel does not capture local realities for a regional readership but constructs a

---

39. See Slaughter, *Human Rights Inc.,* 307; and Anker, *Fictions of Dignity,* 38–43.
40. Shankar, *Flesh and Fish Blood,* xvii.
41. Chaudhuri, "The Construction of the Indian Novel in English," xxix.

symbolic self for Western consumption through recognizably exoticizing literary hermeneutics, with "hybridity worn like a national costume."[42] In contrast, "literatures of the world" include many popular twentieth and twenty-first century literary forms that, even when written in English, are simultaneously constituted by various marginalized indigenous oral, vernacular themes and traditions. These vernacular oralities display a structural resistance to complete commodification because they do not exist as textual objects but as ways of thinking, living, and being that often preexist and exceed the framework of capitalism as a world system. As such, they harness alternative temporalities and ontologies that posit a shared world, undercutting capitalism by sustaining new solidarities through a process that Cheah would call "worlding otherwise."[43] This inherent textual dynamism and relative resistance to commodification, I suspect, is why the contextual universalisms that sustain democratic change, and exceed capitalist hegemony in the process, find their home within these marginalized forms rather than elsewhere.

IV. DIFFERENT KINDS OF UNIVERSALISMS: DELINKING CAPITALISM AND DEMOCRATIC CHANGE

Such a claim about the resistance of contextual universalisms to market forces and ideologies brings up the question of capitalism, which is often read as tied to the universalizing impulses and processes that have accompanied demos expansion. On the contrary, this book distinguishes democratic cultures and processes within modernity from capitalist ones; while the former refer to the diffuse ideas and practices through which the demos expands, the latter encompass a world system marked by the unprecedented global extension of capitalism as a mode of production, economic exchange, and social organization.[44] Capitalism's universalizing processes and discourses are not the primary generator of democratic universalisms, nor are they generated by them, nor are they reducible to each other, for both kinds of universalizing processes work in very different ways. Here, I am not denying the fundamental potency of capitalism in shaping social and political forms of life within modernity, for capitalism is so powerful that it appropriates the contextual and Enlightenment universalisms that drive aspirational representative projects for its own nondemocratic ends. The pervasive power of capitalism also provides the grounds through which democratic universalisms come into their own as

---

42. Ibid.
43. Cheah, *What is a World?*, 17.
44. Lazarus, *Nationalism and Cultural Practice*, 16.

resistance. Rather, in distinguishing between capitalist and democratic universalisms, I am stressing the very different nature of their ideals and processes and the frequently oppositional tendencies of each.

Unlike democratic universalisms, capitalism's universalizing force is limited to its expansion into new markets and to the integration of the world through the logic of abstract equivalence that governs commodity production and exchange. These materialist practices of producing surplus value function as the ends in reference to which capitalism's limitedly universalizing discourses, for instance 'equality of opportunity' within the 'free market,' are developed. The Enlightenment and contextual universalisms of demos expansion, on the other hand, posit an abstract ever expanding and mutually constitutive community of selves and others as the discursive testing grounds through which a whole range of corresponding practices, social arrangements, and actions best suited to realizing these ideals are produced. This is the difference, then, between the universalizing force of capitalism in which "within the act of commodity exchange, all humans are equal as the buyers or sellers of labor and commodities" and the universalizing force of Enlightenment and contextual universalisms in which "everyone is equal and therefore free to build and participate in forms of economic exchange and social organization that they deem most likely to realize these universalizing ideals." When we consider contextual universalisms, we see how problematic is the idea that democratic change is inextricable with capitalism—a claim based on the presumption that both grew out of the same forms of Enlightenment rationalities. This simultaneity of origin, critics note, is the reason for the "Janus faced nature of modernity," in which modernity's freedoms are rooted in the same sources as its ills.[45] The collapsing of political and social freedoms into the market 'freedom' of capitalism is not just a misreading of the way capitalism works, but it also risks the perpetuation of the myth that democratic change cannot be realized without capitalism. In turn, this supposition too often leads to the Eurocentric dismissal of inclusive noncapitalist contextual universalisms as static signifiers of 'tradition,' while simultaneously strengthening exploitative forces of globalization in the postcolonial present. I flesh out these claims below.

The most well-known example of the conflation of democratic universalisms with capitalism is perhaps Max Weber's argument that both capitalism and democratic ideas allegedly arise as products of the same kind of rationalization—that of the state in bureaucratic organization, which leads to the "adaptation to free political institutions" and that of the economy in industrial

---

45. Gaonkar. *Alternative Modernities*, 7–8.

capitalism.⁴⁶ Variations of this particular assumption have been repeated in the work of postcolonial critics such as Dipesh Chakrabarty, whose canonical work *Provincializing Europe* also collapses inclusive democratic change with the spread of capitalism but does so in the context of colonial South Asia. In this account, capitalism enmeshed Enlightenment universalisms into the colonized world, achieving an uneasy syncretization with indigenous tradition to produce unique alternative modernities. To make this argument, Chakrabarty conflates the democratic universalism of equality with capitalism's positing of equivalences between people, the commodities they own, and the money form. Chakrabarty reads Marx's comments on the impossibility of capitalism occurring within a slave-holding society as evidence of the ways that capitalism and aspirational democratic values like 'equality' and 'freedom' necessarily go hand in hand. He concludes that "the idea of abstract labor was a particular instance of the idea of the abstract human—the bearer of rights, for example—popularized by Enlightenment philosophers."⁴⁷ In this account of Marx, the idea of human equality becomes a "bourgeois value" central to capitalism, which has the "vision of the abstract human embedded within it."⁴⁸

But this conflation of the aspirational universalism of human equality with the universalizing force of capital is based on a misreading of Marx's concept of abstract labor as a universalizing force that mediates difference. Abstract labor relates the self to the other not primarily through a transcendent notion of human equality and freedom but through the equation of various commodity forms as products of labor during the act of exchange. Marx explains that within the social act of exchange, one commodity is expressed in terms of another commodity. It is not humans a priori that are equal in this exchange but humans as possessors of abstracted and therefore exchangeable labor power. Equality here is simply the production of equivalence between different forms of human labor in terms of commodity value.⁴⁹ Thus Marx repeatedly clarifies that "free workers" are only free in that, unlike the slave, they can sell their own labor power as a commodity.⁵⁰

Marx, then, is not suggesting that the modern, autonomous, egalitarian subjectivity of the abstract human emerges under capitalism and the bourgeoisie but that these values *become* bourgeois when they are used by capitalists as the ideology that masks their oppression of the worker. The particular treachery of capitalism is that it appears to be freedom:

---

46. Weber, *The Protestant Ethic and the Spirit of Capitalism*, 9.
47. Chakrabarty, *Provincializing Europe*, 52.
48. Ibid.
49. Ibid., 152.
50. Marx, *Capital*, 874.

The sphere of . . . commodity exchange, within whose boundaries the sale and purchase of labor power goes on, is in fact a very Eden of the innate rights of man. It is the exclusive realm of Freedom, Equality, Property . . . Freedom because both buyer and seller of a commodity . . . are determined only by their own free will . . . Equality, because each enters into relation with the other . . . and they exchange equivalent for equivalent. Property, because each disposes only of what is his own.[51]

For Marx, the temporary equivalence created by the money form within the act of exchange does produce a limited kind of ideological freedom and equality—for both parties must meet on equal grounds as exchangers, they must both agree to exchange out of "free will," and both must perceive the exchange as fair. However, Marx claims in a follow-up sentence, that in fact "the only force bringing [buyer and seller] together, and putting them into relation with each other, is the selfishness, the gain and the private interest of each." In other words, the ideological freedom and equality of capitalism is a limited, formal equality compelled by the objective forces of the capitalist mode of exchange, and one which lasts only as long as the moment of exchange itself.[52]

Chakrabarty too readily conflates capitalism's universalizing processes with Enlightenment universalisms throughout his now canonical account. Take his formulation of the different histories that constitute modernity. The first is the history of capital, which he calls History 1, and which he defines as both progressive and hegemonic due to its supposed inextricability from Enlightenment universals. It is "the indispensable and universal narrative of capital . . . which both gives us a critique of capitalist imperialism and affords elusive but necessarily energizing glimpses of the Enlightenment promise of an abstract, universal but never to be realized humanity."[53] Such statements result in Eurocentrism. For having subsumed the cultural transformations central to democratic change wholly within the universalizing drive of capital, and in turn claiming the origins of this drive for Europe (even though capitalism was always a world-historical system), Chakrabarty ends up asserting that the aspirational project of demos expansion itself originates in Enlightenment Europe:

Modern social critiques of caste, oppressions of women, the lack of rights for laboring and subaltern classes in India, and so on—and, in fact, the very critique of colonialism itself as unthinkable except as a legacy, partially, of how

---

51. Ibid., 280.
52. See Draper, "Marx on Democratic Forms of Government," 104.
53. Chakrabarty, *Provincializing Europe,* 254.

Enlightenment Europe was appropriated in the subcontinent. The Indian constitution tellingly begins by repeating certain universal Enlightenment themes celebrated, say, in the American constitution. And it is salutary to remember that the writings of the most trenchant critic of the institution of "untouchability" in British India refer us back to some originally European ideas about liberty and human equality.[54]

Chakrabarty here scripts concepts such as liberty and human equality as "originally" European, thus dismissing Indian versions of these ideals, including the anticaste *bhakti* movements born of local cultures and power relations exemplified by Kabir.[55]

The Eurocentrism of conflating the history of capitalism with these democratic ideals is also reflected in Chakrabarty's formulation of the second kind of histories that constitute modernity—History 2s. These are the local pasts that do not necessarily contribute to the self-reproduction of capital and have the power of interrupting its totalizing thrusts. While such a concept could have included subversive universalisms such as Kabir's, for Chakrabarty, the History 2s that have the power of interrupting capital and producing diverse ways of being in the world can only stem from the encounter of a superstitious/religious colonized native mind with the secular Enlightenment reason of modern political subjectivity. The psychology of the colonized Indian can only be wholly 'other,' such as the astronomer who had no qualms about being an astrologer as well:

> He was a mathematician, an astronomer. But he was also a Sanskrit scholar, an expert astrologer. He had two kinds of exotic visitors: American and English mathematicians who called on him when they were on a visit to India, and local astrologers, orthodox pundits who wore splendid gold-embroidered shawls dowered by the Maharajah. I had just been converted to the "scientific attitude." I . . . was troubled by his holding together in one brain both astronomy and astrology; I looked for consistency in him, a consistency he did not seem to care about, or even think about. When I asked him what the discovery of Neptune and Pluto did to his archaic nine planet astrology,

---

54. Chakrabarty, *Provincializing Europe*, 4–5.

55. In a critique of Chakrabarty's focus only on Enlightenment universalisms, Ghosh thus asks, "Why should we so reflexively assume that the reformist spirit in 19th-century India derived its strength primarily from Enlightenment sources? We know that long before Bentinck, the Mughals as well as many major and minor Hindu rulers did everything in their power to discourage sati. . . . We know similarly that anti-hierarchical thought in India goes back through the bhakti period to the Buddha and Mahavira. Why should we so completely disavow the liberatory potential of these traditions?" Chakrabarty and Ghosh "A Correspondence on Provincializing Europe," 156–57.

he said, "You make the necessary corrections, that's all." Or in answer to how he could read the Gita religiously having bathed and . . . later talk appreciatively about Bertrand Russell and even Ingersoll, he said, "don't you know, the brain has two lobes?"[56]

Chakrabarty follows this quote with an elaboration that History 1 (capital) here is "the scientific attitude," associated with Enlightenment rationalism and political liberty. History 2, meanwhile, is the astronomer's "archaic nine planet astrology." The quote correlates the Americans and English with the History 1 of mathematics and scientific reason and the Indians with an unscientific astrology funded by monarchy. The 'superstition' exhibited by the scientist's astronomy is depicted as somehow internal to his contradictory cognitive nature, a designation that is part of an exoticizing colonial discourse of "gold-embroidered shawls and Maharajahs." In other words, because History 1 (capital) is political modernity's central force here and is conflated with the Enlightenment's progressive as well as hegemonic totalizing thrust, non-European History 2s can only embody a kind of "archaism," replete with "orthodox pundits," sensuality, and Oriental despotism. Such a history can only interrupt but not contribute to the rationalism of political modernity, for without the "elusive" but "necessarily energizing glimpses of the Enlightenment promise of an abstract, universal but never to be realized humanity there is no political modernity."[57]

In their interactions with capitalism, contextual universalisms paint a very different, much more layered picture of power and resistance. Contextual universalisms exist as Foucauldian "potentials" or puissances. Such puissances are capable of constituting new productive possibilities and providing immanent resistance to power, or *pouvoir*. In other words, potential resistance exists as the irreducible ontological condition for the exercise of power relations. Perhaps this is why Foucault notes that "if there was no resistance, there would be no power relations . . . resistance comes first."[58] Power is always responding to potential resistance, trying to capture or divert it. Imperial and capitalist power, then, develops through the productive potentialities generated through countless subjective puissances, rather than only through external, determinative factors. Capitalist *pouvoir* acquires its force within modernity by using available democratic universalisms as the ideological grounds through which to anchor itself into local contexts. But contextual universalisms are also distinct and ontologically prior to such *pouvoir*, challenging its myriad forms

---

56. Chakrabarty, *Provincializing Europe*, 253.
57. Ibid., 228.
58. Foucault, "Sex, Power, and the Politics of Identity," 167.

toward the realization of a greater freedom that exceeds the paradigms of the dominant regime.[59]

Take, for instance, the Kabirian contextual universalism about evaluating humans based not on predetermined identity categories such as caste but by the divinity of the work they do. A very different version of this precolonial puissance is adapted by the *pouvoir* of a globalizing capitalism in postcolonial India, which appropriates this contextual universalism to cement an exploitative work ethic. Nevertheless, Kabirian universalisms also exceed such a nexus of capitalist instrumentality, for they are prevalent among Dalit workers in urban India who use Kabir's idea of an alternative spiritual economy of self-evaluation, coupled with a postcolonial Marxism, to launch very modern social movements of protest against an unfair social order. The contextual universalism of Kabir, working with Enlightenment universalisms, then, is appropriated by, but also challenges and exceeds, capitalism.

Similarly, an encroaching capitalism in the preapartheid colonial moment equated people to one another only as commodity owners within the act of exchange, thereby devaluing the rural South Africans who exchanged through the contextual universalism of *ubuntu,* or "a person is a person through other people." The Zulu populations in the preapartheid novel *The Rich Man of Pietermaritzburg* relate to exchangeable objects—such as cattle, land, and agricultural produce—not as commodities but as objects that cement continuing relationships of reciprocity and political belonging between the chief and the people, and among the people themselves. This brings them into direct conflict with the commodifying logic of the capitalist republic, in which a person is a person only through the property they buy and sell for profit. I show how this conflict between contextual universalisms born of local precolonial power relations and a globalized capital plays out in the postcolonial present when the puissance of *ubuntu* is appropriated by the *pouvoir* of multinational corporations, including FIFA and Coca-Cola, as an advertising tool that helps them capture new markets. Nevertheless, as in Zakes Mda's postcolonial novel *Ways of Dying,* "a person is a person through other people" simultaneously exceeds such an oppressive instrumentalization through indigenous forms of communal, oral storytelling. Together, the conjoined and syncretic universalizing lineages traced in these and other case studies offer a fuller history of the progressive present.

---

59. Such a Foucauldian account of contextual universalisms takes on board his analysis of power and resistance as mutually constituted without his accompanying claims that ideas of 'justice' and 'freedom' are only effects of power and that there is no human agency to realize a greater good or evil, only history amalgamated from "the logic of opposing strategies." Foucault, *Power/Knowledge,* 61.

V. THE CHAPTERS

In light of this analysis, the colonial case studies in the following chapters focus on the interlocking relationships between contextual universalisms and capitalism, as well as the challenges posed to the latter by the former. I examine the late nineteenth century in India and the late twentieth century in South Africa, for these were the respective moments in which the extraction of labor, commodities, and profit had reached its zenith in each location and also the moment when subaltern subversions of these logics become most visible. In India, the peak of colonial capitalism happened in the late nineteenth and early twentieth century because this was the height of primitive accumulation within the history of the Raj. Exploitation capitalism was hard at work buttressing existing divisions in Indian society through capitalist modes of extraction. The late nineteenth century saw the rapid building of Indian infrastructure bankrolled by native tax payers to the tune of fifty million pounds.[60] Yet the transport of raw materials from Indian hinterlands for subsequent transport to England benefitted only elite Indians and the British government. Very little skilled employment was created for Indians. Many small farmers, dependent on the whims of the overseas markets where their raw materials were being exported, lost land, animals, and equipment to moneylenders. More tellingly, the latter half of the nineteenth century also saw an increase in the number of large-scale famines in India, with millions dying. This system of exploitation colonialism, then, resulted in a native population increasingly divided between elite nationalist spheres with access to colonial power structures and the suffering subaltern masses removed from centers of power.

Perhaps not surprisingly, given these depravations, the first steps toward self-rule were also being formulated during this period. The entrenchment of these forms of economic division, however, meant that questions of democratic progress were fought over between native elites and colonizers using subaltern minorities as pawns. The path to demos expansion therefore took shape around questions of the rational organization of a caste-ridden society through nationalist endeavors such as Gandhi's Harijan Uplift campaign. The question of freeing the Hindu woman from patriarchal conventions was another locus of nationalist modernization, with an emphasis on how the high-caste woman would become a fitting subject of a derivative Indian modernity without forfeiting reinvented forms of 'culture' and 'tradition.' My first two Indian chapters on rational social organization and freedom reen-

---

60. Stein, *A History of India*, 258.

vision this history from below by taking the contextual universalisms of the low-caste untouchable and Hindu woman as their starting points. I show how these subalterns had radical philosophies pertaining to their own advancement that preceded colonialism and exceeded colonial capitalist as well as nationalist formulations on their behalf. Yet, significantly, unlike the subjects of my South African chapters, these subjects formulated their own projects of demos expansion through a stress on 'rewriting' rather than 'resistance.' For, unlike black South Africans, Hindu women and lower-caste workers had clear discursive stakes *within* the figurative economy of colonial modernity even as they were materially disenfranchised by it; the nationalist claim to modernity rested, at least symbolically, on the inclusion of these groups within its ultimately falsely universalizing project of national independence.

In South Africa, meanwhile, the height of the colonial moment came much later in the twentieth century, when capital had already entrenched itself completely along the lines of racist social hierarchies. During the last decades of the twentieth century, which were both the apex of apartheid and the moment of its unraveling, South African settler colonialism's modes of primitive accumulation had merged with a simultaneous global moment of late capitalism. Such complicity between land-grabbing settler colonizers and the flows of multinational capital made no space for the rewriting of colonial modernity to accommodate the black self. For, unlike in India, native populations were not divided between elite and subaltern spheres; all colonized blacks were treated in much the same way by apartheid law. There was no elite class comparable to the Indian nationalist bourgeoisie that had its fair share of economic and decision-making power. Blacks were all wholly disenfranchised, with the majority existing as nothing more than commodified labor power. So, unlike Indian subalterns, most blacks could not struggle for liberation by attempting to rewrite colonial modernity in a manner that accommodated them. Rather, black subjects aimed to completely overthrow a wholly exclusionary colonial modernity by reimagining entirely alternative epistemic and economic systems to take its place. The contextual universalisms in these chapters therefore relate to more general issues of economic empowerment through ethical exchange and ideas of rule by the people.

Despite these differences, the case study chapters have a similar structure due to the emphasis on contextual universalisms in both locations; each chapter charts the constitution of democratic struggles—both individual and collective—within the postcolonial present by tracing precolonial and colonial contextual universalisms into the aesthetic forms and philosophies of a contemporary postcolonial text. I choose postcolonial texts—including Bollywood film, the South African novel in English, and vernacular protest poetry—that exceed their divided origins. This structure enables me to illuminate the strikingly different picture of postcolonial modernity that emerges when analysis begins with precolonial universalisms in conjunction with Enlightenment universalisms.

The contextual universalisms within these genealogies of the postcolonial present complicate the narrative of a 'civilized' colonialist modernity imposed on, and appropriated by, a not-yet modern global south. They depict a revisionist picture of democratic progress in which Enlightenment universalisms do not exist as the only significant force of representative change. Contextual universalisms upend the top-down methodology of previous theorizations of democratic progress, pointing us to the forms—both literary and otherwise—of rewriting and resistance enacted by those who were primary agents within local movements of liberation. Rethinking representative change, then, is to locate its core impulses in multiple contexts and overlooked forms, both European and global southern. In doing so, this book seeks to invent a new critical humanism precisely by showing how there is not, and cannot be, any definitive version of it, instead exploring the different lenses through which the world can be imagined—for varied critical frameworks can reveal shifting kaleidoscopic constructions of humaneness and imagining different starting points for universalizing democratic projects uncovers other trajectories of historical progress. In the process, the pursuit of demos expansion emerges as necessarily plural, fragmented, contradictory and ever evolving. The story I tell in the pages that follow is a dynamic one. It continues to unfold as I write, revealing new plot lines in the constantly shifting, ever-emerging tale of a rich and multifaceted human/e world.

CHAPTER 1

Rewriting the History of Radical Rationality from Precolonial to Postcolonial Protest Poetry

STORY ONE: It was a humid monsoon day in July 1997, in the Ramabai colony of Mumbai. Low-caste *Dalit* residents woke up to see that the statue of Bhimrao Ambedkar, the writer of the minority rights enshrined in the national constitution, had been garlanded with shoes. Shoes are a symbol of insult in the subcontinent, so this act represented a direct affront to a man idolized for standing up to the historical discrimination suffered by the *Dalit* community. The offence gave rise to a protesting crowd by the following morning. It did not take long for the police to arrive, but when they did they immediately opened fire, killing ten people and injuring twenty-six. Countering most eyewitness accounts, the police justified their actions by accusing the community of allegedly setting a truck on fire. In the following days, Vilas Ghogre, a revolutionary poet-singer, went around the neighborhood, collecting accounts of what had happened. Then he committed suicide. He died wearing the symbolic headband of the *Dalits,* having written a note on the wall earlier in the day, "Long live Ambedkarite unity."

Ten years later in 2007, poets and activists took up Ghogre's torch and gathered in Ramabai colony for a memorial. Among them was the spirited musical troupe from the neighboring city of Pune, the Kabir Kala Manch (Kabir's Stage of Talent), named after the renowned fifteenth-century saint-poet Kabir (circa 1398–1448). They sang their verses of protest as part of a continuing tradition of *shahirs*, who for centuries had chanted inspirational and educational verses to their audiences:

> There is but one blood in humans
> There is but one
> The bones are made the same
> The bones are but one
> This body, natural, is the same
> Then why this difference?
> How come this division by caste?

The Kabir Kala Manch's songs testify to the continuing importance of music as an essential aspect of *Dalit* politics: the loud *dholak*, harmonium, *ektara*, but also the *pawād*, the rousing, resounding voice. And, most importantly, lyrics that infuse low-caste subjects with pride, inspire them with courage, and reinforce their dignity. Such jongleurs travel from neighborhood to neighborhood with their messages of equality. They are usually armed only with an instrument and trace their art and social message to devotional singers like Kabir, whose *abhanga* (devotional poetry) continues to denounce injustice and oppression through public performances.

Another story, this one going back to the colonial period: On an unusually cool morning in March 1881 in the Orissan city of Puri, located in eastern India, an incident took place that shook the upper-caste religious authorities, as well as the colonial establishment that buttressed them,[1] to the core.[2] A group of fifteen followers of Mahima Dharma, an ascetic religious movement founded in late nineteenth century Orissa by lower-caste and tribal priests, marched to Puri to storm its famous Jagannath Temple compound, which had recently restricted entry only to higher castes. The press and police reports make clear that the Mahima Dharmis, reportedly in Puri under the influence of their *adivasi* or 'tribal' guru,[3] Bhīma Bhoi (circa 1895),[4] tried to remove the idols of Jagannath, Subhadra, and Balarama in order to burn them. In doing so, they placed themselves in the lineage of *nirguna bhakti* (devotion to the

---

1. King, *Orientalism and Religion*, 101–2.

2. Banerjee-Dube, *Religion, Law and Power*, 51.

3. The term 'adivasi' was coined in the 1930s by the British to refer to the original inhabitants of a given region.

4. The Sambalpur District Gazettier only linked Bhīma to the events decades later in 1908 because the instigators marched to Puri from Sambalpur, which is where Bhīma emerged as the main leader of the faith after Mahima Swami's death. See Banerjee-Dube, *Religion, Law and Power*, 53. See also Banerjee-Dube, "Issues of Faith, Enactment of Contest," 149–77.

formless divinity), movements such as Kabir's, reflecting the same uncompromising stand on idolatry, caste hierarchies, and temple rituals. The reports brand the group as rioters, criminals, savages, and fanatics for committing an act so revolutionary that it has been eliminated from the collective memory of an increasingly Brahminized community. This willed forgetting is not surprising given that Bhīma's devotional verses, despite being written by a mere *adivasi*, challenge the authority of the Brahminical priestly and intellectual caste through an emphasis on equality:

> They recite the scriptures and are confused,
> Never finding the path of knowledge.
> I preach the initiation of equality
> And so they call us dogs.[5]

Asserting himself as a writer in the vein of other saint-poets such as Kabir, Bhīma defiantly declares that his poetry is not the result of any scriptural knowledge but of his own bodily experiences as an outcaste: "I mastered no Vedas or Sastras. / I compose my verse with my mind, through my experience, peering into the Void."[6]

And, finally, an origin story: On a hot day in the early fifteenth century, the poor outcaste weaver named Kabir stood in the central marketplace of the holy Hindu city of Banaras. As the square grew busy he declared in the regional vernaculars of the common man instead of the Sanskrit reserved for the higher castes that:

> We're all one skin, one bone,
> One shit, one piss,
> One blood, one intestine.
> All of creation's composed
> From a single point of origin—Then who's a *Brahmin* (upper caste),
> Who's a *shudra* [low caste]?[7]

This was a radical claim for equality and critique of a system that defined people solely by their religious or caste status, with Brahmins occupying the top of the scale and *shudras* the bottom. Kabir thus disrupted the prevalent idea that a person's value was predetermined according to divisive identity categories. He protested against "special" privileges for powerful vested inter-

---

5. Beltz and Baumer, *Bhīma Bhoi*, 131.
6. Ibid., 175.
7. Kabir, *The Weaver's Songs*, 171.

ests who maintained socioreligious divisions at all costs and who even claimed that food touched by lower castes and religious others was impure. It is not surprising, therefore, that during Kabir's own lifetime he reputedly earned repeated death threats for his radical beliefs.

The events in Ramabai colony in the twenty-first century, of Puri in the nineteenth, and precolonial Kabir verses like the one above, are intimately connected. Verses attributed to or inspired by figures like Kabir are not simply literary creations confined to the page. They remain living, breathing social protests, harnessed against hegemonic caste structures as part of a contextual universalism propagated from at least the fifteenth century onward into the postcolonial present.[8] The multiple authors who have used the contextual universalisms associated with Kabir have posited the notion that all humans are equal and part of a universal community, rendering caste and religious divisions among people less important than their fundamental sameness.

This universalism arises from *nirguna bhakti,* meaning "devotion to the indescribable divinity," which was a sociospiritual movement that questioned religious hierarchies on the grounds that the divine lay within the self, in the depths of one's 'atma,' or soul, and was equally accessible to all regardless of social status. For *nirguna* philosophers such as Kabir and Bhīma Bhoi, this universal essence was also contingent, for the divinity within could only be realized through bodily actions that produced ethical cognitive states of mind reflective of such a divinity. In positing such an embodied or 'situated cognition,' these poems suggest that bodily actions have the capacity to change one's subjective feelings, conceptual vocabularies, and cognitive processing. In the context of *nirguna bhakti,* this means that actions that express respect for every human being as a container of divinity, whether it be through engaging in bodily actions that break caste taboos—such as smiling, reciprocal greeting, or touching and sharing food with lower castes—can produce and sustain inclusive thought, knowledge, and emotion pertaining to equality within the individuals engaging in such activity. Similarly, engaging in taboo menial work as if it is socially worthwhile and therefore spiritually valuable has the

---

8. As Indian historian Purushottam Agrawal has argued, Kabir's presence and poetry signaled the beginning of a bhakti public sphere, in which social customs could be publically debated and challenged. Agrawal, *Akath Kahani Prem ki,* chapter 2. The effectiveness of this challenge to social hierarchies is reflected in sixteenth- and seventeenth-century texts from the *nirguna bhakti* Sant movement, in which the great 'sants' or gurus of the fifteenth and early sixteenth centuries were remembered not so much for their ideas about the divine as for their aggressive attack on Brahminical supremacy. Bahuguna, Rameshwar Prasad. "Conflict and Assimilation in Medieval North Indian Bhakti: An Alternative Approach," accessed 20 July 2013, http://jmi.ac.in/upload/departments/history/drs/Conflict%20And%20Assimilation%20In%20Medieval%20North%20Indian%20Bhakti.pdf.

potential to engender this ideal within actors' minds as well as the larger culture within which these actions are situated.

In expressing and making use of such modes of embodied cognition, the *nirguna* poems function as a guide or map for how its universalizing conceptual networks can best be activated through one's daily practices, including one's work. This ontology constituted a direct challenge to the ostracization of lower-caste menial labor, for the latter was seen as just as likely to lead to a life of spiritual salvation as high-caste intellectual labor, thereby promoting the universalizing ideas of rational social organization central to the formation of a democratic nation-state and an open public sphere. If all human beings possessed the bodily ability to be enlightened, all humans were equals and needed to abandon a life of superstition, unreason, and blind obedience to live according to this higher rational truth. Based on this fundamental assertion, *nirguna bhakti* poet-philosophers repeatedly challenged oppressive, hierarchical social systems.

In what follows, I argue that a locally grown universalizing discourse of social equality is legible in colonial and postcolonial verses attributed to Kabir, working with Enlightenment and post-Enlightenment universalisms to challenge an exploitative colonial and postcolonial modernity. The first and second parts of this chapter situate Kabir within the *nirguna bhakti* movement and emphasize the multiple discursive versions of Kabir rather than the elusive historical figure. Here, I investigate the various exclusionary capitalist and Hindu nationalist iterations of the Kabir oeuvre. The third part of the chapter argues that despite these appropriations, the medieval verses as well as current oral versions of Kabir constitute a continuing contextual universalism that helps to produce, coexists with, but also poses a challenge to colonial modernity as well as to hegemonic capitalist orders.

The rest of the chapter traces this *nirguna* journey from the precolonial past to the colonial and postcolonial periods in more detail. The tribal saint-poet, Bhīma Bhoi, mentioned in the second story with which this chapter began, drew on *nirguna* aesthetic techniques and philosophies to protest against both colonial as well as local caste hierarchies. Like Kabir, Bhīma stressed the bhakti message of embodied rationality in which a person's value came from the work they did within their social sphere rather than from predetermined identity categories. In the postcolonial present, the songs of the Kabir Kala Manch continue to challenge oppressive collusions of caste and capital through this contextual universalism as well as through the post-Enlightenment universalisms of empirical and pragmatist rationality and Marxist socialism. Moreover, the Kabir Kala Manch's poems rely on the spirit of the medieval 'upside down language,' a literary device aimed at uncovering a deeper rationality that guides human thought and action. In charting the ways that the upside down language questions accepted realities and incites social change, the chapter plots a partial history of overlooked postcolonial 'literatures of the world.'

I. CONTEXTUALIZING KABIR: THE CONTENT AND FORM OF THE *NIRGUNA* BHAKTI MOVEMENT

Kabir and other gurus (*sants*), including Raidas (circa 1450–1520) and Dadu (circa 1544–1603) among others, were a large part of the *nirguna bhakti* (devotion to the divinity without attributes) movement, a religious and social reformation that spanned centuries and gathered poor, marginalized groups within its fold. The *nirguna* movement was by no means unified or continuous, lending itself to various groups who wanted to denounce the hierarchical caste structure of Indian society. Basing itself in a notion of the divine as equally accessible to all no matter who they were, the *nirguna* movement sought to do away with rituals of worship prevalent in orthodox Hinduism and Islam and declared instead that the divine lived within, to be reached through ethical social practice. Because good actions in life were the most effective acts of worship, people were not to be judged by an irrational and predetermined religious or social status but by the value of the work they did. The latter was calculated against feudal and capitalist calculations as a spiritual measure of one's rational and moral behavior. Ethical actions would bring one closer to the divinity that lay within the self as well as within other beings.

Within *nirguna bhakti*, divinity is indescribable (*nirguna*) and without form (*nirankar*). It is also absolutely pure and flawless (*niranjan*). Since God is *nirguna*, nobody can perceive 'it' within an ordinary state of consciousness. Creation, on the other hand, including the human world, is *saguna*, a realm of describable attributes and qualities that make up the flawed and formed contents, or *maya*, of the human world. Each individual has to achieve spiritual liberation (*mukti*) from these illusory *saguna* trappings by connecting with the *nirguna* divinity within. This tantric concept of union, also known as *Sahaj Samadhi* or *Moksha* (*mukti*), occurs when the individual concentrates his entire being on the 'true' self within her self and becomes identical with only that self, whether through forms of work, meditation, or ethical behavior.

Such an argument about attaining *mukti* has a number of implications for one's daily existence. First, if the divine and human self are so intimately related, for the *nirguna bhakt*, religious rituals and institutions, social orders like the caste system, mediating holy men like priests or imams, scriptures like the Vedas or Koran, and temple hierarchies and kinship rules, are all unnecessary. Furthermore, if everyone contains the same divinity within, and is therefore equally capable of attaining *mukti*, everyone is also fundamentally equal; pre-determined religious, social, or caste statuses are false and individuals must be judged by their actions. These actions must be pure and devoid of selfish concerns, reflecting the divinity within. This is a spiritual rationality in which God is completely accessible to anyone and everyone, regardless of caste, class, birth, gender, upbringing, and status. Such a philosophy, thus, contains a deeply subversive egalitarian potential.[9]

This radical message was conveyed through an equally radical form, a subaltern poetics that buttressed the universalizing project inaugurated by the poems. The Kabir, Bhīma, and Kabir Kala Manch poems use the form or spirit of the "twilight language," or "intentional language," the *sandhya bhasa*, full of paradoxes and contradictions or "upside down" expressions (*ulta—bamsi*). This upside down language is the mystical, paradoxical language of the Buddhist siddhas and nath yogis.[10] It is characterized by spontaneous rhetoric, as described by A. K. Ramanujan. Linda Hess calls it "rough rhetoric," containing a combination of "rudeness and potency" as well as "simplicity and bluntness of style" that illuminates power structures through paradoxical riddles replete with plays on logic.[11]

The Historical Kabir

It is difficult if not impossible to pin down the historical figure of Kabir with any certainty. How does one construct the narrative of his life and identity given that little survives to enable the historian to trace him? The few remaining sources suggest that the historical Kabir most probably lived in and around Banaras from about 1398 to 1448 and belonged to a community of outcast Muslim (*julahas*) or low-caste Hindu (*kori*) weavers.[12] The Kabir verses suggest that he was a poor artisan, a subaltern from the lowest socioeconomic levels of fifteenth-century North Indian society, with no practical opportunity

---

9. Kabir, *Kabir: The Weaver's Songs*, 58.
10. The first known instance of the *sandhya bhasa* or *ulti bamsi* was found in the eighth to twelfth century Vajrayana Buddhist caryagiti, or "songs of realization," from the tantric folk tradition in eastern India. The *sandhya bhasa* literally means the "Twilight Language" in Sanskrit, or *Alo-andhari* (half expressed and half concealed). However, later evidence from a number of Buddhist texts suggests that it was called the "Intentional language," or the *Sandha-bhasha* in Sanskrit. See Mukherjee, "The Sidhacharyas in Orissa," 55.
11. Beltz and Baumer, *Bhīma Bhoi*, 61–62.
12. Kabir, *Kabir: The Weaver's Songs*, 8–25.

in his immediate environment for either education or formal religious initiation. The poems were composed in the oral and musical modes, from a variety of dialects spoken at that time, including elements of the old Avadhi, Braj, and Bhojpuri vernaculars, which transcended social barriers in their use.[13] Moreover, the poems contained such radical condemnations of the powerful groups in his society that it is likely the historic Kabir was persecuted for his bold views while also being recognized as a spiritual leader, intellectual, and poet:

> Slander! Slander!
> People deride me—Folks truly love
> To smear and tarnish.
> Slander's my father,
> Slander's my mother.[14]

What would have made the historical Kabir more susceptible to these kinds of "derisions," "smears," and "tarnishes," is the subaltern nature of his community. Weavers constituted as much as 25 percent of Banaras's population since the thirteenth century, but Muslim weavers were classified as *Mlecchas*, or outsiders, and Hindu weavers as *shudras*, or low-caste servants. These classifications were entrenched religious divisions, with the Hindu scripture, the *Brahmavaivarta Purana*, placing nine types of artisans, including weavers, in the latter categories. Magahar, the town where Kabir probably spent the last part of his life, contained a large population of this sort. It is not surprising, therefore, that the powerful groups within Banaras, including the priestly, business, and administrative classes, described Magahar as a dirty, polluted town for centuries, full of the ignorant, uncultured, and uncivilized. The Kabir poems are full of allusions to poverty and the arrogance of the rich. As part of the underclass of fifteenth-century Banaras, the historic Kabir would have had no route out of this systemic poverty, with no access to literacy. He and the poets who wrote under his name in the following centuries composed their poems orally, singing to largely illiterate audiences.

Discursive Kabirs: Textual Oeuvre and Transmission

Given that a definitive historical account of Kabir is unavailable, this chapter refers to a discursive Kabir that may or may not resonate with the histori-

---

13. Vaudeville in Vaudeville and Kabir, *A Weaver Named Kabir*, 119.
14. Kabir, *Kabir: The Weaver's Songs*, 105.

cal figure. In any case, it is the unstable discourse constituted by the poems that is more significant in terms of influencing democratic protest. This discursive Kabir is not a singular, uncomplicated entity, for the corpus of Kabir poems themselves remains unconsolidated. It is difficult to definitively piece together a body of poems because of their oral composition, their uneven transmission, their appropriation and alteration by different groups within the years following the historical Kabir's death, and the spontaneous addition of various poems to the Kabir canon as his name and works spread. These factors resulted in three major manuscript lines complete with unique dialects and allusions.[15] Adding to this diversity, each tradition composed their own poems, adding Kabir's signature where they saw fit, resulting in thousands of poems currently attributed to Kabir. As Vinay Dharwadker writes: "it is historically impossible to go back to the period between 1448 and 1570 and to somehow reconstruct a unitary origin and a unified body of words from which all subsequent versions [of the Kabir canon] emerged . . . the composition and distribution of the Kabir poems are now radically indeterminate."[16] Indeed, selections and translations of Kabir remain renderings of elusiveness and transformation rather than of a fixed body of work. No manuscript of Kabir's poems that goes back to his lifetime has ever been found. The earliest manuscript, the *Pancvani,* is from 1614 and contains thousands of poems, only a few of which overlap with the other two manuscript lines of the *Bijak* and the *Adi Granth.* Importantly, the poems and the radical messages they contain, then, are by no means the work of one man—they belong to entire groups of people who use Kabir as their penname in their quest to challenge existing social orders and form new ones. As Prahlad Tipanya, a *Dalit* singer of Kabir, notes, this is a deliberately diffuse and pervasive worldview, for it is precisely its lack of boundaries that allows it to sustain its universalizing message: "Kabir is not the name of an individual. We're totally ignorant if we believe that. Kabir is a stream, a flow. Kabir is only a sign, a message!"[17]

My argument draws on a corpus of Kabir poems translated by Vinay Dharwadker from all three main manuscript lines, themselves "radically indeterminate."[18] In recognition of the evolving, unfixed, and multiple nature of the discourse that is Kabir, my other main source is an oral corpus of songs

---

15. The Sikh northern line rejected orthodox Hinduism and Islam to elaborate on Kabir's mysticism instead. The western line in Rajasthan underplayed his social radicalism, especially his harsh condemnations of Hindu and Muslim ritual and practice. The eastern tradition of the Kabir Panth in Bengal and Orissa, meanwhile, sharpened Kabir's satire against religious authorities. Dharwadker in Kabir, *Kabir: The Weaver's Songs,* 25–32.

16. Ibid., 58.

17. Tipanya in Virmani, *Kabira Khada Bazaar Mein.*

18. Dharwadker in Kabir, *Kabir: The Weaver's Songs,* 58.

and poems captured in popular interviews as recorded in Shabnam Virmani's Hindi-language documentaries on Kabir. Journalist-turned-documentary-filmmaker Virmani went on a six-year expedition to discover the essence of Kabir and what he means to South Asians today. Her journey resulted in four films (*Had-Anhad*, or *Bounded Boundless*; *Koi Sunta Hai?*, or *Is Anyone Listening?*; *Kabira Khada Bazaar Mein*, or *Kabira Stands in the Marketplace*; and *Chalo Hamara Des*, or *Come to My Country*). Virmani's films capture the living multiplicity of folk traditions and oral discourses around the Kabir poems and within South Asian social protest movements in a way written texts cannot. For instance, Virmani follows Prahlad Tipanya, who combines singing and explanation of Kabir *bhajans* in the folk style of the Malwa region of Madhya Pradesh, performing a deep engagement with the universalizing spiritual and social thought of Kabir.

I deliberately alternate between the mediated medieval poems and these postcolonial iterations of Kabir to capture their universalizing continuities. Virmani's footage of Kabir devotees in the present, the poems in the manuscript lines, and the poems, songs, and folk traditions derived from the *nirguna bhakti* movement as a whole initiate and sustain a powerful universalism that has survived to confront religious, colonial, and capitalist forms of oppression during various moments of South Asian history.

II. HEGEMONIC APPROPRIATIONS OF KABIR

Yet, as with any popular spiritual figure in the subcontinent, verses attributed to Kabir have also been repeatedly arrogated by multiple groups through the centuries. Following Foucault's conceptualization of the author as a function of discourse, I suggest that it may be useful to think of the Kabir poems as a set of beliefs or assumptions governing the production, circulation, classification and consumption of texts.[19] The complex reception and circulation of the poems attributed to Kabir over the centuries suggests that texts change their meaning according to the different contexts through which they are interpreted. Thus, while this chapter registers the continuing presence of universalizing Kabirian discourses derived from the precolonial period, it first explores some of the poems' more questionable translations and appropriations in service of hegemonic capitalist and exclusionary ends.

One of these appropriations of Kabir is apparent in the recent efforts to increase the productivity of the Indian workforce by The National Acad-

---

19. Foucault, "What is an Author?" 124–27.

emy of Psychology India Congress. In a 2011 Festschrift entitled *Dialogue for Development*,[20] this group reduces Kabir's richly complex universalizing thought to a commodified form of easily marketable 'tradition' that, once combined with post-Enlightenment capitalist universalisms such as Weber's idea of the Protestant work ethic and Fordist notions of productivity, will appeal to the middle classes as a marker of a truly Indian path to development. The text testifies to how claiming universalisms for Europe and capitalism alone results in the reduction of contextual universalisms to homogenized traditional pasts that can be commodified at will. Kabir's multiple democratic and noncapitalist ontologies are simply ignored.

Capitalizing on *nirguna bhakti* as an effective cognitive tool, *Dialogue for Development* begins by noting that the Indian workforce needs to inculcate bhakti values "in which the individual and work are integrated into each other . . . replacing the mind set [*sic*] of 'work as an economic activity' to 'work for work's sake.'" Inculcating this new mindset involves working until one achieves a *bhava* or mood of "euphoria at work," a cognitive state achieved when the worker is "completely immersed into his work through stern renunciation and discrimination [until the worker] finds the meaning of his life in his . . . work." This is apparently a "devotional path" (*bhakti marg*). The text quotes a Kabir line to elaborate: "Jeti man ki kalpana, kaam kahabe soi,"[21] or "whatever the mind imagines, is realized in the work one does" and the text interprets this rational continuity between thought and action as a move toward "work for the work's sake." This is, of course, a capitalist misreading of the Kabirian idea of work as embodied cognition—a rational continuity between one's thoughts and actions, which is a mode of realizing the divinity within. The Kabir poems speak of this kind of embodied cognitive practice as a euphoric experience because it brings one closer to the divine. This is a far cry from the above capitalist description of euphoric work as being the product of such "renunciation and discrimination" that work becomes the only meaning in one's life. As the *Dialogue for Development* elaborates:

> The action of working provides stimulation and impetus because through it, the individual becomes all that he is capable of becoming; Work is an essential part of being alive. Your work is your identity. It tells you who you are. It's gotten so abstract. People don't work for the sake of working. They're

---

20. Pandey and Sinha, *Dialogue for Development*. The book is composed of papers presented at the 16th Congress of the National Academy of Psychology, held in Mumbai in 2006.

21. Singh-Sengupta, "Reconceptualizing the Meaning of Work," 102.

working for a car, a new house, or a vacation. It's not the work itself that's important to them.[22]

In other words, the Indian masses and middle classes should toil not for material sustenance but because work, the commodification of one's labor, is one's whole identity. In service of this message, the text advocates an inculcation of a servile relationship to one's employer and an ethic of increased efficiency and productivity.

Dialogue for Development models the relationship of the ideal worker with her employer through Kabir's description of the relationship between the devotee and her inner divinity. The text quotes a Kabir verse to illustrate this point:

Sevak swami ek mati jo	The servant and master are made of one soil
mati mein mati mili jaye,	Soil mixes into soil
Chaturai rijhe nahin	It is not the cleverness of the servant that pleases the master
rijhe maan ke bhaye.[23]	But only profound love and devotion.

This verse attributed to Kabir is about the inner divinity that each individual contains within the self so that both are made of the same spiritual substance or soil. When an individual achieves salvation through righteous work in the world she becomes identical with this inner divinity so that "soil mixes into soil." Such a state of salvation, moreover, can only be achieved through love and devotion rather than through worldly cleverness. Yet *Dialogue for Development* appropriates this verse toward very different capitalist ends, using it to serve as a metaphor for the employer-employee relationship in a professional setting:

> Saint Kabir beautifully narrates the master-servant relationship. The servant immerses himself in the desires of his master. Dasya *bhava (the mood of servitude)* centers on serving the lord without question . . . with love, not servility. Dasya also cultivates humility, resilience, capacity for hard work and flexibility. These characteristics are essential for a good devotee as well as a worker. The ideal dasa should treat the world as the domain of his Lord, and hence serve everyone with love and devotion. Dasa should serve selflessly, without seeking rewards or recognition. In recognition of this silent service, the Lord protects his beloved servants with great care. Hanumanji is the ideal Dasa. His loving service was rewarded by Rama with such fond words

---

22. Ibid., 95.
23. Ibid., 100. Translation mine.

as 'I am for ever [sic] indebted to you. You are dearer to me than all my relatives, nay; you are more precious than my soul.' For a dasa, such praises are worth more than all the wealth in the universe.[24]

The employer in this account is equated to the divine so that he does not owe the employee anything more than dominance and praise. The employee, meanwhile, owes the employer complete devotion and worship. The verse inadvertently demonstrates that the act of selling one's labor too often extends to the commodification of the entire self for the employer. The text models this bond through a upper-caste Hindu tradition, invoking the relationship of the much-idolized god Rama with his devotee Hanuman to argue that the devotee/employee/servant should work "without seeking rewards or recognition." *Dialogue for Development*, then, uses Kabir to reinforce the same hierarchical, irrational predetermined social divisions that the verses were composed to combat. The text ends with the comments of the controversial American industrialist Henry Ford:[25]

> The natural thing to do is to work—All that we have done comes as the result of a certain insistence that . . . the better we do our work the better off we shall be. . . . As we serve our jobs we serve the world.[26]

Kabir's ideal of work as embodied cognition that elevates the world to the realm of the transcendent divine is replaced with an ideology that is eerily akin to the predetermined hierarchies of the caste system in its reduction of the world to the jobs one does. An individual's identity as a worker is made to subsume all other modes of being.

Another particularly powerful "set of beliefs and assumptions" that has produced a hegemonic iteration of the Kabir poems has been a dominant Hinduism reflected in the Kabir Panth (Followers of the Path of Kabir), which in the postcolonial present is closely tied to the corporatist state and has constituted a rising number of members since the nineteenth century. The website of the Kabir monastery in Varanasi estimates twenty-five million Kabir Panthis and over three thousand Ashrams worldwide.[27] The Kabir Panth has been constituted through a process of gradual state-sanctioned, profit-making 'San-

---

24. Ibid., 101.
25. Henry Ford is credited with Fordism, or the mass production of inexpensive goods. While this included high wages for workers through a system of welfare capitalism, Ford was adamantly against labor unions. See Chapter 18 of Ford, *My Life and Work*.
26. Singh-Sengupta, "Reconceptualizing the Meaning of Work," 101.
27. Kabir Panth Website, accessed May 2015, "Sadguru Prakatya Dham. Kabir Bagh. Lahartara, Varanasi, India," http://www.hajursaheb.com/html/pamphlet.html.

skritization' and 'Hinduization,'[28] reflecting a religious hierarchy that sustains caste divisions, for most of the *mahants*, or abbots, of the Panth are drawn from the higher of the lower castes.[29] Contrary to the poems' universalizing emphasis on equal access to a divinity within, the Panth regards monks, who preside over a new set of ritual profit-making practices called *chauka aarti*, as the only true source of knowledge about the teachings of Kabir. As an attendee to the Kabir Panth's annual festival put it: "This is a marketplace. In this marketplace, people buy the goods they want. Some want sweets. They buy those. Some buyers want the saints' words. They buy that."[30] This is an incisive critique of the commodification of religions, which are seen primarily in terms of their exchange value.

This hegemonic Hinduization of Kabir has its roots in the nineteenth-century colonial construction of Hinduism as a world religion, formed by the religion's translation into English as it shuttled between East and West.[31] The transformation of the Kabir poems is apparent in Rabindranath Tagore's English translation of Kabir titled *One Hundred Poems of Kabir*. Tagore's translation of Kabir was one of the first and, due to Tagore's own position as a transnational figure and because it has been continuously in print since it was published in 1915, has had a significant impact on popular images of Kabir in the West. Tagore's Kabir,[32] however, reflected his own political and religious beliefs, grounded in what Charlotte Vaudeville has called neo-Hinduism. The latter was characterized by an exclusive nationalist and upper-caste Hindu and Christian monotheism, formulated in response to the British characterization of Indian religion as irrational and superstitious. Neo-Hinduism arose first from "a process which located the core of Indian religiosity in certain Sanskrit texts (the textualization of Indian religion), and second by an implicit (and sometimes explicit) tendency to define Indian religion in terms of a normative paradigm of religion based upon contemporary Western understandings of the Judeo-Christian traditions."[33] This new episteme created the rising perception that Hinduism had become a corrupt shadow of its former Vedic self and needed to be "salvaged from the morass of superstition, polytheism and idol-worship," making it "into a strongly monotheistic faith, spiritually and

---

28. Gold, "The Dadu-panth," 249–50; Lorenzen,"The Kabir Panth: Heretics to Hindus," 151–71.
29. Lorenzen, "The Kabir-panth and Social Protest," 300.
30. Virmani, *Kabir Khada Bazaar Mein*.
31. See Aravamudan, *Guru English*, 26–62.
32. See Tagore and Underhill in Kabir, *Songs of Kabir*, vi.
33. Nandy, *The Intimate Enemy*, 24; King, *Orientalism and Religion*, 105; Sen, *The Indispensable Vivekananda*, ix.

ethically acceptable to the new western educated Hindu elite."[34] A key component of this colonialist religious revival was the Brahmo Samaj or "Society of God," founded by Ram Mohun Roy in 1828 but then led by Tagore's father, Debendranath Tagore, after Roy's death. Under the leadership of Roy and then the elder Tagore, the Samaj represented a conservative Brahminical Hinduism with European religious and philosophical influences. Roy himself was an orthodox Brahmin, but his theology was drawn from eighteenth-century Deism (rational belief in a transcendent Creator God) and Unitarianism (belief in God's essential oneness).

The Brahmo Samaj, and the neo-Hinduism they formulated, saw the Brahmin upper castes and their religious text, the Vedas, as representative of Hinduism as a whole. And ironically, given Kabir's anticaste protests, this upper-caste worldview appropriated Kabir's *nirguna bhakti* for his theorization of the divine as a formless and unified entity. Such a *nirguna* understanding tallied well with the Vedic doctrine of nonduality, or *Advaita*, which argues that the self does not exist separately from, and must unite with, the divine. In line with the upper-caste monotheism of *advaita*, Tagore and Underhill's translation introduces Kabir to the West as a figure whose thought was partly derived from an adapted version of "the traditional theology of Brahminism."[35] This is a singular Kabir that greatly simplified a diverse, plural, and complex spiritual landscape for a Western or elite upper-caste educated audience, exhibiting ignorance of the living vernacular tradition of Kabir's followers in India.

One of the most prominent members of the Brahmo Samaj was Swami Vivekananda, a figure whose life and teachings perhaps best represent such a neo-Hinduism and its effects on interpretations of Kabir. Born Narendranath Dutta in Calcutta, a colonial metropolis, in 1863, Vivekananda is considered a key figure in the introduction of Vedanta and Yoga in Europe and America and is also credited with raising interfaith awareness, bringing Hinduism to the status of a world religion during the end of the nineteenth century. As Richard King and Ashis Nandy have pointed out, Vivekananda's reform of Hinduism was devoted to representing Indian spirituality to the West as rational within a transnational "Parliament of Religions"; a universal religion for world consumption that was free of transnationally illegible practices such as idol worship, tantrism, and symbolic, ritualistic aspects. While seeking out the West as its main influence and audience, Vivekananda's neo-Hinduism also bolstered the cultural hegemony of the upper-caste Hindus who financed him. It is not surprising, therefore, that one of Vivekananda's references to Kabir

---

34. Vaudeville in Vaudeville and Kabir, *A Weaver Named Kabir*, 27.
35. Tagore and Underhill in Kabir, *Songs of Kabir*, vi.

complains that the latter was not able to "raise the lower classes" because he did not teach them the value of upper-caste knowledge. According to Vivekananda, Kabir should have

> applied his energies to the spreading of the Sanskrit language among the masses. . . . Knowledge came, but the prestige was not there. Knowledge is only skin deep, as civilization is, and a little scratch brings out the old savage. Teach the masses in the vernaculars, give them ideas; but something more is necessary; give them culture. Until you give them that, there can be no permanence in the raised condition of the masses. . . . The only safety, I tell you men who belong to the lower castes, the only way to raise your condition is to study Sanskrit, and the fighting and writhing and frothing against the higher castes is in vain, it does no good, and it only divides the race. . . . The only way to bring about the leveling of castes is to appropriate the culture, the education which is the strength of the higher castes. That done, you have what you want . . .[36]

Remarkably, this statement advocates the eradication of deep social divisions through a perpetuation of the same Vedic Sanskritic culture that was responsible for these inequalities in the first place. Vivekananda characterizes subaltern religiosity and vernacular knowledge as nothing but "savagery" and appropriates Kabir's entire vernacular discourse, which derided Vedic knowledge and linguistic hegemony for its oppressions, *for* this upper-caste culture. This formulation of Kabir not only ends up preserving caste hierarchies but also turns Kabir himself into a very different figure from the discursive Kabir of the poems.

These were the lenses through which cosmopolitan colonial figures were translating Kabir and other *nirguna bhakti* saints for consumption by a transnational, elite audience. Given these various ideological appropriations, it becomes imperative to study *nirguna bhakti* figures such as Kabir through the versions that continue to be harnessed by the subaltern groups who remain their main audience and conveyers. The next section does so by tracing the discursive Kabirs that have sustained consistently subversive, universalizing messages over the centuries by positing a very different idea of the value of one's work as well as of oneself.

---

36. Vivekananda, *The Indispensable Vivekananda*, 77.

III. KABIR'S DEMOCRATIC CONTEXTUAL UNIVERSALISM IN THE PAST AND PRESENT

While these exclusionary neo-Hindu iterations of Kabir remain powerful in the postcolonial present, inclusive universalizing principles associated with his oeuvre consistently reappear in manuscript lines, folk traditions, and movements of social protest, reflecting what Dharwadker has called a "remarkable thematic and imaginative consistency at their core."[37] This section traces this core by alternating between resonant messages in the precolonial and postcolonial verses. We will see that within Kabir's poems in the past and present, daily activities and forms of work—domestic or otherwise—are elevated to modes of realizing the divinity within. One's bodily practice must correspond to one's inner divinity, thus constituting a rational link between the thoughts that reflect such a divinity and one's bodily work.

This ontology of work differs markedly from the conceptions of labor within the feudal system in which Kabir lived, from the system of colonial capitalism, as well as from the capitalism of the postcolonial present. The economic system in which Kabir lived was primarily agricultural and hierarchical, having spread to the whole of the subcontinent via a system of land grants, or *brahmadeyas,* which buttressed the deep-rooted ideological interests of the upper castes. These land grants consisted of a grossly unequal distribution of land and its produce, with lower castes often being transferred into the keeping of upper castes when the lands they lived on were reassigned by the *brahmadeya* system.[38] Within the medieval feudalism of Kabir's time, then, lower-caste labor as well as the lower-caste self was an alienable form of property tied to the land he or she worked, with both the self and one's labor belonging to upper castes. The colonial system was to reform some elements of this system while retaining and even consolidating Brahmin landholdings. Within the capitalist postcolonial present, meanwhile, human labor power—or a person's capacity for work—her abilities and attributes—are considered to be her "property in the person," a fiction that conceptualizes a person's abilities as commodities to be used as alienable goods while ignoring the ways that such an assumption too often commodifies and subordinates the self. In each system—caste-based feudalism, colonial crony capitalism, as well as postcolonial capitalism, then, the laboring self is alienable, though considered autonomous in the latter period.

---

37. Dharwadker in Kabir, *Kabir: The Weaver's Songs,* 77.

38. The practice of land grants as *brahmadeyas* was initiated by ruling dynasties and feudal lords. *Brahmadeyas* were exempted from various taxes and also endowed with privileges (*pariharas*). Kumar, *Medieval Indian History.*

Within the universalism of Kabir, however, only the products of one's labor are alienable, for the labor itself serves a double function. The first involves the completion of a finite task whose commodified product is appropriated by one's lord or employer. But there is also the other product of the finite task—that of spiritual meditation—or *sadhana*—which is a consolidation rather than an alienation of the true self because it realizes the divinity within. Within this spiritual ontology, one's labor is not alienable, for it is put toward the completely different ends of spiritual salvation, and the self is not alienable, for the true divine self is in fact realized through the embodied worship that is work.

As Saba Mahmood has written following Judith Butler and Foucault, such an idea of embodied worship inverts the understanding that a disembodied mind, or "an abiding interior depth . . . core or static essence" produces one's actions.[39] Rather, one's bodily practices and actions equally determine one's desires and emotions; as theorists of cognition have argued, action creates the substance of thought and interiority rather than vice versa.[40] The Kabir poems harness this process to suggest that through repeated bodily acts and social demeanor one must train one's memory, desire, and intellect in accordance with virtuous goals, for the divinity within is realized through the outward behavior of the body.

The Kabir poets thus promote an embodied spiritual practice in which virtuous goals are produced by corresponding bodily actions rather than via rituals mediated through temple hierarchies. The medieval verses repeatedly denigrate the irrationality of religiosity that is simply organized according to prescriptive and oppressive social categories instead of being accompanied by a synchronization between ethical thought reflective of one's inner divinity and one's worldly praxis.

> They forget the true words
> And the songs of witness
> The moment they've sung them—
> They haven't heard
> The news of the Self.
>
> When learned priests

---

39. Mahmood, *Politics of Piety,* 19.

40. Cognitive scientists have explored how perceptual symbol systems, formed from interaction with one's environment, may influence conceptualization. People engaging in certain actions and dealing with certain items tend to develop representations that reflect the nature of their interactions with them. Medin et al. "Categorization and Reasoning among Tree Experts," 49-96.

Forget their stuff,
They read the good old Vedas—
Without their books,
They don't have a clue
To the secret of things.[41]

The Kabir poem points out that within many rituals of medieval Hinduism, there is no connection between ritual actions and the deeper understanding of divinity they are supposed to give access to. As such, they are meaningless actions. That is why the devotional songs are forgotten as soon as they've been sung. And even if they are heard, "the news of the self" they contain does not register in the core of the devotees' being where the divine truth lies. The lack of a rational connection between the why and the how of ritual practice is also why wisdom, by definition something that is felt and understood within the self, is reduced to knowledge, constantly and pointlessly looked up in a reference book. The verse continues:

They begin to worship
Brass and stone—
They're so proud
Of their pilgrimages,
They forget the real thing.[42]

Ritual worshippers are not worshipping the divine but only "brass and stone" because they have not been able to connect their bodily modes of worship with the divinity within the "true self" that the idols are meant to represent. Similarly, "they're so proud of their pilgrimages, they forget the real thing." During the fifteenth century, pilgrimage towns such as Puri developed into centers of trade and commerce resulting in a flourishing pilgrimage economy. The verse's critique, then, is also aimed at the commercialization of religious rituals in which "brass" and "stone" are evacuated of any meaning other than their worth as saleable items.

The condemnation of such irrationality is transmitted through the radical experimentalism of the *ulti bamsi*, the upside down language of sensible nonsense. Its use suggests that the accepted norms of the world, sanctioned and set up by organized religion, are in fact highly nonsensical, for they are not capable of reaching the ultimate rationality of *nirguna* God. The formal features of these literary expressions, intentionally containing plays on logic, are

---

41. Kabir, *The Weaver's Songs*, 149.
42. Ibid., 162.

contiguous with the verses' emphasis on logical continuity between thought and praxis.

> The fish in the water
> Is racked by thirst:
> I hear about it
> And burst out laughing.
>
> What you're looking for
> Is right at home:
> And yet you roam from forest to forest,
> Full of gloom.
>
> Without self-knowledge
> The world's all make believe:
> What's Mathura,
> What's Kashi?[43]

A fish, an entity that lives in water and feels thirsty, is a nonsensical image, an impossibility. Yet the Kabir poems use the upside down language to point out that this is the kind of nonsensical unnatural state prevalent in the illusory world of maya for those who live without self-knowledge. And if this whole world is illusory nonsense, then even the idea that the purported holy places—Mathura and Kashi—contain the divine is logically incoherent. The divine, the one who lies outside worldly matters, lives within, "right at home." For the Kabir poets, unenlightened mortals understand only the reality they are trapped in and cannot reach a higher order of understanding concerning the divine truth within. The Kabir poems, then, use the *ulti bamsi* to highlight the illogic prevalent in a world accepted as logical and rational.

While dismissing institutionalized rituals, Kabir poems in the past as well as the present propagate the development of an unmediated link between ethical thought and bodily action, especially in the context of one's labor, whether domestic or professional. Many verses forcefully etch out the universalizing philosophy that a person's value comes from the socially useful work they do rather than from predetermined, divisive identity categories. And all work deserves recognition and reward provided it is productive of the thought processes that lead to union with the divine. This, then, is a spiritual evaluation of work very different from an appraisal of labor in terms of its use value to a feudal upper-caste lord or in terms of its exchange value within the crony

---

43. Ibid., 200.

capitalism of the colonial moment or the hegemonic capitalism of the postcolonial present. Thus, the medieval Kabir poems equate even menial labor, disparaged by the upper castes, to spiritual work that leads to salvation:

> Put the bulls
> Of Love and Detachment to work:
> Plough, plough
> The field of nirvana.
>
> The man who comes home,
> Harvest and husking done,
> He's the happy farmer
> With real skill.
>
> With equal servings
> On their plates,
> Both sage and scholar
> Eat their fill.[44]

The verse describes the bodily work done by laborers as spiritual practice so that "ploughing" the fields becomes equivalent to harvesting the "love and detachment" crucial to reaching a state of spiritual salvation. Here, the equation of plowing a field with the harvesting of love and detachment elevates feudal menial labor to an activity of spiritual communion.

This verse, however, is also a spiritual and political critique of the commodification of lower-caste labor power by the upper castes, who unfairly extracted and accumulated the value of lower-caste menial work. The verse thus makes both a political and spiritual point; it highlights the alternative unalienable spiritual value of menial farm work done by lower castes, equating it to an embodied religious practice that deserves to be remunerated with the richest of rewards: salvation. Moreover, the verse presents this salvation through a metaphor regarding the material satisfaction of bodily need; such people will be recompensed for the extracted value of their labor "with equal servings on their plates." This process applies to the sage who understands things wisely and the scholar who understands things intellectually—both "eat their fill," becoming one. The verse, then, functions as a metaphor for the oneness of bodily practice and spiritual thought. It valorizes a rational social outlook in which spiritual praxis is not just intellectualized by religious scholars in books but embodied. Through meaningful labor, this understanding is

---

44. Ibid., 205.

deeply lived and felt with the wisdom of a sage and must be rewarded accordingly with equal material compensation.

The conception of work as an embodiment of spiritual value is also present in a medieval verse where the Kabir poet stresses labor done by all castes as equal:

O saintly men,

Don't ask the man
Devoted to the God without qualities
What his caste is.

The brahmin's good,
The warrior's good,
The trader's caste is good.
The thirty-six clans, they're all good—
It's your question, then,
That's crooked.
The barber's good,
The washerman's good,
The carpenter's caste is good.[45]

The verse orchestrates demos expansion through dissensus, pitting the ethnos (the upper castes) against the demos (the barber, washerman, and carpenter) only to unite them within a new shared space of community where all are equal. The poet names the castes: the Brahmin, Kshatriya (warrior), Vaishya (trader), and lower-caste workers, and affirms all these social ranks in the same terms. The next verse emphasizes the fact that these should not be regarded as predetermined social identities but judged according to the work they do. This was a revolutionary statement to make at a time when organized religion played an influential role in shaping economic activities. The castes and subcastes ensured a rigid division of labor that restricted the lower castes from changing one's occupation and aspiring to an upper caste's lifestyle. Thus, a barber could not become a goldsmith and even a highly skilled carpenter could not aspire to the lifestyle or privileges enjoyed by a Kshatriya (person from a warrior class). This barrier to mobility on labor restricted prosperity to a few castes. The poet critiques this state of affairs by highlighting the work of the "barber," "washerman," and "carpenter" as equal to that done by other castes. No one's identity is to be predetermined as inferior, and those who

---

45. Kabir, *The Weaver's Songs*, 196.

believe so are "crooked." The "devoted" should have their work validated and recognized as ethical action, for such "good" men have no place within the discriminatory categories of the caste system. The Kabir poet claims, in other words, that even if the products of lower-caste labor are alienable, the labor itself is not, for it is a mode of connecting to the divinity within.

Similar connections between meaningful bodily work and spiritual thought are expressed in the postcolonial present in the film *Kabira Khada Bazaar Mein*. In one scene, the current guru of the Kabir Panth declares:

> Those who clean gutters and the shit of others . . . people avoid them. They don't touch them. Why? Only because he cleans shit? And who makes that shit? If he stopped his work, those big people would choke on their own shit and die. If you're so special Brahmin, why didn't you take birth from a special door? Why be born from the same door as the low caste *shudra*? There should've been a special door for you! Kabir hammers them with his verse! People are worshipping idols. They pray to stones, give respect to them. But they disrespect the living people around them.[46]

In line with the above Kabir verses from the medieval manuscript lines, this speech validates the work of lower castes who "clean shit" for a living as equal to that of *bade log* or 'big people' who are assumed to be above *shudras* in both class and caste status. Shabnam Virmani documents another validation of menial work as embodied spiritual thought in her filming of Tipanya. In one interview at his home, Tipanya's wife Shanti expresses dissatisfaction at her husband's brief spiel within the Kabir Panth, for, in her opinion, in that capacity Tipanya's bodily practice no longer remained one with his universalizing spiritual teachings:

> I have only one thing to say to him [Prahlad Tipanya] . . . Leave the panth! And instead search quietly for the master who lives within your body. Singing these *bhajans* [religious songs] and making people happy—all this is fake, it's shallow. This is all a way of pandering to your own ego. In any case, reflection is not possible in a crowd. I don't know anything at all. But I do know that I must stay within the home and do *atam puja* [soul/inner worship]. First that, then everything else. *Atam puja* is serving everyone. Giving tea to one, milk to another, food to another, fodder to the cattle. This is my *atam* worship. I know nothing else.

---

46. Virmani, *Kabida Khada Bazaar Mai*. Translation mine.

Prahlad: see, she's the true Kabir. Because Kabir has said—whatever I see and do are acts of worship. All my daily actions—worship!⁴⁷

Within this ontology, *atam puja* consists of the daily acts of labor that form Shanti's domestic routine. These are also embodied acts of spiritual worship, for they are continuous with the recognition that the *nirguna* divinity lives within her body and the bodies of all whom she serves, whether they be her family members or even her cattle. And if all these bodies contain the same breath of divinity, no type of bodily work should be valued more than another; Shanti's uneducated domestic labor is just as valuable within this spiritual economy as the exchange value of an educated person's labor, and even more so than what she sees as her husband's bombastic and empty promotion of Kabir for a hierarchical Panth.

Precapitalist vs. Spiritual Economies of Valuation in Kabir

While the above philosophies are equalizing, in validating menial and domestic labor as modes of worship, the universalism posed by the Kabir discourses may also be read as preventing social mobility in practice—for rather than critique the larger patriarchal economic structures that confine Shanti to domestic labor as a *Dalit* married woman, or that keep lower castes in dirty, low paid jobs, they simply provide a discourse that allows these marginalized groups to come to terms with, and even celebrate, the forms of labor they are restricted to. These philosophies may, in other words, do something akin to the capitalist appropriation of Kabir explored above, sustaining a system that has much to gain from caste and domestic labor exploitation. However, the Kabir verses offer a very different—even subversive—way of being from that encapsulated by the *Dialogue for Development* because they simultaneously highlight a spiritual economy of work that is at odds with the ideals of a money economy, for each values work and selfhood in very different ways. This disconnect between the precapitalist economy of medieval India and the spiritual economy of *nirguna bhakti* is portrayed in a verse from the precolonial northern manuscript line that imagines an individual's death summons by *nirguna* God:

Hari has sent summons—
COME INSTANTLY.

---

47. Virmani, *Kabida Khada Bazaar Mai*. Translation mine.

> Your time to act is up—
> You have to submit a written account of your deeds.
> Death's brutal messengers are here
> To take you away.
> What have you earned?
> What have you spent and lost?
> Come quickly, now—
> The Divan has sent for you.[48]

The verse uses fiscal metaphors such as a "written account," "earned," "spent," and "lost" to convey the point that within a spiritual economy, "deeds" are what will be calculated and weighed up, rather than money. God is a "divan" or accountant who will count up the individual's good actions and bad. The verses convey the inability of the higher castes to comprehend this kind of unworldly accounting by depicting a dying wealthy individual's pleas to delay leaving his worldly attachments:

> You beg and plead:
> I still have a few things
> Left to do in the village.
> Let me wrap them up—
> Give me a few hours—just tonight.
> I'll cover your expenses.
> We'll stop at a rest house for our morning prayers,
> When we're on our way tomorrow.[49]

The worldly attachments valued within a precapitalist economy do not mean anything within the higher rational truth of the divine, yet the foolish individual described in the verse insists on finishing "a few things left to do in the village," even offering to cover the "expenses" of "death's messengers" and ridiculously offering to "stop at a rest house for our morning prayers." The verse critiques the wealthy higher castes who live according to irrational and unethical religious guidelines and do not grasp that a relationship with the divine cannot be exchanged in the way that money is in the world of maya. The verses convey an alternative rational social order in which, by contrast,

> All the folks who've kept
> The company of good men,

---

48. Kabir, *The Weaver's Songs*, 117.
49. Ibid.

And hence are imbued with Hari's colour—
They share in the Lord's substance.
They've found perennial happiness,
In this world, in that one—
They've won the priceless object.[50]

The "priceless object" is the true wealth, beyond the material entrapments of money, theorizing another kind of genuine wealth accumulation within a spiritual economy of meaningful work. This is the wealth of "good" life practices, borne of sharing in "the lord's substance." The Kabir poet articulates an idea of rational social organization in which good deeds add up to spiritual wealth, resulting in successful union with the divine.

Kabir Panthis, worshippers, and popular folk singers of Kabir's verses in the postcolonial present also repeatedly express versions of this universalism when they critique unjust wealth accumulation. If virtuous thought and practice need necessarily be one in this ontology of embodied divinity, a system in which people accumulate wealth in a manner in which they alienate others from their labor is also one in which their relationship with the divine is necessarily commodified. Tipanya's postcolonial Kabir songs repeatedly stress that being a capitalist—or making profit by extracting surplus value—is inconsistent with the quest for internal divinity. In another folk song captured by Virmani, the capitalist, as opposed to the true seeker of the divine, is equated to a "wandering trader":

> True religious seekers are walking with you.
> Your way lies clear in front of you.
> So why, oh trader, have you lost your way?
> Oh market after market you roamed, greedy fellow.
> I had to wander these markets with you.
> Now you've been wise deal-maker, you've struck the right bargain.
> But you fool, in the process you've also lost all your capital.
> Oh trader, why have you lost your way?[51]

In this song, superficial seekers of divinity are equated to wandering traders who trade spiritual goods for material goods. Rather than understand the truth of the divine through meaningful, embodied work, they are "greedy," for they follow capitalist principles of seeking "right bargains" in order to sell at a higher price and make a profit. However, the verse notes that to do so is

---

50. Ibid.
51. Virmani, *Kabira Khada Bazaar Mai*. Translation mine.

to emerge a spiritual "fool," for such a "wise" capitalist ends up losing spiritual "capital," which is a priceless entity that transcends all other measures of value and cannot be exchanged or traded through the easy equivalences of the money form. Thus, the songs equate the exercise of capitalist trade to an inadequate spiritual practice in which there is no synchrony between one's quest for divinity and one's bodily work in the world.

Attention to the discourses surrounding *nirguna bhakti* in colonial and postcolonial South Asia reveals a contextual universalism that has filtered down through the centuries to present a universalizing philosophy of social equality. How do these alternative ontologies of valuation continue to influence social protest movements that work toward realizing ethical, universalizing social orders? While medieval bhakti had provided the possibility of salvation for all and thus implicitly promised social equality, its radical social message, as C. J. Fuller points out, was fleshed out largely in the course of the social and religious reform movements of the last couple of centuries. Through these more recent movements, Fuller argues, a particular "devotionalist ethic comes to be widely reinterpreted as a charter of egalitarianism."[52] This is why, as David Lorenzen asserts, anticaste and anti-Brahminical movements of the nineteenth and twentieth centuries have, in one way or the other, drawn on the bhakti movements for their radical politics.[53] The following sections flesh out this claim through the examples of Mahima Dharma and the Kabir Kala Manch.

IV. A CONTINUING *NIRGUNA* UNIVERSALISM: COLONIAL RULE AND BHĪMA BHOI

What did the *nirguna* universalism of which Kabir was a part look like during the colonial period? How did collusions of caste and colonial capitalism reinforce social hierarchies, and how did *nirguna* contextual universalisms present democratic alternatives to these forces? This section explores how, during the colonial period, a *nirguna* universalism not only survived but was intensified alongside the structure of exploitation colonialism, which "created much of what is now accepted as Indian 'tradition,' including an autonomous caste structure with the Brahmin clearly and unambiguously at the head."[54] Within this kind of colonialism, the British ruled from above, employing and training an entire class of largely upper-caste native administrators who "may be

---

52. Fuller, *The Camphor Flame*, 29.
53. Lorenzen, "The Kabir-panth and Social Protest," 281–303.
54. Dirks, *Castes of Mind*, 12.

interpreters between us and the millions whom we govern; a class of persons, Indian in blood and color, but English in taste, in opinions, in morals, and in intellect."[55] Brahmanic texts provided transregional and metahistorical modes of understanding Indian society that clearly appealed to British colonial interests and attitudes, consolidating caste as a recognizable and pervasive social phenomenon. It is not surprising, therefore, that by the mid to late nineteenth centuries, caste histories began to predominate, with the colonial state feeling increasingly compelled to collect, organize, and disseminate caste-related designations in preparation for a wide variety of governmental initiatives and activities relating to "almost every form of executive action."[56] Yet, as this chapter explores, during the colonial period, poets such as Bhīma Bhoi were subverting these ossifying social hierarchies within *nirguna* movements such as Mahima Dharma.

Nirguna challenges to caste proliferated relatively independently of nationalist discourse, the Gandhian version of which sought to elevate the lower castes by glorifying them as harijans, the children of God. This was a formulation that nevertheless insisted on their difference from the rest of caste society. Yet, as this section shows, many of India's subalterns, or laboring classes, peasants, and workers, were also following an alternative genealogy of liberation in the form of the universalisms of *nirguna* saint-poets such as Kabir.

This section turns to these contextual universalisms in the context of Orissa, a state neighboring Bengal where reformist ideologues such as Vivekananda were most active. Orissa offers an interesting case study because, like the colonial cosmopolis of Calcutta, it was also home to a vast number of reformist movements. Yet, unlike Calcutta's bustling reformist sphere, the former were not derived from colonialist or nationalist discourses of subaltern upliftment. This was largely due to the fact that, along with upper-caste elites, vast swathes of Orissa were also occupied by large populations of subaltern groups, including the tribal peoples, or *adivasis,* who formed *nirguna* universalisms of their own in response to caste hierarchies. These aboriginal subjects had been the targets of feudal practices throughout the nineteenth century. They had to pay *bethi*—or forced menial labor—to upper castes and local rajas. They were also systematically targeted by the British under colonial legislation such as the 1871 Criminal Tribes Act. As Henry Schwarz describes, this invented classification supposedly referred to a "community of people predisposed by birth to commit crime and basically incapable of reform."[57] To make matters worse, the great famine of 1866, the worst that Orissa suffered in the century and one caused largely by the self-interested 'free trade' policies

---

55. Macaulay, "Minute on Indian Education," 237.
56. Dirks, *Castes of Mind*, 48.
57. Schwarz, *Constructing the Criminal Tribe*, 2.

of the British, wiped out one-third of the population of the province, mostly lower castes and tribals. Miseries born of scarcity were exacerbated by the upper castes' discriminatory attitudes. Many caste elites reacted to missionaries' relief operations during the famine with furor; lower castes and tribals who accepted cooked rice from non-Hindu relief houses were punished by ostracization.

Moreover, colonial policies were also gradually making tribal conditions worse by causing the increased encroachment of upper castes on to *adivasi* lands. When the British took away the kingdoms of local rajas, they often drew on the symbolic authority of Jagannath, the central deity of Hinduism in Orissa, to justify their actions. In retaliation, local rulers such as the Raja of Puri hung on with greater fervor to their own connections with the deity by building Jagannath temples near their palaces. To do so, they demanded more *bethi* and land from *adivasi* subjects to grant to upper-caste priests. The British report of the land revenue settlement of the area of Sambalpur thus mentions the excessive alienation of land to priests, temples, and rajas from 1829 onwards, reporting in a massive understatement that "the power of the aboriginal owners of the soil is gradually being broken."[58] The same was true of other areas of the state. In Dhenkanal, the local rajas gifted Brahmins extensive grants of rent-free lands to "induce them to settle down in the State with a view to raise the standard of public morality."[59]

Colonial rule strengthened caste to such an extent that, by the late nineteenth century, the cult of Jagannath, who had begun his journey as a tribal god and who had been defined by his accessibility to all people, had become an upper-caste god. In 1882, a British commentator tellingly noted that "the temple of Jagannath in which every creed obtained an asylum and in which every class and sect can find its god now closes its gates to the low caste population."[60] These social trends led to a proliferation of *nirguna* sects in colonial Orissa, a state that had precedents for *nirguna* movements since the eleventh and twelfth centuries even before the emergence of medieval *sants* like Kabir. One of these faiths was the Mahima Dharma movement.

Mahima Dharma, literally the "glorious dharma," was a sect that advocated devotion to an all-pervasive, formless Absolute, equally accessible to all, as the way to salvation. Mahima Swami, the founder of the faith, preached in the distant territories of the tributary states, inhabited predominantly by lower-caste, untouchable, and indigenous peoples. Mahima Dharma's followers included members of the Khond, Santhal, and Pan tribes, many of whom were categorized as criminal tribes. Mahima Swami actively contested the power of rajas,

---

58. Quoted in Banerjee-Dube, *Religion, Law and Power*, 42.
59. Ibid.
60. Hunter, "A Statistical Account of Bengal," 61.

Brahmins, the colonizers, and deities on behalf of such systematically marginalized peoples, launching campaigns to feed starving tribals en masse. The faith rendered the worship of idols (*murtipuja*) redundant, including that of Jagannath, and questioned hierarchies of caste and kinship (*jatigata bibheda*) and the role of Brahmins as mediators between gods and men. Mahima Swami's successor, the saint-poet Bhīma Bhoi, was himself a member of the heavily policed Khond tribe and rejected the ritual use of the *tulsi* (basil) plant, a high symbol of Brahminic Hindu identity. In a radical reversal of social conventions in which upper castes usually reject food prepared by lower castes, he also refused to accept food from Brahmins. It is not surprising, then, that Bhīma had frequent conflict with the local ruling elite, resulting in imprisonment and ongoing harassment.[61]

Mahima Dharmis were also repeatedly condemned within popular opinion. In 1873, the local newspaper, the *Utkal Deepika*, stated that Mahima Dharmis were out to destroy *jati dharma* (caste) by contravening caste rules, compelling the ruler of Madhupur to drive them out of his territory and Brahmins to demand repentance from them. The newspaper expressed upper-caste loyalist sentiments by declaring that the sect better not challenge British rule.[62] Colonial officials in turn characterized Mahima Dharmis as gullible barbarians who "never learnt or understood what the new religion was but adopted it and had blind faith in it, in ignorance being misled by the show of extraordinary qualities which they took to be superhuman and divine."[63] Mahima Dharma, then, was "doubly subaltern"; not only geographically and epistemologically separate from the colonizing powers but also separate from powerful groups within Indian society.[64]

The Mahima Dharmis' siege of the Jagannath temple, which I describe in story two at the beginning of this chapter, was a defining incident; the temple takeover provided evidence of the radical social movement that Mahima Dharma had become by the late nineteenth century, as well as of the challenge the sect posed to upper-caste religiosity and the colonial powers that buttressed them. Responses to the siege crystallized the discrimination faced by lower castes and tribals. Law keepers of the colonial state underscored the irrationality of Mahima Dharmis by defining them as a lunatically inclined band of fanatics, with the *Utkala Deepika* harping on the lowly origin and filthy habits of the attackers. They were denigrated as extreme *mlechhas* who neither bathed nor cleaned themselves after defecation. When the police were

---

61. Satpathy, *Bhīma Bhoi, Prayers and Reflections*, 19–20.
62. *Utkala Deepika*, September 6, 1873, part 8., no. 36, quoted in Banerjee-Dube, *Religion, Law and Power*, 35.
63. Ibid.
64. Banerjee-Dube, *Religion, Law and Power*, 8.

called to the temple to intercede, one tribal was killed and his death ruled an accident even though he had bruises on him. The deputy magistrate squarely blamed the *adivasis*, declaring, "The evidence of the witnesses proves that the Defendants . . . are also guilty of trespassing into a place of worship . . . low caste people and barbarous people who have no distinction of caste . . . are not allowed to enter the temple of Jagannath."[65] Colonial officials were clearly supporting discriminatory upper-caste attitudes.

The leader of the faith at the time of the siege was Bhīma Bhoi, who, after the death of Mahima Swami, had acquired a huge following of his own. Just like Kabir, Bhīma's origins are uncertain, with a number of hagiographic legends circulating about him. Yet, also like Kabir, Bhīma's poems provide written evidence of egalitarian bhakti politics and beliefs, dissolving distinctions between the lower-caste self and upper-caste other by describing both as issuing from the same divine realm. One of his verses unequivocally declares:

> In the realm of the indescribable no one is big or small.
> He sees all creatures with equal eyes.
> Says Bhīma, the lowly servant.[66]

Bhīma articulates a continuing *nirguna* universalism from his standpoint as a "lowly servant," just as Kabir did so from his position as an outcaste weaver. I explore Bhīma's iteration of this *nirguna* universalism, pitted against local, colonial, and caste hierarchies, in the rest of this section.

Bhīma Bhoi was voicing his challenge to Brahminical authority from the peripheral tribal regions of Orissa at the same time that Swami Vivekananda was bolstering Brahminical, Vedic interpretations of Hinduism for the colonialists and educated nationalists in metropolitan regions of India and the Western world. Unlike Vivekananda, however, Bhīma derived his "criticism of the Hindu tradition directly from the tradition itself,"[67] drawing from the diverse intellectual lineages that tribal Orissan society was steeped in. His devotional verse collections, the *Stuti Chintamoni* and *Bhajan Mala*, identify him with a number of regional intellectual and narrative traditions, rather than with the Sanskrit Vedas and Shastras of high-caste Hinduism. Most significantly, Bhīma's language of bhakti, that of devotion and total surrender to the guru who embodies the divine, drew on the influence of Orissa's bhakti poets. In particular, his various influences included the *nirguna* poems of Kabir, which had spread to the east in the decades following his death. Kabir poems, like Bhīma's, contain the descriptor 'alekh,' a variation on 'nirguna'

---

65. Quoted in Banerjee-Dube, *Religion, Law and Power*, 35.
66. Bhīma in Beltz and Baumer, *Bhīma Bhoi*, 59.
67. Eschmann, "Mahima Dharma," 375.

that suggests that the Absolute divinity cannot be represented. 'Alekha' comes from the Sanskrit root 'lekh' or 'likh,' which means to write. 'A lekh,' then, means "that which is 'unwritten,'" constituting an implicit challenge to the educated Brahmin religious authorities and the colonial institutionalization of their written texts. Like Kabir, Bhīma also drew on symbolic tantric cosmology, the *panchasakha*, the group of sixteenth-century poet-saints who wrote for the masses in vernacular Oriya rather than in Sanskrit for the educated elite, as well as the fifteenth-century farmer Sarala Das, widely revered as *shudra muni*, or low-caste sage, who produced vernacular Oriya versions of the Sanskrit ancient Hindu epics, the *Mahabharata* and the *Ramayana*. Bhīma's universalizing assertions of equitable and rational social organization, then, were contextually grounded in local, precolonial intellectual cultures.

This section focuses on Bhīma's collections of popular devotional verses, the *Stuti Chintamoni* and *Bhajan Mala*,[68] sung even today during the ritual worship of the divine. The context of its recitation is a song filled-ritual called *dhuni*, devoted to Alekha, and sung fervently by often illiterate devotees and *babas*, although their content is full of highly philosophical and mystical ideas that are far from simple. The verse form of the text activates its universalizing conceptual network of rational social organization in the mind of the devotee by mirroring the logical, 'rational' sequence of its philosophizing. Bhīma Bhoi's verses are obsessive about formal patterns; the manuscript of *Stuti Chintamoni* contains one hundred *bolis* (oral poems) with forty lines in each. Every two lines make a stanza, with each *boli* containing exactly twenty stanzas, and each line containing exactly twenty letters. Like other bhakti poetry, the verses start with a *ghosa*, or refrain, repeated by the entire group of devotional singers, and end with a "signature line," expressing a prayer or an intense feeling. This text was and is still largely transmitted orally, though a number of palm-leaf manuscripts still exist. Moreover, Bhīma's language is Kabir's *ulti bamsi*, or upside down language, full of the spontaneity and "rough rhetoric" of grassroots vernacular religious poets and used to emphasize the 'nonsensical' illogic of caste society.

Bhīma's *Stuti Chintamoni* and *Bhajan Mala* are not just counterhegemonic texts in form but also in content. Bhīma articulates his subaltern consciousness and calls for social change by highlighting the hypocritical, exploitative, and irrational structure of caste organization. It is not surprising, therefore,

---

68. Bhīma Bhoi's Oriya text is very popular, but there are only three accurate translations in English. I use the latest complete and scholarly 2010 translation by Johannes Beltz and Bettina Baumer, longtime scholars of Mahima Dharma, and supplement it with Sidharth Satpathy's 2006 translation of *Stuti Chintamoni*. For other *bhajanas* not in the above translations, I use Sitakant Mahapatra's 1983 translations. See Beltz and Baumer, *Bhīma Bhoi*; Satpathy, *Bhīma Bhoi, Prayers and Reflections*; and Mahapatra, *Bhīma Bhoi*.

that his radical ideas were dismissed by elements at the top of the colonial and religious hierarchy who found them threatening, including neo-Hindu Sanskritized versions of his own sect.[69] Very differently, Bhima Bhoi theorizes rational social organization through a *nirguna* conceptualization of identity that relied on an individual's embodied actions (karma), rather than their fate (*bhagya*.) Karma is the Hindu law that proclaims that one's past actions determine one's social status, the good or bad events in one's life, as well as one's capacity for salvation:

> What you have written I enjoy,
> Following the unseen karma.
> I fill my belly with a morsel of food
> That I earn from daily toil.[70]

The verse begins by referencing the widespread belief that karma is linked to fate; the divine has "written" "unseen karma," therefore determining a soul's fate without the soul being able to see its destiny, let alone change it. Bhīma, however, turns this on its head, transferring a theological point that generally refers to how actions in one's past life decide one's static and rigid caste identity in the next to a notion of identity in which one can change one's current circumstances according to one's own actions in the present. Thus, the karma Bhīma is referring to is not "unseen" after all; it is the result of carefully calculated rational action. Bhīma highlights the fact that he fills his belly with food that he "earn[s] from daily toil." The word "earn" reinforces the notion that the food he eats is directly the result of his actions, stressing the link between the realization of inward spiritual goals and righteous bodily work.

Other poems elaborate on this connection between bodily practice and the realization of spiritual goals by arguing that one's value comes from one's work rather than from fixed and unconditional identity categories. The verses stress the rationality of this idea through a logical tracing of the relationships between cause and effect:

> If the pandit or a poet does not study,
> Knows not the auspicious and inauspicious times,
> If he is without his almanac or chalk or betel-nut,
> How can he understand virtue and vice?
>
> If a yogi is mad for sense-objects
> And cares not for yoga-sadhana,

---

69. Beltz and Baumer, *Bhīma Bhoi*, 39–40.
70. Ibid., 103.

> If he has no faith in the practice of mind-and-breath,
> How can he perform his tapasya?
>
> If a Brahmin does not fulfill his ritual duties,
> And follows not the Vedas, if he repeats no mantra,
> If he does not practice the three times of prayer,
> And offers oblations to the dead, then he is of no use.[71]

The verse explores the logical links between a person's actions and the outcomes of those actions; if a yogi is mad for sensual objects, how can he perform his *tapasya*, or spiritual practice, since the very definition of *tapasya* is to detach oneself from the pleasures of the senses? And if a Brahmin does not fulfill his ritual duties, he "is of no use" as a Brahmin since the very definition of Brahmin is to fulfill these rites. Apart from the logical consistency in these statements, they also make a radical social point. A Brahmin is not a Brahmin unless he does his duty, just as a pandit or a poet cannot understand virtue and vice if they do not study these things. There is no such thing as an identity that one is born with; identities are constructed through one's bodily actions. The radical corollary of this, then, is that Brahmins do not deserve their place at the top of the social hierarchy anymore than anyone else does.

Bhīma also posits a continuity between spiritual thought and bodily practice through the *ulti bamsi*. This form enacts a practice of overcoming opposites that, in the Kabirian mode, stresses a rational continuity between ethical thought and the spiritual practice that can produce such thought.

> When you measure the measureless and eat the inedible,
> The company of saints destroys past sins.
> If you meditate on the unimaginable divinity day and night,
> The body is transformed anew.
>
> If you can see the essence of the unseen,
> You can recite the unuttered prayer.
> Know the unknowable
> And worship the formless.[72]

In these verses, Bhīma speaks of a knowledge beyond duality involving the overcoming of opposites so that their contradictions are dissolved. The first verse refers to the bodily act of "eating the inedible," alluding to the ritual practice of offering food to the gods to be blessed, which is then eaten by wor-

---

71. Ibid., 107.
72. Ibid., 304–5.

shippers after prayer ceremonies to imbibe the divine blessing. For Bhīma, such food is "inedible" because a divine blessing cannot be literally eaten but only received through an altered state of cognition. The second verse refers to the bodily act of "reciting the unuttered prayer" and meditating on the "unimaginable" "unknowable" divinity. These opposites invoke certain rituals only to negate them, suggesting that the divine is solely knowable and imaginable through meditative practices that employ an alternative cognitive state. If one embodies these other modes of cognition, Alekha will become reachable or "measurable," a process that will destroy past sins." Bhīma's creative transformation of language through the mystical upside down language ends up transcending all opposites in the same way that the devotee's mind has to overcome the duality of maya in order to achieve salvation.

A Spiritual vs. Capitalist Economy of Valuation in Bhīma Bhoi

Just as in the Kabir verses, such a journey of embodied worship highlights a spiritual economy of value over a precapitalist or capitalist one. The devotee's quest for spiritual wealth is suggested by the title of Bhīma's verse collection itself. *Stuti Chintamoni* literally means "eulogy to the thought jewel," which pointedly ascribes the name of a precious object, a jewel, to a philosophy containing the teachings and virtues of "the enlightened one" who has reached *Moksha*. As part of this spiritual economy, Bhīma advocates overcoming one's maya by acquiring spiritual capital instead of the material goods that are valuable within capitalism. Addressing the divine, one verse declares that

> What you gave me is merely a glance.
> Of compassion, grace and mercy.
> I paid you back with my devotion and service.
> What remains of my debt or its interest?[73]

Bhīma measures material riches through spiritual metaphors such as "compassion, grace and mercy," which he "pays back" not in monetary terms but through "devotion and service," which render the question of "debt and interest" redundant. The use of fiscal metaphors conveys that the riches of spiritual enlightenment are much more valuable than financial rewards or external signifiers of wealth.

Such an emphasis on valuing a person according to their actions rather than by their material wealth and social status is reinforced by verses that

---

73. Ibid., 215.

criticize the "ignorance," "pride," and "wickedness of the high born" as well as verses that stress the Kabirian point that if one's material wealth should derive from one's spiritual actions, *adivasis* should not be mistreated and consigned to poverty:

> I get easily neither food to eat
> Nor clothes to wear.
> My life is lowly, I am an outcaste.
> I know not when I shall receive your grace.
>
> You are the great Lord and Creator, yet all is in vain.
> You have given me this body,
> Yet my most basic needs you have not met.
> What justice is this, Oh Lord?[74]

In the Oriya original, "basic needs" refers to *manda*, the word for gruel. Bhīma, then, is not talking about his desire for the Lord to grace him with material wealth, a desire he often dismisses as sinful, but simply asking for basic clothing and for enough food to eat, and that, too, of the minimal quality needed for him to survive. Asserting his basic rights, Bhīma demands "justice," arguing that there are some things that deserve to be satisfied just by virtue of his humanity. Within this spiritual economy, tribals deserve the basic staples of existence by virtue of their righteous action in the world. These bodily actions rather than a precapitalist or capitalist system of value define a person's worth.

V. SPIRITUAL ECONOMIES OF VALUATION IN KKM'S POSTCOLONIAL PROTEST POETRY

The representative cultures of the medieval and postcolonial Kabirs, as well as of Bhīma Bhoi, are fragmented yet evolving. They are alive. The continued emphasis on embodied cognition and the value of spiritual economies over precapitalist ones endures as this "radical charter of egalitarianism" transforms into postcolonial processes of demos expansion. The songs of the Kabir Kala Manch evidence this. KKM is a protest poetry troupe formed in 2002 in Pune, a neighboring city to Mumbai. The timing of the KKM's inception was crucial—the state-orchestrated Gujarat riots against Muslims had shredded the fabric of Indian democracy and the KKM took it upon themselves to stitch it back together again through messages of equality. The troupe was made up

---

74. Ibid., 123.

of students and young professionals who performed protest poetry and plays in slums and streets to give voice to the voiceless. This was threatening to the state authorities; it was not long before its most prominent performers and poets were accused of being Maoists and *Naxalites* under the Unlawful Activities (Prevention) Act. In May 2011, a crackdown by the Anti-Terrorism Squad led to members such as Sheetal Sathe going into hiding, inciting protests from youth all over the country.

This arrest and the resulting protests testify to the ways that caste and related forms of religious discrimination continue to define India, even in urban, cosmopolitan spaces such as Mumbai, the 'financial capital of India,' where the Kabir Kala Manch is most active. As Salil Tripathi puts it, the state of Maharashtra forms a line of demarcation between the relatively progressive South, in which a large proportion of college seats and government jobs are reserved for Scheduled Castes and Tribes, and the conservative north, where upper castes revolt at the mere hint of a challenge to their supremacy. As recently as the 1970s, human excreta was being flung into low-caste wells and grinding stones were being thrown at lower castes from high-rise buildings. Violent retribution continues to follow those who marry someone from an upper caste. Low-caste *Dalit* women are regularly the targets of violent unpunished rape.[75] Significantly, Dr. Ambedkar was based in Maharashtra, and this was where he urged *Dalits* to reject Hinduism in its entirety. This also meant turning one's back on Gandhi's renaming of untouchables as harijan, or the children of God, a designation that in the eyes of many *Dalit* critics would only consolidate difference. As Anand Patwardhan captures in his renowned film, *Jai Bhim Comrade,* those that did not follow the Ambedkarite path of leaving Hinduism for other religions such as Buddhism often regret it. A *Dalit* man speaking of the rape of his granddaughter by upper-caste men declares: "We are responsible for this. We never got organized or converted to another religion. Had we done it, we could have mentally discarded caste and made others understand we are humans. We bear the brunt of injustice. . . . it happens to Buddhists too but they now have the strength to retaliate. We lack that strength."[76] KKM builds on these historical legacies of caste discrimination.

The need for KKM and the unjustified state response to it also arises out of an increasingly corrupt and fractured political landscape. In May 2014, Narendra Modi of the right-wing Hindu nationalist Bharatiya Janata Party (BJP)

---

75. A *Dalit* demanding rights is often violently punished. An infamous example includes the Khairlanji episode of September 2006, in which all four members of the *Dalit* Bhotmange family in Bhandara district were lynched, with the two women being paraded naked before they were killed. Rao, *The Caste Question,* 237–38.

76. Patwardhan, *Jai Bhim Comrade.*

FIGURE 2. A poster demanding the release of members of the KKM. Source: Democratic Students' Union (DSU), Jawaharlal Nehru University Unit.

was elected prime minister of India. The rise of the BJP had for decades consolidated increasing caste divisions, splintering *Dalit* political consciousness. The main *Dalit* party, the Republican Party of India (RPI), disintegrated into factional disputes, with each leader attempting to claim supremacy by forging alliances with mainstream political parties. Ironically, this often involved *Dalit* alliances with Hindu supremacists who stood behind the caste system. Most famously, Namdeo Dhasal, a legendary *Dalit* activist-poet and founder of the

Dalit Panthers,[77] did the unthinkable when he allied with the Shiv Sena leadership, writing a column for the Shiv Sena mouthpiece, *Saamana*, and sharing a platform with prominent Shiv Sena personalities. In 2009, a BJP election candidate canvassed for votes in Ramabai Nagar—where the firing took place under the rule of the Shiv Sena–BJP alliance. And, yet, public memory is so short that even some *Dalits* think that the Congress Party was in power at the time of the firing. This historical amnesia is particularly ironic considering the history of low-caste violence incited by the Shiv Sena in the past. In 1974, riots broke out between upper-caste Shiv Sena supporters and the Dalit Panthers in the Bombay Development Department Slums of Worli in Bombay.[78] Ghogre thus took his own life at a time when the future of *Dalit* politics in Maharashtra looked dismal. As Tripathi puts it, "the inclusive, cosmopolitan city Bombay had shrunk into the narrower identity of 'Mumbai.'"[79]

Perhaps because of these distasteful divisions, the Kabir Kala Manch has followed a very different kind of political engagement more consistent with the *nirguna bhakti* principles of saint-poets such as Kabir, which they articulate within conjoined conceptual networks that include post-Enlightenment universalisms such as Marxism and empirical rationalism. As the troupe's name would suggest, among the most prominent of these universalisms is the *nirguna* contextual universalism that claims equality for all human beings on the basis of their shared divinity, itself realized through ethical action in the world. The Kabir Kala Manch Defense Committee, launched after the poets' arrests for alleged Maoist activity, places the poets in the continuing lineage of such a universalism, stating, "The 20th century in Indian history is marked by a significant occurrence—the struggle for freedom by the slaving Shudras. The foundation of this great struggle was led by Gautama Buddha, Kabir, Ravidas, Tukaram and like-minded abrahmins, who had a rational . . . approach. The struggle reached its zenith of human liberation due to the stellar efforts of Phule–Shahu–Ambedkar."[80] The sentence stresses direct connections between saints such as Kabir and emancipatory political figures such as the anticaste activist, B. R. Ambedkar, who have now been superseded by hypocritical politicians like Namdeo Dhasal. Members of the KKM themselves claim this

---

77. The Dalit Panthers are a social organization that was founded by Namdeo Dhasal in April 1972 in Mumbai and were most active in the 1970s and '80s. The organization was inspired by the Black Panthers of the U.S. civil rights movement.

78. Sharma, "Group Violence in a Neighbourhood," 419–42.

79. Tripathi, Salil, "The Revolution Will be Sung," *Caravan Magazine*, last modified 1 May 2012, http://www.caravanmagazine.in/reviews-and-essays/revolution-will-be-sung.

80. Kabir Kala Manch Defense Committee, "Freedom of Speech," https://kabirkalamanch.wordpress.com/tag/freedom-of-speech/.

bhakti heritage of "the vidrohi voice (the counter culture, the voice of opposition), drawn from a long history of Dalit literature and activism that prompted social betterment." They elaborate that "our performances come from our folk culture. They tell our audience, primarily tribals and Dalits, about the oppression they face and why such things happen." The KKM, then, harnesses liberating contextual universalisms to renounce majoritarian Hinduism, thereby placing itself directly at odds with the increasingly Hindu state. As a newspaper article declares, in June 2013, members of the KKM were arrested in Pune for allegedly singing "inflammatory songs, banned by the State government" in efforts to prevent the development of the Bhamchandra and Bhandara hills associated with another bhakti saint, Tukaram.

However, even though the KKM's ideology can be traced to a fragmented bhakti lineage, the group's protest poetry is not recognizable as 'religious' in twenty-first-century India, where religion is equated with social divisions, aggressive claims on public space, demonstrative forms of idol worship, publicized pilgrimages, and loud fervor. Instead, the KKM have extracted the humanist and egalitarian essences of *nirguna bhakti* poets, propagating the rational message that a person's value comes from the righteous work they do in the world rather than from predetermined identity categories such as caste, even while they do not make the spiritual claim that such mindful action is the path to *Moksha*. The KKM's appreciation of *nirguna* ideals translates into a poetic program of anticaste politics. Building on the *nirguna* tradition of embodied spirituality in which righteous bodily action and work in the world defines human value, one verse protests:

> And if we are the same humans
> Then why are we outside the village?
> The outsider cleans up the waste
> Then why do we have to bow and beg
> "Curtsey oh my lord, I am passing through
> Curtsey oh my master, I bow to you
> Curtsey oh my lord, I am passing through
> Curtsey oh my master, I bow to you"
> Our shadow is untouchable, our touch nauseating
> This disgust in your faces, this shit in your thoughts
> This nausea of your beliefs
> Is hanging from our necks, from our settlements' necks[81]

---

81. Sathe, "Ek Maitra Raangadya," https://kractivist.wordpress.com/2012/08/20/sheetal-sathe-sings-a-song-penned-by-her-ek-maitra-raangadya/.

Just as Bhīma does in many of his poems, this verse lays out logical links between one's actions and the outcome of those actions to condemn the illogical state of affairs in which subaltern work is devalued and not rewarded with just treatment or compensation. The verse highlights the irrationality of lower-caste treatment: "the outsider cleans up the waste / then why do we have to bow and beg?" As various Kabir poets also point out, "cleaning up waste" is work that deserves appreciation rather than the punishment of "bowing and begging," for *Dalits* are the "same humans" as upper castes. Even menial labor is dignifying, provided it is embodied, or produced through a rational link between righteous thoughts and one's bodily actions. In line with the Kabir and Bhīma poems, this is an observation that values a person by recognizing the work they do for a larger social whole rather than through oppressive religious designations such as *Dalit*.

The KKM fights for rational social organization not only by harnessing bhakti contextual universalisms but also through other syncretic universalizing traditions, which are apparent in another verse critiquing organized religion and its irrationalities:

> Let's kick this stupidity away
> Let's keep our heads about us
> Let's think scientifically
> That legion of 330 million gods—
> We can't find a single one,
> We find it a bit odd
> This so called incarnate holy man,
> That so called incarnate holy woman
> Incarnations, Miracles, Their claims of divination
> Sun signs moon signs,
> Astrological charts
> Mars and Saturn are acting smart
> These priests are versed in the cheating art
> So we are sweeping aside the temples here
> We are sweeping them aside.[82]

Urging fellow *Dalits* to "keep our heads about us," the verse harnesses an empiricism grounded in multiple humanist lineages to "sweep aside the temples," pointing out that they have not been able to "find a single one of Hinduism's 330 million gods." If there are so many gods, the hypothesis of their

---

82. Ibid.

existence should be easily proved through evidence of at least one. Yet, a sarcastic "we find it a bit odd" proclaims that this "claim" is not supported through physical proof, so the priests must be "cheating," and "acting smart" in a way that precludes "thinking scientifically" and that does not embody a rational continuity between spiritual thought and righteous action. The verse ends with "we are sweeping aside the temples here" to represent such a continuity even as it simultaneously equates the *Dalit* vocation of sweeping as the epitome of such rationality. Kabir's views on rational social organization here collude with a discourse of partly post-Enlightenment and partly Charvakian scientism in which 'claims' must be supported by pragmatic inquiry and experimentation in order to be socially realized. Charvaka was an ancient Indian philosopher who is frequently invoked in KKM's poetry. He was the founder of a school of Indian materialism that holds direct perception, empiricism, and conditional inference as proper sources of knowledge, embraces philosophical skepticism, and rejects the Vedas and Vedic ritualism as sources of divine truth. This verse, then, is an example of how contextual and post-Enlightenment universalisms are harnessed together toward genuinely democratic ends.

Other post-Enlightenment universalisms, including Marxism and the Buddhist secularism of Ambedkar, also appear within KKM's verses to enhance the message of Kabir. These influences are evident in the words of the group's lead singers and poets. Dhengle speaks of having immersed himself in Marxist theory, stating that "the college students who are joining us now already know Marxism. They don't have to study the ideology first like we did." He adds that "if Ambedkar was alive today, maybe he would have accepted the Communist party."[83] It is clear why Marxism would appeal to someone like thirty-eight-year-old Dhengle, a working-class poet who toils as a small-time motor mechanic. This experience of poverty combined with the discrimination he faced as a *Dalit* led him to join the KKM in 1996 after the communal Gujarat riots when the group seemed to be the lone voice singing about the removal of caste, class, and community differences. The Marxist influence is apparent in much of Dhengle's analysis of social inequality. For instance, he points out that "the capitalist media's brainwashing causes even a grassroots person living in a shanty to be preoccupied with the same thoughts as a mansion-dweller. We're forgetting the world around us."[84] This is a dissensual statement in that it points out the ways that the upper castes, the ethnos, occupy a separate world than that of the lower castes and seeks to construct a new shared world where

---

83. Dhengle, "Aisa Kyon Hai?" in "Armed with Revolutionary Poems, Kabir Kala Manch Activists Want to Fight Against State." http://indiatoday.intoday.in/story/revolutionary-poems-and-kabir-kala-manch/1/310788.html.

84. Ibid.

this disparity does not exist by uncovering unfair social divisions. Dhengle's statement, moreover, is also a trenchant application of the Marxist conception of ideology, or the "ruling ideas" that constitute the "ideal expression of dominant material relationships," to postcolonial India."[85] According to Marx, these ideas consolidate the hegemony of the dominant classes by obfuscating the violence and exploitation involved in their power. Dhengle uses the Marxist concept of 'ideology' frequently to describe how capitalism's limited, falsely universalizing ideologies derived from the formal 'equality' and 'freedom' of laissez faire capitalism hide the very real obstacles that a low-caste shanty dweller faces in ever becoming a "mansion dweller."

The KKM's Marxism coupled with bhakti contextual universalisms as well as the syncretic universalism of Dalit Buddhism combat an undemocratic capitalism in a bid to expand the demos. Dalit Buddhism was itself intertwined with B. R. Ambedkar's *nirguna bhakti* upbringing as well as his English and American education in the post-Enlightenment tradition. For Ambedkar, the caste system had rendered Hinduism inherently corrupt so that the only hope for an emancipated social order lay outside of it. In his essay "Buddha or Karl Marx?" Ambedkar thus argued for a joint bhakti Marxist-Buddhism. Dismissing the French and Russian revolutions for "failing to produce equality" in conjunction with "fraternity and liberty," he insisted that "the three can coexist only if one follows the way of the Buddha. Communism can give one but not all. Man must grow materially as well as spiritually."[86] These strands of diverse post-Enlightenment universalisms, forged in the crucible of the colonial encounter, collaborate with the contextual universalism of Kabir within KKM's activism.

The poem partly quoted above, penned by Dhengle, embodies these Ambekarite universalizing lineages and their joint critiques of the power of global capital:

So we are sweeping aside the temples here
We are sweeping them aside
My Bhima has reaffirmed the Buddha
Pandhari, Shirdi-Tirupati, all are snares
The trustees of temples are now billionaires[87]

---

85. Marx and Engels, *The German Ideology*, 64.
86. Ambedkar, "Buddha or Karl Marx?," www.drambedkar.co.in/books/category1/8buddhaorkarlmarx.pdf.
87. Pandhari and Shirdi-Tirupati are names of famous pilgrimage temples in the subcontinent that are also known for the staggering amount of profit they make every year. For instance, in 2011, Tirupati's Balaji temple netted an income of $260,576,000 from the donations of rich devotees and politicians. Press Trust of India, "Balaji Temple Nets 1700 Crore Rs Income," last

> It's a business, it's one all right
> All Mathas pretend that black money is white[88]
> So we are sweeping aside the temples here
> We are sweeping them aside
> My Bhima has reaffirmed the Buddha
> They made religion the opium of masses
> Through the politics of religion, these gangs of asses
> Are committing genocide
> Behind the religions, they all hide
> So we are sweeping aside the temples here
> We are sweeping them aside
> My Bhima has reaffirmed the Buddha.[89]

This song expands on one of Kabir's central messages, denouncing the irrationality of organized religion and its oppressive hierarchies by critiquing upper-caste Brahmins and religious capitalists for turning worship into a business. Yet Kabir's diatribes against the business of organized religion and his statements on human equality gel seamlessly with a Marxist activism that speaks of religion as the "opium of masses" as well as Dalit Buddhism, with the verse also speaking of "my Bhima (Ambedkar's first name) as reaffirming my Buddha." Together these strands critique a global capitalism that, through donations to hierarchical, discriminatory religious institutions and strategic inventions of tradition, turns "black money into white." Despite their ideological dissimilarities, these diverse discourses collaborate with each other to produce a more equitable democratic public sphere against a repressive capitalist state, insisting as Kabir did that, as humans, "We're All One."

Another example of a syncretic conceptual network of rational equality is found within the KKM's song "You can destroy the body," composed to protest the February 2015 and August 2013 murders of Govind Pansare, the left-wing anticaste politician of the Communist Party of India, and Narendra Dabholkar, a self-described "rationalist" who criticized the country's "godmen" and campaigned for the eradication of superstition and the caste system. The song places these murders in a long line of attacks on rational truth that began with Charvaka:

---

modified 31 December 2011, http://www.ndtv.com/article/andhra-pradesh/balaji-temple-nets-rs-1-700-crore-income-162329.

88. A *matha* is a hierarchical religious ashram.

89. Mahabal, Kamayani Bali, "The Best Songs and Poems of Kabir Kala Manch," last modified 28 September 2012, http://kabirkalamanch.wordpress.com.

Even if they destroy the body, they can't destroy thought.
O religious mercenaries can you stop the wheel of progress?
You killed the ancient materialist, Charavaka.
You wiped him from the pages of history.
But how many children of Charavaka shall I show you today?[90]

The song extends this lineage of rational truth to other murdered activists who are the "children of Charavaka," including the bhakti vernacular poet, Tukaram, as well as nationalist reformers such as Gandhi. Then the poet describes a break in this endless stream of violence: the birth of the "sun of wisdom" in the form of Ambedkar:

Remember Tukaram whose books you drowned
and hid news of his murder.
That same Tuka's poems fill you with fear today.
To behead Buddhist priests you paid 100 gold coins.
Religious fanatics murdered Gandhiji.
After cutting their throats did their principles die?
By trampling upon truth, religionists have grown.
O religious mercenaries can you stop the wheel of progress?
Manu's ancient laws created terror.
Ignorance ruled with an iron fist.
A caste hierarchy imposed cruelty.
Then rose the sun of wisdom. Bhima.
And set fire to the Manusmriti.[91]

The rupture within this continuing lineage of violence comes in the form of Ambedkar destroying the manusmriti, the scriptures that set out a Hindu hierarchy and delineated the inferior role of women and lower castes. The centering of Ambedkar within this poem is significant because it places the poem's universalizing democratic impulses at direct odds with the 'democratic' modernity the Indian state itself professes. The latter dominant modernity is one that, as M. S. S. Pandian points out, relegates the language and practice of caste to the private sphere so as to disallow any mention of continuing caste discrimination in the public sphere. This move allows upper-caste modernity to hide its caste practices while continuing to exercise them. Ambedkar cannot figure in this hegemonic history of modernity because of

---

90. Sathe, Sheetal and Sachin Mali, "You Can Destroy the Body," https://www.youtube.com/watch?v=BtJoJ53ieoQ.
91. Ibid.

his perceived sullying of the secular-modern with the language of caste.[92] The KKM, in placing Ambedkar at its center, interrupts and rewrites this dominant Indian modernity to claim another beginning, the dawn of a new day. In inaugurating this fresh start, the KKM reclaims comparative secular democratic universalisms for the particularity of the *Dalit* struggle, invoking the continuing salience of caste while refusing to cede universalisms to the obfuscating discriminatory practices of upper-caste democracy. The KKM's refusal to jettison universalisms altogether belies Pandian's other claim that a sphere of subaltern politics that continues to invoke caste is "one step outside modernity," separate from the other strand of "lower caste politics which mobilises modernity and speaks a language of universal freedom."[93] For the KKM is a subaltern counterpublic that speaks a language of universal freedom from the standpoint of caste, and it does so to oppose a hegemonic Indian modernity that only pretends to universalizing in order to obscure its own exclusions.

The centering of Ambedkar serves to highlight the KKM's own universalizing vision, which ends by temporally expanding Ambedkar's inception of a local lineage of emancipation to include global events and figures that came before him, thereby composing a transnational and syncretic conceptual network of rational truth:

> For truth, Socrates drank poison.
> Copernicus invoked the wrath of the pope.
> Martin Luther was deemed a heretic and Galileo rotted in jail.
> See how these flowers of light mock death.
> How many such flowers have you murdered?
> What is the final death count of your religious cruelties?
> Let your darkness clash with our light.
> Ignorance will come to an end.
> Untruth will turn to dust.[94]

In placing these pre-Enlightenment European "flowers of lights" after Ambedkar, the verse theorizes rational battles for equality as comparative struggles born in multiple contexts. These fights include the efforts of pre-Enlightenment scientists like Copernicus and Galileo as well as reformers such as Martin Luther who incited the protestant reformation, which, like *nirguna bhakti*, espoused a divinity that lay within and was equally accessible to all. The last verse is performed with a backdrop of images of religious and racial violence,

---

92. Pandian, "One Step Outside Modernity," 1739.
93. Ibid., 1740.
94. Sathe and Mali, "You Can Destroy the Body."

including a Ku Klux Klan (KKK) lynch mob during the American civil rights struggle. All of these struggles for rational social organization occupy a comparative position within a truly syncretic genealogy that includes parallel struggles in transnational contexts, but the KKM traces this unified lineage by starting from a very particular locale, the bhakti-Ambedkarite Marxist *Dalit* lens that colors the KKM's view of the world.

These allied universalisms acquire force because of their frequent use of an aesthetic derived from the spirit of Kabir's upside down language. The verses use their form to invert the accepted rationalities of hierarchical social orders, thereby activating their *nirguna* concepts of rational being. The upside down language posits illogical, nonsensical statements only to highlight an inner sense apparent only to those who think against the currents of worldly existence. The KKM songs reverse this order, beginning with seemingly logical social truths only to point out how illogical they are. Consider these lines from a verse quoted above: "Our shadow is untouchable, our touch nauseating / This disgust in your faces, this shit in your thoughts / This nausea of your beliefs / Is hanging from our necks, from our settlements' necks." The first line matter-of-factly repeats the upper-caste belief that *Dalits* are so polluted, impure, and unclean that their touch is nauseating. However, the rest of the lines highlight the illogical nature of this statement by pointing out that they are only "beliefs" and "thoughts," not accurate descriptions of reality. And so vile are these notions that they deserve the signifiers of "nausea" and "shit" attached to them. The images of nausea thus reveal the irrationality of upper-caste discrimination through multiple opposing semantic levels that are finally resolved; first, they suggest that untouchables are nauseating. But then they reverse this meaning by clarifying that these thoughts, and not anything about the *Dalit* body, are what makes upper castes nauseous when they encounter a *Dalit* touch. Finally, the images affirm that the world should recognize the nauseating nature of these antihumanist thoughts.

Another verse uses the same upside down technique and the imagery of nausea to highlight *Dalit* oppression:

> The nausea is served in the plate, the untouchable nausea
> The disgust is growing in the belly, the untouchable disgust
> It's there even in buds of flowers, its there even in sweet songs
> That man should drink man's blood,
> Which is the land where this happens?
> This is the land of this hellish nausea[95]

---

95. Sathe, "Ek Maitra Raangadya."

The verse condemns the high-caste practice of refusing to eat food cooked by a *Dalit*. It starts by describing such a meal as nauseating in a way that suggests neutrality or even an effort to sustain the discriminatory status quo. However, the poem then highlights the illogical nature of this belief by noting that such a practice is akin to "a man drinking man's blood." Halfway through the poem, then, the first sentences are revealed to be operating on two distinct semantic registers, each opposing the other—that food cooked by *Dalits* is nauseating and conversely that the people who believe this are nauseating. Finally, the poem comes down heavily on the latter side. While eschewing the exact form of the upside down language, these poems are also devoted to posing opposing standpoints only to collapse them in favor of an alternative ontology of being that highlights the irrationality of antihumanist social systems.

This emphasis on a spiritual embodied cognition constitutes an alternative history that interrupts and critiques the exploitations of the global capitalist system. A verse points out the upside down nature of the social order, addressing itself to *Dalits* who are reduced to begging by a society that allows little or no access into the demos for lower castes:

> Your world involves standing in the blistering heat of the traffic signal
> While dogs drive around in Indica cars
> While dogs drive around in Mercedes.
> They give you the alms of a biscuit.
> Why is it this way? Why is it this way? Why is it this way?[96]

The verse seeks to construct a new shared community in which the demos includes lower castes by reversing the assumption that the *Dalit* beggar, handed a biscuit in the way of alms, is the one deserving of dog food. Thus, the KKM point out the illogical reality of a capitalist society in which the real dogs drive around in fancy cars while worthy humans are reduced to the status of animals, highlighting a universalizing economy of value instead.

In tracing continuities between Kabir's verses as recorded in the main manuscript lines and those sung by postcolonial folk singers, colonial gurus such as Bhīma Bhoi, and urban protest activists in the present, this chapter traces a *nirguna bhakti* contextual universalism that arose from within 'religion' itself and, in the process, challenges many of the binaries set up by the categories 'modern' and 'tradition' and the 'religious' and 'secular.' If we resist reading these literary legacies wholly according to a Eurocentric narrative of democratic progress as Enlightenment universalisms coupled with capitalism,

---

96. Dhengle, "Aisa Kyon Hai?" Translation my own.

these poems emerge as democratic universalisms in their own right that cannot be reduced to commodified 'tradition.' Indeed, while the Kabir poems have been repeatedly appropriated, often in hegemonic ways, many subsequent iterations also stress a consistently universalizing philosophy of equality that resists commodification. These contextual universalisms constitute an alternative theorization of embodied worship that exceeds and interrupts the power of global capital, even as capital provides these ontologies with the grounds for their resistance and becoming. Together with post-Enlightenment universalisms, contextual universalisms produce a vast array of local narratives from all corners of the world conflicting, intersecting, and arising in response to one another, all contributing to the universalizing thrust of representative cultures and practices. More importantly, though, different kinds of world-making are able to coexist with European thought rather than be dominated and humiliated by it. Democratic progress is turned into a simultaneously local and global legacy. The next chapter extends this revisionist account of demos expansion by turning from subaltern lower-caste and tribal universalisms within the public sphere to feminist universalisms within the domestic sphere.

CHAPTER 2

Restaging Freedom from Precolonial and Colonial Theater to Contemporary Bollywood Film

STORY ONE: In Karan Johar's 2001 superhit blockbuster film, *Kabhi Khushi Kabhie Gham* (*K3G*) or *Sometimes Happiness, Sometimes Sadness,* one of the female protagonists is depicted as a *pativrata,* or a wife who worships her husband as a god, thereby completing a religious duty. Several scenes promote this dominant Hindu discourse, showing Nandini praying simultaneously to God and to her husband, Yash, during religious rituals. Yet, the film also challenges the idea of *pativratadharma,* tracing the breakdown of a close family and the departure of the adopted eldest son, Rahul, due to Yash's authoritarian tendencies. Throughout the film, Yash shuts down any counteropinions that Nandini expresses: "My word is final. I've spoken haven't I? That's it then." However, in a game-changing moment, Nandini finally stands up to her husband and decides that outrage is a better response to her husband's misbehavior than submission to his will:

> NANDINI: Mother always told me that a husband is a god. No matter what he says—no matter what he thinks—he is always right. Whatever he does is right.
> You brought Rahul home one day. Right.
> But then one day Rahul left. Wrong.
> You let him go. Wrong.

You separated a mother from her child. Wrong.
Our family shattered to pieces. Wrong.
Then how does a husband become god? My husband is just a husband, just a husband, not god. Not god.
YASH: Nandini, listen. . . .
NANDINI: My word is final. I've spoken haven't I? That's it then.[1]

For the first time, Nandini directly challenges the patriarchal discourse of *pativratadharma*, stating that Yash's actions do not deserve godly status. These words form part of a chain of events that eventually lead to Rahul coming home again.

Another story: In late-nineteenth-century colonial Bengal, the stage actress Binodini Dasi (1863–1942) lamented her helplessness as a lone woman in the public sphere, forced to earn money through her acting when to do so was regarded as being the equivalent of a prostitute. In her autobiography, she notes the structural abuse faced by women, referring to her relationships with men as ones of "complete surrender" that nevertheless result in them "abandoning her."[2] In response, Binodini rages at these repeated betrayals, referring to men who seduce women like her as "tempters of the helpless who become leaders of society and pass moral judgment on these insecure women in order to crush them at every step of their existence!"[3] Binodini eventually leaves the theater in a refusal to subjugate herself to their power any longer.

And an origin story: In a climactic scene of the precolonial Indian play by Kalidasa, *Abhijnana Sakuntalam* (circa 400 CE), or *The Recognition of Sakuntala*, the pregnant eponymous protagonist rebukes her husband, Dushyanta, for refusing to recognize her as his wife and their child as his own. She angrily exclaims: "Wicked man! You see everything through the distorted lens of your own heart. Who else would stoop so low? You cover yourself in virtue like a derelict well, overgrown with weeds."[4] Then, rather than follow her kinsmen's suggestions that she throw herself at her husband's feet until he accepts her, for "a husband's power is absolute," Sakuntala chooses to keep her dignity and leaves.[5]

Nandini's fury with her own husband, Binodini's rage at the multiple men that have deceived her, and Sakuntala's wrath at Dushyanta are all examples of

---

1. Johar, *Kabhi Khushi Kabhi Gham*. Translation mine.
2. Dasi, "Amar Katha," 105.
3. Ibid., 66.
4. I am using W. B. Johnson's recent translation of *Sakuntala* into English because of its emphasis on producing a performable translation of Kalidasa's play. Kalidasa, *The Recognition of Sakuntala*, 66.
5. Ibid., 67.

women exercising resistance to patriarchal mistreatment in a way that liberal feminists would clearly categorize as autonomous. Although describing very different female subjectivities in varied historical contexts, these actions are all carried out according to the protagonists' self-interest and in opposition to oppressive conditions rather than in line with dominant discourses such as *pativratadharma,* a frequent theme in all three stories. What interests me about these stories is that none fit neatly into existing discursive paradigms surrounding Hindu women's emancipation from oppressive patriarchies, which was a defining theme of nineteenth-century colonialism and Indian nationalism. The structure of exploitation colonialism resulted in upper-caste elites occupying a space of power left open by "British dominance without hegemony." Yet, even as the British granted power to upper-caste Hindus, they simultaneously had to reaffirm their own dominance by undermining the claims to self-rule of these indigenous elites. They did so by using upper-caste Hindu women's allegedly wretched condition as an excuse to justify their conquest of India. In response, Indian nationalists also placed women at the center of their own ideological struggle for independence,[6] but too often did so by seeking 'liberation' for women within the domestic realm of the *pativrata*. In this schema, the pure Hindu wife served as a symbol for the path to a uniquely Indian modernity. Despite these pervasive ideological strands, the three texts this chapter examines belie the all-encompassing hegemony of such colonial and nationalist discourses, for the above stories are also partly constituted by an embedded conceptualization of freedom in which the subject acts against constraints through an agentive process constituted through the dramatic contextual universalism "human actions are produced by the capacity to feel the emotions of others."

This conception of agency is universalizing because it locates itself in the human body, no matter who possesses it or where they possess it and because truly free actions are not, in fact, 'individual' but produced through interrelational affects between the self and others within a larger community of humans. 'Affects,' as I will show, are those emotions that register in the body as physical sensation, such as crying, a fluttering heart, or a throbbing arm. Such affects extend the body outwards into intersubjective relationships, triggering corporeal modes of cognition, decision making, and agentive action. These affects, moreover, are ideally 'felt' by all who witness them, schooling the audience to identify with marginalized others, including the female subaltern subject. This conception of affective agency is also contextual because it is rooted in the culturally and historically located episteme of Sanskrit dramatics,

---

6. Mill, *The History of British India,* 309–10.

because it theorizes agency as arising in response to the body's embedded-ness within local structures of power, its environment, and various intersubjective relationships, and also because what 'moves' the audience away from hierarchical ideologies is itself contingent on the different historical moments within which affective agency is put to work. Such an affective agency works with, and alters, post-Enlightenment ideas of individual freedom to sustain a composite genealogy of representative change in the postcolonial present. Affective agency, moreover, operates independently of and even resists capitalism by positing relationships between the self and the other in terms of emotional ties that transcend capitalist notions of social status as well as patriarchal and caste-ist kinship ideals.

The first part of the chapter traces affective agency back to precolonial forms of Sanskrit drama, which exemplifies one originating repository of the contextual universalism traced in the rest of the chapter. Although produced within structures of upper caste, patriarchal power, I suggest that Kalidasa's *Sakuntala* reworks these structures to posit a universalizing conception of free action located in the body and harnessed against divisive social hierarchies. The second part of the chapter then considers the ways in which this affective agency is instrumentalized on the late-nineteenth-century Bengali stage through the autobiography of Binodini Dasi, which uses Kalidasa's *Sakuntala* as an important subtext. Binodini was one of India's first female theatre actresses and harnessed affective agency to resist conservative colonialist and elite nationalist constructions of Indian women, thereby expanding the demos to include marginalized women. Binodini uses affective agency to shore up a self caught between the evaluating metrics of a new colonial capitalism—which created oppressive and totalizing equivalences between Binodini's labor power and the money form—and a patriarchal native *bhadralok* that equated any working woman to a prostitute. Finally, I expand on my analysis of $K3G$, arguing that while the film cannot be read as a purely progressive or oppositional text, its partial constitution through dramatic forms of affective agency testifies to the filtering of democratic contextual universalisms into otherwise hegemonic texts.

I. CHALLENGING HIERARCHIES IN KALIDASA'S *SAKUNTALA*

Kalidasa's *Sakuntala*, itself a story adapted from the Hindu epic the *Mahabharata*, was a central text for German romanticists such as Schlegel and Herder who used it to rearrange philosophical patterns and offer a new genealogy of modernity.[7] However, the text is equally interesting for its unique theatrical notions of freedom, formulated through and against local and precolonial relations of power and resistance. This section begins with a situating of *Sakuntala* and its author, Kalidasa, in upper-caste, patriarchal structures of power, before noting romanticist and colonial interpretations of the play. I then highlight the very different understandings of the play espoused by precolonial literary commentators and viewers. The latter responses recognize a pedagogical message of affective agency for its protagonists, which are articulated through the Sanskritic aesthetic device of *rasa*. *Rasa* aims to transfer moods or emotions from characters and actors in a play to its audience, thereby also activating universalizing concepts of freedom within spectators. Drawing on Sanskrit literary commentaries, including the influential classical treatise on drama, Bharata Muni's *Natya Shastra* (100–300 CE) and the eleventh-century criticism of *Sakuntala* by philosophers such as Abhinavagupta, I show that the text posits an affective agency because characters' affects actively change their actions in line with the realization of a particular mood or *rasa*, thereby catalyzing major plot turns in decisive directions. This means that actions are not predetermined by patriarchal discourses encompassed within *pativratadharma* but revised in relation to the protagonist's affects and the new interpretational frameworks her affects draw her attention to—including, for instance, too often marginalized Hindu discourses asserting a wife's ownership of her self and right to act in her own best interests. This is an ontology of free action that emphasizes and makes use of a process described by the cognitive scientist Joseph LeDoux, in which the emotional states we subjectively experience are the end result of information processing that occurs in response to stimuli and which then shape appropriate behavior and action.[8] In line with this understanding, the play depicts how the characters that do not revise their choice of action in line with their affects, who only heed dominant ideologies in choosing how to act, go wrong. These characters' morally flawed actions hinder the play's eventual realization of the generalized experience of joy that Sanskrit dramatists called *shanta-rasa*. For, within *rasa* dramatics, the affective states that spur actions are generalized rather than individual, ideally being transmitted to all observers along with their accompanying messages.

Sakuntala is written in the form of a heroic romance that concerns itself with a royal hero, King Dushyanta. One day Dushyanta, out hunting in the forest, comes across Sakuntala, a beautiful half-divine, half-human woman who is the adopted daughter of a forest sage. Dushyanta falls deeply in love

---

7. McGetchin, *Indology, Indomania, and Orientalism*, 58–62.
8. LeDoux, *The Emotional Brain*, 19.

with her, they marry by promise (*gandharva vivah*), and he tells her that he will soon call for her to join him at his palace. A pregnant Sakuntala pines for him for months, during which a wandering holy man comes to their ashram. When Sakuntala ignores the sage, lost in her thoughts of Dushyanta, the sage curses her, pronouncing that the one who has caused her to lose her sense of reality will himself forget all about her. Her companions beg the holy man to repeal the curse but the sage gives them a ring instead, proclaiming that when Dushyanta sees the ring, his memory of Sakuntala will return. Sakuntala takes this "ring of recognition" with her to meet Dushyanta but loses it on the way so that Dushyanta fails to recognize her. During the ensuing confrontation, Sakuntala asks the earth goddess to take her rather than live humiliated in the palace of a man who has forsaken her. She resides up in the heavens with her son, Bharata, until Dushyanta finds the ring and recalls his missing wife. Lamenting and heartbroken, he goes in search of her, and they are eventually happily reunited.

Not much is known about Kalidasa today, even though he was the most renowned poet and playwright of the classical Gupta Empire and was likely to have lived in Ujjain, the capital and a center of arts and learning in the fourth to fifth century CE. Kalidasa was well versed with the *Natya Shastra* and its theorizations of dramatic devices such as *rasa*, which he used to write not just *Sakuntala* but at least six other poetic plays under the patronage of the royal court. He was reputedly the favorite poet of King Chandragupta II, also known as Vikramaditya, under whose rule drama "emerged as a sophisticated form of public literature" meant to both educate and entertain.[9] Nevertheless, as J. A. B. van Buitenen points out, classical India and its dramatic literature in this period were not homogenous entities by any means: "drama straddled several language barriers in northern India, and yet became the most lofty expression of a typically Sanskritic culture. It provided a spectacle for all classes of the population, yet at the same time it was mainly directed to the highly educated. It drew on epic and folklore which was the common heritage of all, yet . . . could be savored only by the connoisseur. At once accessible to all and impervious but to the few, the theater was the image of civilization itself."[10] These insights reveal Kalidasa's own imbrication in ever-changing, heterogeneous local relations of power, preventing a reading of this text in line with culturally essentialist—whether nationalist, nativist or Orientalist—fetishizations of ancient Indian literatures as representative of a pure golden age that must be revived in the present day. *Sakuntala* is itself a

---

9. Stoler Miller "Kalidasa's World and His Plays," 13.
10. Van Buitenen, *Two Plays of Ancient India*, 3.

text composed by a man to be performed in a royal setting for the pleasure of other powerful men. This is apparent from the text's differentiation of its royal characters from commoners and females, the latter of which speak in coarse prose, *prakrit,* as opposed to the refined Sanskrit poetry that spills from the lips of the royal male protagonist and his compatriots. The author's privileged location as a male court poet is also apparent in the play's subjection of the eponymous, female protagonist to an eroticized gaze, a common feature of the *kavya* genre of Sanskrit poetry. As Simona Sawhney argues, Kalidasa's love story is invested in patriarchy even as it critiques it; through Sakuntala's suffering it "reveals the place of violence in this economy of love, for though the violence must be transformed, it cannot be erased. Its memory sustains the very structure of patriarchal romance."[11] Other aspects of the play also signal its positioning as a text performed for powerful elite groups within a monarchical state. Dushyanta is depicted as an emperor with connections to the upper castes and gods who fights off an army of *asuras* (demons) depicted with supposedly lower-caste characteristics. Similarly, the *Natya Shastra* was itself a document partly formulated to raise supposedly inferior lower castes to holier thoughts in the form of a "fifth veda." As the play was taken up during the colonial era it came to manifest traces of these local hierarchies as well as new ones.

The story has been the subject of rich reappropriations since its first appearance, prior to Kalidasa's adaptation, in the religious Hindu epic, the *Mahabharata.* As Romila Thapar has shown in her exegesis on the story's permutations through changing historical circumstances, Sakuntala herself has undergone extreme alterations; from a self-reliant, defiant woman (as in the oral popular tradition of the *Mahabharata*), to the "child of nature in German romanticism," to a symbol of the primitive, unevolved psychology of an unchanging Hindu civilization (British Orientalists), and finally as the "ideal Hindu wife from the perspective of Indian nationalism and its reactionary perceptions of Hindu tradition."[12] Before the advent of colonial rule, the various versions of the *Sakuntala* story appeared in regional languages, including Braj Basha and Urdu, but still manifested traces of continuity with earlier versions of the story. However, as English translations of the Kalidasa play became an Orientalist focal point, regional versions of *Sakuntala* receded even if, as this chapter as a whole argues, their embedded theorizations of affective action remained constitutive of various colonial and postcolonial subjectivities.

---

11. Sawhney, "Who is Kalidasa?" 295–312.
12. Thapar, *Sakuntala: Texts, Readings, Histories,* 257.

Reading Sakuntala's Affective Agency through Sanskrit Commentaries

In the centuries after Kalidasa's death, and in the centuries leading up to the colonial period, *Sakuntala* remained preeminent all over the subcontinent, recognized as the best extant example of the *nataka* form and the subsequent basis for major new forms, translations, and commentaries. Significantly, from the turn of the first millennium, further commentaries became more extensive than before and kept the text alive, often assessing Kalidasa's play from the perspective of Sanskrit literary theories which, by the end of the first millennium CE, had a wide geographical reach. The Sanskrit literary texts in translation considered here include Bharata Muni's treatise on drama, the *Natya Shastra,* or *A Manual of Dramatic Arts,* Anandavardhana's *Dhvanyāloka,* or *Illuminating Dramatic Suggestion*"(circa 820–890 CE), Abhinavagupta's commentary on the *Natya Shastra*—the *Abhinavabharati,* or *Aesthetic Experience,* and his *Dhvanyālokalocana,* or *Commentary on the "Interpretation of Illuminating Dramatic Suggestion"* (circa 950–1020 CE), and finally, Raghavabhatta's interpretation of *Sakuntala,* the *Arthadyotanika* (circa 1300 CE).[13]

Read alongside these dramatic treatises and commentaries, Kalidasa's play can be interpreted as positing a theorization of autonomous agency for its protagonists that is affect based. This is because the plot, including the major decisions and actions of the characters, are driven and determined by affects, aimed at the consequent realization of a particular *rasa. Rasa,* a concept described in the *Natya Shastra* (circa 100–300 CE), is a key characteristic of the *kavya nataka,* a genre that flourished between 400 and 1200 CE and which aimed to aestheticize the body in emotive terms, thereby giving the reader or spectator an exciting sensual involvement in the events of the epic. The word *rasa* itself means sap, juice, fluid, or semen, and is connected to the essence, flavor, and core of experience, to the universal emotions that bring a work of art to life. Poets recognized eight *rasas*: erotic, comic, grievous, angry, heroic, fearsome, odious, and marvelous, with a good poet able to include them all, thus giving voice to the fullest range of human experience. The performance of *rasa* aimed to produce these emotions not just in its players but in its audience, ending the production with a generalized experience of joy, the *shanta-rasa* or *rasa* of peace—an intensification of sorts comparable to the spiritual experience of achieving moksha or salvation.[14] *Rasa,* then, refers to an aesthetic taste experienced by an audience after witnessing the portrayal of

---

13. There are four major recensions of the *Abhijnanasakuntalam,* listed as Bengali, Devanagri, Kashmiri, and Dravidian largely on the basis of the scripts used.

14. Abhinavagupta, *The Dhvanyaloka of Anandavardhana,* 226.

emotional components, or *bhava,* onstage. It is the transferring of emotions or moods evoked by the poetry to the audience through empathic witnessing and listening.[15] A playwright could achieve the eight *rasas* by arranging their eight corresponding *bhavas* (emotional moods) harmoniously. The different *bhavas* were linked to situations or actions that either produced each *rasa* or that were produced through the evocation of a *rasa*.[16] For example, the essence of comedy, a *rasa* could produce a feeling of jest, a *bhava,* and vice versa for the audience. Or *rati,* the *bhava* of love, could produce the *sringara rasa to* do with erotic sentiment. The *kavya nataka,* then, operates according to known aesthetic codes, each of which function as triggers for particular emotions in the audience. Andrew Schelling therefore notes that *kavya* "relies on the assumption that aesthetic response depends as much on the expectations and conditioning of the audience as it does on poetry, theatrical conventions, and styles of acting."[17] As such, *rasa* poetics draws on a form of what cognitive psychologists have called "emotional contagion," which describes the ways that people, in this case audience members, unconsciously and automatically mimic the expressions of emotion they witness on other people, in this case actors, and often come to feel pale reflections of these feelings. The perception of emotion activates the neural mechanisms that are responsible for the generation of emotions. Viewing facial expressions triggers emotions and expressions on one's own face, even in the absence of conscious recognition of the stimulus.[18] This is an account of emotional cognition that tallies with Massumi and Brennan's definition of affect as the intersubjective capacity of the body to affect and be affected. Audiences of *rasa* drama are attuned to this process and attend to the stream of tiny moment-to-moment reactions expressed by actors on stage, thereby "feeling themselves into" the emotional landscapes inhabited by the actors.[19]

Kalidasa's text is structured through these *rasa* principles; the plot, including the major decisions and actions of the characters, is driven by performed yet genuinely felt affects, which register in characters' bodies as physical sensation. These affects work to transfer emotional states to spectators with the aim of a consequent realization of *rasa.* The *Natya Shastra* calls these affects *sattvika anubhava,* referring to both volitional corporeal actions such as raising the eyebrows or gesturing with the hand as well as comparably involuntary bodily states such as perspiring or developing goose bumps, having one's voice altered,

---

15. Buchta and Schweig, "Rasa Theory," 624.
16. Kuritz, *The Making of Theatre History,* 65.
17. Schelling, *Dropping the Bow,* 11.
18. Dimberg et al. "Unconscious Facial Reactions to Emotional Facial Expressions," 86–89.
19. See Hatfield, Cacioppo, and Rapson, "Emotional Contagion," 96–97.

shivering, changing color, crying, and fainting.[20] Bharat Muni identifies eight of these *sattvika* states, with these not just being acted but manifested by the actor in his identification with the role.[21] The following close reading suggests that Kalidasa's *nataka* plays with these conventions of *rasa*, subverting dominant patriarchal discourses of the era by undermining their conventional emotional triggers and replacing them with new corresponding *rasas* in the audience. In doing so, the text rewires the audience's perceptions of patriarchal structures, hopefully inaugurating them into a *rasa* universalism.

As Raghavabhatta's eleventh-century commentary points out, the two *rasas* the play is concerned with are the *sringara rasa* (the erotic mood pertaining to romantic love) and *vira rasa* (the heroic mood pertaining to social and dharmic duty). Raghavabhatta analyzes the structure of *Sakuntala*'s plot on the basis of the interaction between these two *rasas*.[22] The resolution of the tension between love and the fulfillment of social obligations results in the generalized feeling of peaceful joy, the *shanta-rasa*. The goal of uniting these two *rasas* determines the actions of the characters and the plot. Following Bharata Muni, the eleventh-century philosopher Abhinavagupta writes that the particulars of a given situation in a play are 'determinants' or 'causes' that combine with affective 'consequents,' or *anubhava*, experienced by an actor onstage. This combination of elements leads to a character's actions and subsequent plot turns that result in the final realization of a particular *rasa*: "thus where the death of a close relation is the determinant, wailing, shedding, tears, etc. the consequent, and anxiety, depression (*dainya*) etc., the transitory feelings, then the permanent sentiment (the *rasa* transmitted to the audience) cannot be other than Sorrow."[23]

In line with these affective principles of plot development, the play begins by depicting Sakuntala's major actions as the results of her emotive and affective reactions (consequents) to particular experiences (determinants). Her "consequents" or *anubhavic* affects register in her body as physical sensation to work in service of *sringara rasa*. Thus, when Sakuntala meets Dushyanta (the determinant), Kalidasa expresses her feelings as a physical love sickness (the consequent). Dushyanta notes that

> Sakuntala seems to be very ill. (Pondering) Now, is it the heat, or is it the heart, as it is with me? (Gazing with longing) But there's really no question:

---

20. Bharata Muni, *Natya Shastra*, 145–49.
21. Ibid., 146.
22. Raghavabhatta, "Arthadyotanika."
23. Abhinavagupta, *The Aesthetic Experience*, 78.

> Her breasts are smeared with lotus balm,
> Her fiber bracelet slips her wrist,
> Her body's racked—and lovely still,
> The summer sears her—but so does love,
> And love with greater skill.
>
> Her cheeks are drawn, her bosom shrinks,
> Her waist contracts, her shoulders stoop,
> Her color drains. Love strikes her down—
> A beauty sad as spring's young leaves,
> Shriveled in the furnace of the summer's breeze.[24]

Sakuntala does not acknowledge or 'know' that she is in love except through her body. The experience of falling in love registers in her body as physical sensation, as painful, erotic affect. Kalidasa depicts the experience of erotic pain to elicit the *rasa* of *sringara,* one meant to effect erotic sentiments in the audience. Thus, the verse simultaneously takes on the role of the voyeur, moving, through Dushyanta's gaze, over Sakuntala's breasts and cheeks, only to once more gaze at her waist and shoulders. Sakuntala's emotions are inseparable from and visible on her body, causing her to physically shrivel. In service of the *sringara rasa,* Dushyanta, too, experiences affective responses to his emotions and talks of "love's cruel wastage of my bow scarred limbs" so that his "golden bracelet . . . shuttles up and down my arm."[25] These are 'bodily signs,' affective markers, objects, and clues arousing, in the characters, actors, and the audience, a 'true' interpretation of the romantic encounter. Through his evocation of a physical manifestation of love in his protagonists and in the audience, Kalidasa conveys that their decisions and actions are affectively determined and produced.

The text does not simply school the audience to pay attention to characters' affects as central to unlocking the meaning of the play. It also highlights the ways that the protagonist's actions, and therefore major plot turns, are actively changed by affective consequents in line with a particular *rasa.* Kalidasa's text shows that the subject's processing of the events that befall her is interpreted through her physical sensations. These affects may actively determine the discourses through which she interprets events, as well as the actions she decides to take in light of those interpretations. Through this process, the text rewires the audience's ideological structures by consistently conveying a disconnect between the patriarchal narratives that surround and partly produce Sakuntala and the texture of her affective experiences. For instance,

---

24. Kalidasa, *The Recognition of Sakuntala,* 35.
25. Ibid., 36.

when Sakuntala leaves for the palace where she hopes her husband is waiting for her but where he will shortly reject her, the text replaces the *bhavas* during an archetypal bridal farewell—joyful anticipation of married life, and simultaneous sadness at leaving one's kin—with foreboding *anubhava* or affects that signal to her and the audience that the expected *rasas* of joyous grief are not, after all, apt moods through which to interpret the unfolding events. Here, Kalidasa describes an unusual and disruptive divide between the determinant—the situation of a bridal farewell and its accompanying discourse of bridal anticipation and modesty—and the consequents—Sakuntala's actual bodily signs or affective *anubhava*:

> SAKUNTALA: (Showing that she feels an evil omen.) Ah why does my right eyelid tremble so?
> GAUTAMI: My child, may every evil be averted, and your husband's family gods grant you happiness![26]

Sakuntala's affective *anubhava* of a nervous ocular twitch tells her and the audience that all is not right with their previous understanding of her marital contract and introduces them to the alternative *rasa* of fear. In doing so, Kalidasa disrupts the formulaic causal chain set up by Bharata Muni between determinants, consequents or *anubhava,* and *rasa,* for the determinants in this situation do not produce the anticipated consequents/*anubhava* or *rasa.* At this moment, the text incites both Sakuntala and the audience to realize that unquestioning wifely devotion as prescribed by *pativratadharma* will not necessarily result in her husband's acceptance and love. This dawning understanding comes to Sakuntala as other unexpected affective *anubhava*:

> SAKUNTALA: (with her hand on her bosom she speaks to herself.) Why is my heart fluttering? I know my husband's love so I should be calm.[27]

If Sakuntala and the watching audience are supposed to greet the dominant discourses of patriarchal conjugality with an emotional participation that signals an acceptance of these events, the text uses *anubhavic* affects to undo this participation. Instead, the play reeducates its protagonist and the audience, through the *rasa* of fear, into thinking critically about patriarchal conjugalities and replacing them, if necessary, with new ideas about the experiences women are subjected to.

In portraying this disconnect between a wife's knowledge of her "husband's love" and Sakuntala's contradictory affective consequents, Kalidasa is not just

---

26. Ibid., 61.
27. Ibid.

engaging in an act of literary foreshadowing about the disheartening events to come. Rather, Sakuntala's affects actively change her actions and therefore the plot of the *nataka,* thus highlighting the body as the key interpreter of the events that befall his protagonist. The text demonstrates that Sakuntala's agentive responses to painful events are revised and readjusted through her affective physical sensations. Sakuntala's nervous despondence, affectively registering in her body as a fluttering heart, causes her to arrive at a more appropriate response to her experiences than unquestioning wifely devotion. When Dushyana rejects her, she has been worked up to such an eventuality by her affects, demonstrated by her words: "My heart knew what was coming!"[28] As a result, the text's chosen *bhava* is anger (*kroda*) and the *rasa* and action it produces is outrage rather than quiet submission to Dushyanta's will:

> SAKUNTALA: (angrily.) Wicked man! You see everything through the distorted lens of your own heart. Who else would stoop so low? You cover yourself in virtue like a derelict well, overgrown with weeds.[29]

She continues sarcastically:

> It becomes you very well to disown a naïve and innocent girl with meager words, after you used them so richly to deceive me in the hermitage.[30]

These words are notable for their power. Nowhere else does Sakuntala use such strong language. In fact, thus far she has functioned as little more than a stock character, a woman of ethereal beauty who spends her time either in docile obedience or fawning over Dushyanta in lovesickness. In light of her past behavior, it would be almost unimaginable that these words are Sakuntala's. That they are hers is testimony to the shift in her discourses and narratives of self—and corresponding *rasa*—that her affective responses to her experiences have occasioned. As a result of these affects, Sakuntala's chosen action is angrily leaving for the heavens rather than following her kinsmen's demand that she live discarded and humiliated within her husband's palace walls. Because of Dushyanta's betrayal and Sakuntala's resulting departure, the audience is left adrift, far from the stated goal of achieving the generalized experience of *rasic* joy, the *shanta-rasa,* they have been promised through a unification of the *sringara* and *vira* rasas.

---

28. Ibid., 63.
29. Ibid., 66.
30. Ibid., 64.

Discursive Traps and the Truth of Affective Signs

The text's strategic revisions of *rasa* through Sakuntala's affective *anubhava* demonstrate that Dushyanta is unable to invoke the *vira rasa* of heroic duty sufficiently until the end of the play because he does not trust his own affects and bodily signs but *only* preexisting patriarchal ideologies. He therefore cannot hope to arrive at accurate understandings of experiences and is therefore at risk of taking inappropriate action. This is indeed what happens to Dushyanta when he acts according to chauvinist notions that, in fact, do not correspond with the invocation of *vira rasa*, despite what his own and others' affects are telling him. The text thus depicts the choices of interpretive frameworks that Dushyanta finds himself with before foregrounding why his eventual action of rejecting Sakuntala reflects inaccurate readings of his own affects and, therefore, his experiences.

Dushyanta has the choice of heeding affective *anubhava* to 'feel' the truth of Sakuntala's claims, or of only using dominant ideologies about women's deceitful nature to guide his actions. At first, Dushyanta seems to be observing the affects that will lead him to a more accurate understanding of events. For instance, in response to Sakuntala's outburst at his rejection, Dushyanta thinks: "her anger seems real. It almost makes me doubt myself."[31] The texture of Sakuntala's anger clearly comes across to the king as defensible; it is not arrived at through patriarchal ideas of conjugality that would tell Sakuntala to accept even "slavery at her husband's hearth," as her kinsman instructs her to, but in accordance with a new narrative of self that she chooses directly in affective response to the circumstances she finds herself in. Dushyanta's reading of Sakuntala's outburst as "real" is telling because it also lends credence to Sakuntala's words as being 'autonomous,' derived from active choices between multiple narratives of the self, rather than simply being predetermined by a hegemonic discourse.

Furthermore, the text suggests that the process of interpreting an experience correctly that so eludes Dushyanta is a cognitive process that is inseparable from the body's affective knowledge. Dushyanta acts wrongly because he does not pay attention to the perceptive powers of his anguished heart, his visceral longing for Sakuntala, or Sakuntala's "real" anger. Dushyanta relies too much on one interpretive framework, that of dominant patriarchal ideologies that insist on a woman's devious nature, rather than Sakuntala's genuine and *felt* arguments testifying to their marriage:

---

31. Ibid., 66.

SAKUNTALA: Very well! If you really think you're in danger of taking another man's wife, let me show you something that will refresh your memory.
KING: An excellent idea.
SAKUNTALA: (feeling her ring finger.) No! It can't be! The ring has gone from my finger! (She looks at Gautami in despair.)
GAUTAMI: It must have fallen off when you were bathing at Indra's crossing in the Goddess's holy waters.
KING: (smiling.) What a nice example of women's proverbial quick thinking.
SAKUNTALA: Fate may have taken a hand here, but I have something else to tell you.
KING: Now it's a matter of *hearing* something. These are the kinds of lying, honeyed words that women use, for their own ends, to lure over-excited youths.
Cuckoos get other birds to raise their chicks
And teach them flight. Females of every kind
Have natural cunning to perform these tricks,
But women, in addition, have devious minds.[32]

Dushyanta's responses to Sakuntala here are tinged with sarcasm. Rather than pay attention to the genuineness of her despair through sensual cues including "seeing" and "hearing," which are supposed to incite guiding affects in him, Dushyanta immediately resorts to interpreting Sakuntala's words through negative cultural stereotypes. Females have "proverbial quick thinking" that suggests "natural cunning" and "devious minds." They use "lying, honeyed words" to lure men. In its depiction of Dushyanta's unnecessarily malicious invective here, Kalidasa's text revises one of Bharata Muni's primary conditions for a *nataka*—that the hero is a "model of virtue."[33] As Simona Sawhney puts it, "the entire text becomes deeply and fundamentally ambivalent. It is both an exoneration of the king (due to his forgetting not being deliberate), and a most pointed critique of his character and world."[34]

The text depicts these pejorative stereotypes only to juxtapose them to Sakuntala's poignant, despairing attempts to convey the truth of her claims. The text thus lends force to the argument that Dushyanta's interpretation of the situation is flawed because he does not *feel* the tangible evidence that she is trying to show him. In the above exchange, Sakuntala asks him to experience the truth of her words through his senses, "hearing" and "seeing" her

32. Ibid., 65.
33. Krishnamoorthy, *Kalidasa*, 18.
34. Sawhney, "Who is Kalidasa?" 302.

evidence for what it is. In other words, she asks him to affectively experience the truth by understanding it palpably and emotionally. As Dushyanta later says himself:

> I am like a man who disbelieves
> The evidence of his eyes: For all its obvious size,
> He doubts the elephant exists—
> Such was the miasma that poisoned my mind.[35]

Here Dushyanta acknowledges that certain ideologies poisoned his mind and made him disregard the tangible truth, which he refers to as the elephant in front of his eyes. This tangible truth can be grasped through the emotional experience of its perceptual details. The "ring of recognition" serves as Kalidasa's symbol of the "truth" of such direct, perceptual experience embodied through affect, and Sakuntala attempts to make up for its absence by trying to arouse other affective clues for Dushyanta. Yet Dushyanta misinterprets the situation because he pins meaning to existing discourses rather than the details that reveal the situation to him.

Such a reading aligns with the eighth-century literary philosopher Anandavardhana's concept of *dhvani* or suggestion/resonance and Abhinavagupta's eleventh-century development of *dhvani* in terms of *rasa* poetics. Drawing on Anandavardhana, in his interpretation of Kalidasa's play, Abhinavagupta argues that Dushyanta suffers on account of his separation from Sakuntala without *knowing* why because he ignores his latent bodily knowledge, which eventually works to remind him of his past with Sakuntala. Such an argument bases itself on the concept of *rasadhvani*, which, as Patrick Colm Hogan elaborates, is an affective memory felt by the actor, character, and audience that is invoked by a sentence, phrase, or sensory experience.[36] *Rasadhvani* is created because whatever our senses perceive leaves latent impressions on our mind. Memory occurs when a latent impression is awakened. This account of memory is close to a process described by cognitive scientists Kevin Labar and Roberto Cabeza, within which the recollection of personal episodes from the remote past is directly connected to the reactivation of latent emotional associations.[37] Abhinavagupta interprets *Sakuntala* to elaborate on this principle: "For, as Kalidasa said: 'often a man, though happy, becomes uneasy of mind on seeing beautiful objects and hearing sweet musics. Surely, he remembers

---

35. Kalidasa, *The Recognition of Sakuntala*, 103.
36. Hogan, "Toward a Cognitive Science of Poetics," 164–78.
37. See Labar and Cabeza, "Cognitive Neuroscience of Emotional Memory," 54–64.

in his soul, though vaguely, associations of former births deeply implanted in him.'"[38] The passage from *Sakuntala* that Abhinavagupta cites presents Dushyanta's thoughts on hearing a love song after he has rejected Sakuntala:

> Why should this song fill me with desire,
> when I'm not even separated
> from someone I love? But perhaps
> It's what survives of love from other lives,
> Trapped in certain forms and sounds,
> And then released by song,
> That keys my mood
> From happiness to longing.
>
> Seeing rare beauty,
> Hearing lovely sounds,
> Even a happy man
> Becomes strangely uneasy . . .
> Perhaps he remembers,
> Without knowing why,
> Loves of another life
> Buried deep in his being.[39]

Here, Kalidasa elaborates on the ways that latent experiential traces are affectively embodied and then revived by sensory perception. For Dushyanta's relationship with Sakuntala, though wiped from his mind, still lives on in his body and is reawakened in his mind affectively by the song he is hearing. The episode reminds the actor playing the king, the character of the king, and the audience of Dushyanta's previous affective engagement with Sakuntala. That this much-awaited achievement of *shanta-rasa* can only happen affectively illustrates an idea of an affective conscience. In doing so, Kalidasa's text lays out a universalizing theorization of affective agency that revises accepted exclusionary attitudes about women's roles, personal freedom, and ethical behavior. Centuries later in the colonial period, a Bengali actress would take up this contextual universalism to negotiate and challenge a system that reduced her worth to the value of her labor power while simultaneously judging her as a prostitute for selling her labor.

---

38. Abhinavagupta, *The Aesthetic Experience*, 60.
39. Kalidasa, *The Recognition of Sakuntala*, 58.

II. CONTINUING AFFECTIVE AGENCIES IN COLONIAL INDIA: BINODINI DASI'S *SAKUNTALA*

In 1896, centuries after Kalidasa penned *Sakuntala,* the thirty-three-year-old Bengali theater actress Binodini Dasi composed a poem she named after Kalidasa's eponymous protagonist. In it she entreated her lover, in the voice of Sakuntala, "You must keep my word. Nor darken my life."[40] Binodini, in the voice of Sakuntala, entreats her lover to keep *her* promise to *him.* This interesting turn of phrase was a request, in other words, not to create circumstances in which she would be forced to leave him. This was a radical rewriting of Sakuntala as passive victim into Sakuntala as a woman reacting to mistreatment. Yet, just as in Kalidasa's play, Binodini's faith in fulfilled love and respect was to be repeatedly dashed by the men in her life. Significantly, this poem is not the only mention of Kalidasa's protagonist in Binodini's writings, for Sakuntala haunts and structures Binodini's works. This section argues that Binodini's life, career, and autobiography instrumentalizes the constructions of affective agency present in Sanskrit drama on the late-nineteenth-century Bengali stage, thereby resisting conservative colonialist, capitalist, and elite nationalist constructions of Indian women. Binodini's autobiography never takes nationalist debates on the woman's question as its primary discursive frame. The controversy surrounding the Brahmo Marriage bill (1868–72) or the Age of Consent bill (1890–92) and the Swadeshi movement of 1905–06, which must have been in the recent memory of her readers, are not even referenced in her writing. Instead, Binodini's textual self-constitution is carried out through universalisms, particularly colonial post-Enlightenment ideals of individual freedom as well as through embedded *rasa* based ontologies and epistemes regarding the emancipation of women. This syncretic conceptual network testifies to a continuing if fragmented contextual universalism that utilized but also exceeded colonialism's capitalist structures and conceptions of subjectivity.

Binodini was one of the first generations of actresses on the Bengali stage, which was inaugurated as a public institution in 1872 and began recruiting women to play female roles in 1873. She joined the theater in 1874 at the tender age of eleven and very quickly shot to fame in the title roles of a spate of bhakti plays written and produced by her mentor, Girish Chandra Ghosh (1844–1912). The most significant of these was *Sri Chaitanya,* based on the life of a bhakti saint whose life had profoundly influenced Bengali literature and culture. Her performance was so effective that Sri Ramakrishna, a renowned

---

40. Dasi, "Shakuntala," viii.

holy man who was in the audience, blessed her. In Binodini's own lifetime, the blessing served not only to 'redeem' her in the eyes of the masses but also to rescue theater itself from its reputation as a morally degraded colonial import. So powerful was the narrative of Binodini the redeemed "fallen woman" that it continues to appear repeatedly in films and plays. Overall, Binodini played over eighty roles during her twelve-year career. She also had a large role in the formation and construction of the Star Theater, although she was denied both credit for and association with it on account of the persistent social classification of her as a public actress, a figure regarded as the equivalent of a prostitute. Perhaps due to this mistreatment by her male colleagues, by 1887, while still in her early twenties, Binodini quit the stage and began living as the co-wife by *gandharva vivah* of a scion of one of the royal families of Calcutta. During this time, Binodini bore and also lost to illness a daughter she named Sakuntala. Upon her husband's death at the end of a twenty-five-year relationship, Binodini left his home on account of her socially degraded status as a 'public woman.'

Binodini's autobiography *Amar Katha*, or *My Story* (1912), rewrites nationalist and colonialist versions of Sakuntala to re-center an embedded affective agency for women. Binodini was cognizant of the fact that both her public life and that of Kalidasa's protagonist had significantly similar plot points, and both were therefore being read in the public sphere through the trope of the 'fallen woman' in need of redemption through a penitent Hindu piety. Yet Binodini's text is resistant to these interpretations of her life; she uses the dramatic devices of *bhava* and *rasa* grounded in the precolonial *kavya nataka* to contest conservative colonialist and elite nationalist constructions of Indian women. Binodini's use of *bhava* and *rasa* stages the actress self as a rewritten Sakuntala, not a figure in need of redemption but one who was made to suffer unfairly as a result of social structures loaded against women's interests. In line with *rasa* principles, Binodini harnesses the pain of patriarchal mistreatment into instances of affective action for her and the reader, thereby revising the oppressive colonial, capitalist, and nationalist ideologies of upper-caste Hindu womanhood through which she was judged.[41]

This section first explores the intertextual context within which Binodini was writing as a woman in the late nineteenth and early twentieth centuries as well as the construction of the nationalist stage of which she was a

---

41. I read Binodini Dasi's autobiography *Amar Katha*, or *My Story* (1912), through Rimli Bhattacharya's relatively recent translations, which I supplement with my own for the Bengali words that Bhattacharya leaves untranslated or for which I prefer another word.

FIGURE 3. Photograph of Binodini Dasi. Source: *Roop o Rang*, 1st year, no. 18, 16 Falgun 1331.

part through reformist issues surrounding upper-caste womanhood. Binodini's own position within these exclusionary discourses was contradictory; she was counted on to perform reformist roles even as she was marginalized as a woman working in the public sphere within upper-caste Hindu nationalism. I then show that Kalidasa's *Sakuntala* had become an illustrative example of good Hindu womanhood within this discourse; the play was increasingly being read to support conservative notions of female purity and degradation. Binodini challenges these interpretations by presenting a continuum of rewritten Sakuntala figures in response and, primarily, *Sakuntala* as her own autobiographical text, *Amar Katha* (*My Story*). The next sections argue that *Amar Katha* harnesses post-Enlightenment liberal ideas of freedom as the absence of coercion or constraint as well as an embedded notion of freedom as affective agency performed through *rasa* principles. Affective agency performs a kind of dissensus by uniting the female self with the upper-caste male other within a shared space. The device 'moves' Binodini and her privileged audience/readership away from exclusionary tropes of the 'fallen woman' within two performative scenes: Binodini's exclusion from the Star Theater and her 'redemption' by bhakti saint Shri Chaitanya. *Amar Katha* shows that contextual universalisms did not disappear or change unrecognizably during the colonial encounter. Affective agency was an embodied dramatic form and cognitive framework that suffused and partly produced Binodini's subjectivity, helping her to resist the simultaneously capitalist and nationalist patriarchal metrics through which she was judged.

Binodini's Intertexts and Contexts

Binodini's writings, consisting of *Amar Katha* (*My Story*) as well as an account of her career, *Amar Abhinetri Jiban* (*My Life as an Actress*), began to appear in theater journals from 1885 onward and continued to be published until 1925. *Amar Katha* was first serialized in the popular theater journal *Natya Mandir* (*Temple of Theater*) as *Abhinetrir Katha* (*An Actress's Story*). These texts are best understood when placed in relation to other women's writing in the same period in Bengali newspaper articles, journals, poems, pamphlets, tracts, novels, short stories, autobiographies, and memoirs as well as a surprising number of rarely performed plays.[42] Unlike Binodini, however, these writers were generally *bhadramahila,* or women from the respectable urban, propertied, upper classes.[43] Binodini, by contrast, was a public figure, dubbed by the contemporary press as the "flower of the native stage," who had received very little formal education. Yet her writings follow the conventions of other 'feminine' writing, falling into the categories of the private lament and the *charit sahitya* (character literature) that was largely modeled on the Western biographical tradition rather than on the Persian or Arabic *nama*. Yet, while the *charit sahitya* most often mandated the establishment of a patrilineal genealogy (*pitri parichoy*) and family affiliations (*kula parichoy*), Binodini deliberately flouts these conventions, structuring her text around a series of the absent men in her life. Her writing in this genre was part and parcel of her larger self-constitution by, but also resistance to, late-nineteenth-century discourses surrounding respectable Hindu womanhood. Binodini conceptualized herself as a woman alone, forced to act in a society that could not understand her except through oppressive nationalist notions of feminine innocence and corruption.

---

42. See Mukherjee, *Staging Resistance* for a collection of other women's plays from this period.

43. Binodini was writing for a different readership founded and edited by the theater community rather than popular upper-middle-class women's journals such as that edited by Rabindranath Tagore's sister, Swarnakumari Devi.

Such discursive constructions surrounding nationalist womanhood were developed in reaction to British ideology, which used the supposedly wretched condition of India's women to affirm the need for colonialism to emancipate them. In response, Indian activists such as Ram Mohan Roy placed women at the center of their own ideological struggle for independence. As the historian Partha Chatterjee has argued, nationalists were divided between those who regarded the Indian woman as a repository of Hindu "tradition," untouched by empire and a pure symbol of the domestic sphere, and those who insisted that the anticolonial struggle required the addressing of the woman's question through social reform to modernize Indian society. What was common to both groups, however, was the setting up of binaries within nationalist discourse that defined the inner/outer and spiritual/material worlds as respectively feminine/masculine. Indian women were therefore represented as the soul of the inner, spiritual, and Hindu world of the home.[44] At the heart of this burden of representing an authentic national identity lay the figure of the perfect wife, who was to be educated in Western-style conjugality while simultaneously being a *pativrata*, a woman who embraced devotion to her husband as the ultimate dharma.[45] A domesticated, heterosexual, conjugal, and, by extension, religious femininity, then, has long been at the heart of nation building in South Asia. As Janaki Nair points out, the result was the sidelining of the popular female cultural worlds that did not fit this frame of femininity and had long been the location of a robust critique of patriarchy, as well as expressions of female desire.[46] For example, upper-caste women's eroticism in song was attacked by the Bengali *bhadralok*, the upper-caste middle class, who wished to minimize contact between the women in their families and such subversive subcultures. Chatterjee thus suggests that "the new patriarchy which nationalist discourse set up as a hegemonic construct culturally distinguished itself not only from the West but also from the masses of its own people."[47] As a stigmatized actress, Binodini was placed squarely in the midst of these masses.

The Nationalist Stage

The nationalist stage played a large part in the making of a homogenous Hindu culture that sidelined any subversive subcultures. This upper-caste Hindu theater developed between the 1830s and 1860s under the patronage of

---

44. Chatterjee, "Nationalist Resolution of the Woman Question," 251.
45. See Rabindranath Tagore's novel, *Home and the World*, for a literary representation of the tension between these ideals.
46. Nair, *Women and Law in Colonial India*, 149.
47. Chatterjee, "Nationalist Resolution of the Woman Question," 251.

three groups, the gentry, social and religious reformer figures who used the theater to espouse a particular social or religious cause, and youngsters from upper-middle-class families. The period between the 1850s and '60s was one in which private theater, through the involvement particularly of the first two groups, became host to a growing bourgeois public sphere, with vibrant dispute and debate between reformists, traditionalists, and reactionaries in journals, public meetings (*sabhas*), and newspapers. As Binodini notes: "numerous men, educated, respected gentlemen, would also come because they were all so excited about the theater. The theater in those days was a place for . . . so much discussion on so many varied topics—I understood very little of it then, but I did realize that theater was in those times a meeting ground for a distinguished group of *bhadralok*."[48]

The heated discussions Binodini describes at these gatherings revolved around the construction of a nationalist public theater, the *sadharon rangalay*. This was a project gathering much steam during the latter half of the nineteenth century. It involved the construction of a unified Indian cultural identity against British influences and the establishment of the upper class as representative makers of a pure Hindu culture different from what was considered the 'vulgar' entertainment of the streets or of the Muslim population. It is not a surprise that this incipient nationalism was derived in part from the Orientalist construction of Hinduism, celebrating a predecadent, even pre-Islamic, wonder that was India.

Much of the construction of this Hindu nationalist identity was falsely universalizing; it took up major reformist issues of the time that revolved around the role of the upper-caste Hindu woman, including the promotion of widow remarriage,[49] but reformers did not seek to take radical stances vis-à-vis the emancipation of women. Instead they reformed selectively, endorsing issues such as widow remarriage only within conservative frameworks of upper-caste Hinduism. This meant that the public theater simultaneously occupied a space in which it espoused conservative reformist beliefs about the didactic purpose of a public stage but also a radical space in its employment of women in public roles, such as the actress. This contradiction explained why famous Hindu reformists and writers such as Ishwar Chandra Vidyasagar and Bankim Chandra abandoned the theater when women were hired from the prostitute quarters in 1873 to perform in reformist plays. The main contradiction representing this gap between theater's purported role to provide a

---

48. Dasi, "Amar Katha," 206.
49. See Sarkar and Sarkar, *Women and Social Reform in Modern India*. The Hindu Widows' Remarriage Act of 1856 legalized the remarriage of Hindu widows, which had been previously disallowed by a particular construction of Hindu tradition.

righteous education and public perceptions of it as a spectacle of moral degradation lay in the person of the public woman—the actress. The actress was targeted because she disturbed nationalism's foundational moral distinction between the home and the world, moving onto the public stage to enact the most private social relations.[50] She thus occupied the contradictory position of being both a sexual object and a performer of domestic reformist virtue.

Binodini's Life as an Actress: The Nexus of Colonial Capitalism and Nationalist Patriarchy

What was it like to be a young woman actress in Calcutta in the last decades of the nineteenth century? Binodini suffered much for being a woman employed at a time when an incipient colonial capitalism was just embedding itself into Bengali society. In this period, working for money and to appear in public was synonymous with being a prostitute. Her ostracization, then, was in part due to the unusual nature of a working woman in colonial Bengal, where colonial capitalism had resulted in a decline in the number of women who worked for money. As Nirmala Banerjee has shown, the British were investing in selected industries for processing local raw materials and agricultural products into commodities for overseas markets. Simultaneously, in order to promote their political, administrative, and economic interests, they were building a network of transport and communications institutions for imposing British systems of administration, commerce, education, and judiciary while also setting up support industries for training and building up professional services. This establishment of a capitalist economy destroyed the structure and organization of skilled traditional occupations within which women had been previously occupied.[51] At the same time that women were being sidelined as earners and participants in the public sphere, Binodini had no choice but to work for a wage, for she did not belong to the dominant native *bhadralok* class with its ties to the colonizers and was not yet married to a man who could provide her with the means to live.

Significantly, Binodini herself initially saw the limited freedom afforded by being a waged laborer as a bid toward achieving complete autonomy—a state in which she would not have to rely on and pander to upper-caste men to satisfy her material needs: "I had always worked for money. My mother believed that theatre work had finally put an end to our poverty—in the theatre was

---

50. Singh, "Foregrounding the Actress's Question," 272.
51. Banerjee, "Working Women in Colonial Bengal," 269–70.

enshrined our Lakshmi . . . working without wages did not make sense . . . if I am capable of taking care of myself and the expenses of my family through my exertions, I need not add to my burden of sins by selling my body, and torment myself besides."[52] For Binodini, selling her labor was an elevated act that was very different from the act of selling her body; for one was an act of autonomy and the other of compulsion. Yet, Binodini was soon to discover that working for a wage in this context would not earn her the deeper equality and respect she yearned for. The limited, formal, and ideological equality of capitalism lasted only as long as the moment of exchange itself, leaving her vulnerable to nationalist judgments of her acting as equivalent to prostitution.

Nationalist ideologies of upper-caste womanhood derided a woman who worked as an actress on the public stage. Actresses were regarded as the despicable opposites of the nationalist ideal of high-caste Hindu womanhood, who remained within the domestic sphere as a paragon of purity to be viewed only by her husband. A woman who worked in a profession that relied on the public gaze of men was the farthest one could get from such an ideal. By the late nineteenth and throughout the twentieth centuries, Binodini was scripted in public discourse as 'nati,' a word for public dancing woman that was increasingly a comment on sexuality rather than a primary indicator of occupational identity. The 'nati' became emblematic of the degraded morals of the metropolis. The derision received by actresses within public discourse was compounded by the fact that most actresses were recruited from the prostitute quarters, seeing the theater as a way out of prostitution in exchange for a reasonable if uncertain income. Although Binodini herself was not one of these, she did belong to an *a-bhadra* or 'disrespectable' household—usually those of women abandoned by husbands or those of widows without any source of legitimate male support. Calcutta was becoming known as a city of *a-bhadra* women, a *beshya shahar*, for widows as well as destitute *kulin* women flocked to the city from surrounding rural areas to make a living.[53] Sudhir Chakraborty points out that in 1853, prostitutes numbered 12,419; by 1867, the number had gone up to 30,000.[54] As both groups were considered *a-bhadra*, the terms prostitute-actress or *barangana-abhinetri* came to be used interchangeably. Thus Binodini was already read as a "fallen woman," outside of the nineteenth-century colonial and nationalist projects being constructed for women.

The interchangeability of the designation *barangana* and *abhinetri* is perhaps better understood when one considers that due to this marginalization, Binodini and other actresses often found themselves requiring a 'protector,' or

---

52. Dasi, "Amar Katha," 84.
53. Bhattacharya, "The Nautee," 191.
54. Chakraborty quoted in Bhattacharya, *My Story and My Life as an Actress*, 11.

ashroydata, a 'theaterer babu' from a respectable household who patronized the theater and who was also entitled to sexual liaisons with the actress with whom he was associated. Sometimes, the *ashroydata* would marry the actress according to the norms of *gandharva vivah*, as Binodini's *ashroydata* did for the twenty-five years they were together. Nevertheless, even as an *ashrita*, or one who is protected or sheltered, who was also the co-wife of a wealthy protector, Binodini as well as other women performing in the public theater thought of themselves as outcasts. As one of the actresses herself observed, they lived under the shadow of an accursed birth, a *janmashap* from which there was no escape. Binodini refers to herself as a *janmadukhini*, or one who is wretched from birth. *Amar Katha* contains repeated invocations of herself as a *patita*, or "fallen woman," undeserving of spiritual salvation or material advancement. She also refers to herself as "one abandoned by fate"—"*ei abhagini,*" "*naroker keet*"—literally "pest from hell," and "*khudro,*" or "little" and "tiny."[55] As Bhattacharya puts it, Binodini's *Amar Katha* testifies to how "the metropolitan theater, the most modern of dramatic representations in colonial India, paradoxically, came to house the most conservative statements about women."[56] Yet Binodini's autobiography can also be read against the grain as seeking to regain agency through embedded theatrical modes such as *rasa*. And such a reclamation of agency is carried out affectively through a rewriting of her life story, via the lens of Kalidasa's play, and in terms of extant dramatic models of freedom. This was not a far-fetched project, for both Binodini and Kalidasa's protagonist were being read through the trope of the fallen woman in need of redemption through a penitent Hindu piety. Binodini challenges this trope as well as the capitalist and nationalist notions of value that supported it.

Contesting the Nationalist Stage, Rewriting Sakuntala

In line with Victorian values and the process of constructing a homogenous national culture in which the Hindu wife was the *grhlakshmi*, or 'goddess of the home,' nationalist readings of *Sakuntala* laid an emphasis on female virtue, including the qualities of self-sacrifice, benevolence, devotion to her husband, religiosity, and sexual chastity. Thus, while criticized for her eroticism, Sakuntala would simultaneously be characterized by members of the *bhadralok* as a model of the "ideal wife."[57] This ambivalence toward Sakuntala is reflected

---

55. Dasi, "Amar Katha," 49–53. Translation mine.
56. Bhattacharya, *My Story and My Life as an Actress*, 38.
57. Tagore, *Sakuntala, Its Inner Meaning*, v–xiii.

in Tagore's 1907 interpretation of the play, which condemns Sakuntala's willing exercise of sexual desire and her *gandharva vivah,* an agreement to marry Dushyanta without parental sanction, as a "fall." However, Tagore also needs to reconcile this view with the nationalist notion of Sakuntala as an ideal wife, so he stresses the 'natural' innocence and 'simplicity' that led to Sakuntala's "fall," emphasizing "the deeper purity of her character—her unimpaired innate chastity . . . like the simple wild deer, the mountain spring, she stood forth pure in spite of mud." According to Tagore, it is precisely this "natural innate chastity" that enables Sakuntala to develop "into the model of a devoted wife, with her reserve, endurance of sorrow, and life of rigid spiritual discipline."[58] The moral imperative to make up for unrighteous behavior here falls on Sakuntala despite it being Dushyanta who seduced and then betrayed her. In fact, Tagore justifies Dushyanta's betrayal as a deserved response to Sakuntala's surrender to sexual desire.

Binodini's autobiography was published only five years after Tagore's essay characterized Sakuntala as a fallen woman and was likely a text she was familiar with. In any case, she would definitely have been familiar with the sentiments expressed by Tagore, for she herself had also married by *gandharva vivah* and had been accorded public censure for it. Significantly, echoing Tagore's categorization of Kalidasa's protagonist, the word 'patita,' or 'fallen' was also the one that Binodini used to describe herself repeatedly within her autobiography.[59] Such invocations of her own 'fallen' nature are not surprising; *Sakuntala* was perhaps the most famous theatrical text in late-nineteenth-century Bengal when Binodini was acting, and, given the pervasiveness of Jones's translation of *Sakuntala,* Binodini would have identified with the version of Kalidasa's protagonist as she had filtered down within colonialist and nationalist discourse. However, Binodini also deploys a very different Sakuntala than the 'fallen' child-woman, rewriting herself and Kalidasa's character through her autobiography. Binodini's text itself functions as a reincarnated *Sakuntala* through which she can reclaim an affective agency and critique the nationalist reformist discourses that subjected her to much misery over the course of her lifetime.

Amar Katha focuses on the pain of being judged as a "fallen woman" through a retelling of Binodini's own life story in terms that mirror Kalidasa's depiction of his female protagonist. However, unlike Orientalist and nationalist readings of *Sakuntala,* Binodini's focus is not on Sakuntala's and, by extension, her own 'fall' and subsequent elevation to wifehood, even though her own life story could and was being read through these plot points. Instead,

---

58. Ibid.
59. Dasi, "Amar Katha," 222.

Binodini critiques the men who have repeatedly taken advantage of and wronged her.

Binodini sets up this critique by establishing parallels between herself and Sakuntala as a "child of nature," casting herself as the playful holy river Ganga and evoking her own purity and sacredness. Binodini also offers an extensive commentary on a play in which she performed, *Prakrita Bandhu*, or *Nature's Friend*. Despite its relative lack of popularity and banal storyline, the play interested Binodini because it was also a weak imitation of Kalidasa's text. Binodini writes that the "role suited me perfectly," for the Sakuntala figure she played, Bonobasini, or 'forest maid,' was "simple and innocent and quite wild." Invoking Tagore, Binodini asserts that such an admission of simplicity rejects the idea that either she or Sakuntala need to practice penance for their 'fallen' natures:

> As to repentance! My entire life has been wasted in repentance. I have been repentant at every step; had there been the means to correct my life I would have realized the fruits of repentance. But has repentance borne anything? Even now I am swept along like a bit of grass overwhelmed by the current. I do not then know what you mean by repentance. Why do I not receive mercy when I lie at His vast doors, my heart burdened with pain?[60]

Here, Binodini sustains the metaphor of herself as a divine and pure 'child of nature,' while suggesting that calls for her to practice 'penance' have reduced her from the holy river Ganga to nothing more than "a bit of grass overwhelmed by the current." In an exceptionally bitter passage that rejects any responsibility for her degraded status within society, Binodini asserts that her position is not her fault. Women like her become "prostitutes forced by circumstances, lacking shelter, lacking a space."[61]

Binodini also presents a second reworking of Kalidasa's character—not only was Binodini herself a wronged Sakuntala figure, but so was her deceased daughter, a figure who repeatedly acts as a structuring device for her autobiography. Binodini named her own daughter Sakuntala and characterized her through the same natural metaphors that Kalidasa used to describe his protagonist: "In that loving, trusting heart of hers was manifested the purity of the goddess Devi, the exquisite splendor of flowers, the pure sound of the gurgling waters of the river Jahnavi. Like a blossoming

---

60. Ibid., 57.
61. Ibid., 105.

lotus, the purity of her sweet nature brought constant happiness to my life."[62] The continual repetition of 'purity' stresses the extent to which mother and daughter were innocent yet wronged.

Finally, Binodini's *Amar Katha* features another Sakuntala to replace nationalist versions of the character, the autobiographical text itself. The *gatha* form included the fairly common reference to one's work as a daughter, as opposed to the more neutral *santaan* or 'child.' Within this convention, a woman writer (mother) was allowed to express the kind of hope for her book (daughter) that she may not have on behalf of her real-life daughter. The text births words to rebirth these two overwritten or lost figures (progressive iterations of Kalidasa's protagonist and Binodini's deceased daughter), aiming to transport the author's feelings to others. Through this new Sakuntala as text, Binodini carries out a dramatic recuperation of Kalidasa's heroine, drawing on Sanskritic dramatic theory to cast defining episodes in her life in the language of *rasa* and *bhava*. In doing so, she causes the audience to affectively identify themselves with her experiences rather than through the judgmental discourse of the 'fallen woman.' Binodini's investing of this continuum of Sakuntala figures—Kalidasa's precolonial heroine, herself, her daughter, and her autobiographical text—with an affective agency suggests that Binodini's text is not just a response to and rejection of nationalist readings of Kalidasa's play. It is also constructed and constituted partly through indigenous dramatic principles to render herself as possessed by an affective agency.

The assertion that *Amar Katha* can be interpreted as a dramatic rewriting of *Sakuntala* that performs an affective agency through *rasa* dramatic principles recognizes the prevalence of a continuing, if uneven, precolonial dramatic tradition. The latter had survived the colonial influence on Bengali theater, which resulted in a "systematic reorganization of theater . . . generating hierarchies that relegated indigenous forms to a "low" status, as opposed to the high and privileged status accorded to European drama, notably Shakespeare."[63] Yet Binodini refused such divisions, imbibing post-Enlightenment ideas of individual freedom while also harnessing the contextual universalism of affective agency within *rasa* dramatics. In the following sections, I show how Binodini connected both concepts of freedom in resistance to the colonial capitalist and nationalist ideological and material structures that oppressed her.

---

62. Ibid., 106.
63. Bhatia, *Modern Indian*, xv. See also Bhatia, *Acts of Authority/Acts of Resistance*, 17; and Chatterjee, *The Nation and Its Fragments*, 7–8 on this split.

Post-Enlightenment Conceptions of Negative Freedom in *Amar Katha*

By the late nineteenth century formal English education had become widespread, creating a substantial intelligentsia that could read English texts in the original. As Sudipta Kaviraj elaborates, Bengalis developed an insatiable curiosity about European political and social theory, which almost entirely replaced Hindu scriptures. Individualist liberalism had the deepest influence in colonial Bengal, and young people and intellectuals eagerly debated the arguments of John Stuart Mill.[64] Thus the prominent Bengali novelist Bankim Chandra Chattopadhyay wrote a widely discussed essay called *Samya* (*Equality*), in which he drew heavily from Rousseau and Mill to mount a strident critique of social inequalities. Mill was among the first to recognize the difference between what Isaiah Berlin would later call positive and negative freedom, or between liberty as the freedom to act on the basis of a rational will and liberty as the absence of coercion. Mill propounded the latter, stressing "the importance, to man and society, of a large variety in types of character, and of giving full freedom to human nature to expand itself in innumerable and conflicting directions."[65] Hypocritically for a colonial official, Mill argued against the coercion of people's opinions and behavior, contending that a person should be free to do whatever he chooses, provided that he does no harm to others. Binodini's immediate environment was made up of the young men who were reading these texts and imbibing principles of moral and cognitive autonomy from them. It did not take long for these men to extrapolate from these ideals and take up the causes of widow remarriage and companionate marriage. As Kaviraj points out, young men increasingly began thinking about their moral right to decide whom they wished to marry rather than allow their families to arrange their marriages.[66]

Binodini's autobiographical account testifies to these social trends and points to the failure of these ideas to extend to figures like her. Several of the wealthy young men who became Binodini's 'protectors' were part of this educated *bhadralok* class and yet treated her as an inferior being who did not deserve the benefits of familial life that were due to high-caste womanhood. In one passage, Binodini thus describes the deceit of one of her protectors who had promised to marry her but then betrayed her by entering into an arranged marriage with a social equal. Binodini explains:

---

64. Kaviraj, "Ideas of Freedom in Modern India," 105, 107.
65. Mill, *Autobiography of John Stuart Mill*, 249.
66. Kaviraj, "Ideas of Freedom in Modern India," 110.

> This was the time when I fell into the direst of circumstances. Unfortunate and fallen women, prostitutes such as us, have always to endure changes in fortune. The path that we are destined to take is always condemned but it seems to be a rule of our life that whenever we want to walk on the path of virtue, evil will inevitably appear to waylay us. . . . Do we not desire a husband's love? But where are we to find it? Who will give us their hearts in return for our own? Is there one who would put his heart to the test and find out whether we have anything like a heart?[67]

Binodini's words point to the ways that within the nationalist patriarchy she lived in, all labor exchanged for a wage—whether it was prostitution or acting—was judged in the same way. Binodini describes oppressive social mores as "the rule of our life," "the path we are destined to take," terms that highlight her lack of choice. Any sort of enactment of her free will is made impossible and preemptively smothered by "evil." Binodini's transference of the way that freedom was being discussed among the colonized liberal intelligentsia to describe the coercive pressures on a 'fallen woman' suggest that she was likely internalizing the abstract European theorizations of individual autonomy that pervaded her intellectual and social environs.

Binodini recognized such systemic oppressions as the result of collusions between a newly forming capitalist economy and nationalist patriarchal ideologies—both of which excluded women such as her from respectably participating in a profession in a truly equal way. The equivalence between prostitution and acting because of their similar reduction to the money form led to her 'protector' asking her to refuse her wages. This demand was itself ironic and hypocritical considering that the young man in question 'kept' her by paying for her upkeep. Moreover, it highlights colonial Bengal's opposing and ultimately irreconcilable views of capitalist waged labor, especially for women—one as the path to true autonomy and the other as complete commodification of the self. This state of affairs caused Binodini to be continually shuttled between opposing ideals: she was the famed actress as romantic love interest, deserving of a companionate marriage, but she was simultaneously also nothing more than a prostitute whose acceptance of payment from her professional work demeaned her as well as her 'protector.' Aware of these dichotomous pressures, Binodini harnessed a post-Enlightenment ideal of freedom as the absence of coercion and clearly labels any demands that she not work as forms of compulsion: "If I had once set my mind on doing something, no one could persuade me to change it . . . forbidding me with vehe-

---

67. Dasi, "Amar Katha," 84.

mence or force never served to deter me from my purpose." True to these words, Binodini insists on living free of constraints and refuses the young man's money as compensation for her not to work:

> I was enraged at his words. I stood up and told him "you can keep your money. It is I who have earned the money and not the other way around. Leave me now!"[68]

This response refuses her own commodification as an object to be bought and sold. Instead, Binodini highlights an agentive self, an 'I' that precedes exchange and who "earned the money and not the other way around." This positing of a universal human subject who can act independently of social constraints testifies to Binodini's constant striving to act against the twinned nexus of patriarchal-nationalist and capitalist-colonialist constraints. She consistently harnesses a liberal conception of freedom as the absence of coercion to argue for the right to fulfillment through work as well as the right to escape being designated a polluted fallen woman. In the process, Binodini went radically beyond the boundaries of the more prominent nationalist and colonialist agendas for the new women.

Performing Affective Agency within an Embedded Dramatic Tradition

Significantly, the conceptual network of freedom in Binodini's lifetime did not just include the liberal notion of absence from coercion but also a notion of positive freedom as one that resulted from self-mastery, involving reasoning through what path would be best to choose and then acting on the basis of such a rational process. While Enlightenment thinkers of such a 'positive freedom' were also being read in colonial Bengal, positive freedom within Binodini's syncretic conceptual network took the form of the emotional rationality of affective agency, a contextual universalism that arose out of Binodini's deep immersion in indigenous dramatic traditions.

Amar Katha is replete with references to indigenous dramatic and literary traditions, including the Sanskrit dramatic, bhakti, and *puranic* literatures. As Bhattacharya notes, in the actual process of interpreting and producing a play, traditional and folk performance forms exercised more influence than did Western models. These indigenous mediations need to be placed alongside

---

68. Ibid.

rather than simply against the English literature materials that Binodini was familiar with. Indeed, to read her dramatic self-representation as having been constructed primarily by a colonial grid is to ignore whole domains of being. A significant range of these other domains can be successfully traced to a precolonial Indian dramatic tradition in its late-nineteenth-century iterations, which, following the *Natya Shastra,* divided texts into sections entitled *ankur* (seed or germ), *pallah* (leaf), *kusum* (flower), and *phal* (fruit). Binodini makes use of this convention in her account of her professional career as a performer, signposting in the process the history of the public stage. She uses headings such as "Seed," "The First story: From Bud to Lead," and "The Second Leaf: On Stage" to map her career as it moved through stages of apprenticeship to fame.

Moreover, Binodini's informal education relied largely on the dramatic teachings of Girish Ghosh, who would couch his instruction in the vocabulary of English literature but also of Sanskrit dramaturgy, in particular, of *bhava.* Referring to Ghosh's mentoring, Binodini writes: "His was a wonderful teaching method: first, he would explain the *bhava* of the role in question; then, he asked me to memorize the lines."[69] As noted earlier, in acting a role, an actress was required to embody a particular *bhava* completely so as to successfully give birth to and transfer its corresponding *rasa,* or mood, to the audience. Indeed, the actress was to be a vehicle for feelings—a *patra* (literally, a vessel), for the translation of *bhava* into expression, gesture, and movement. This process defined Binodini's response to any text she encountered, including European literatures: "I did not merely listen to these stories, but absorbed from them whatever I could of their *bhava* and then constantly meditated on it."[70]

This kind of self-constitution through indigenous as well as European dramaturgy was very different from what Vasudha Dalmia describes as the nationalist Sanskritization of the Indian stage in which historical plays were used to establish the "historicity of the national past, seen primarily in Hindu terms, as contained and perpetuated within the frame and conventions of classical Sanskrit drama, and as filtered through the various influences of the times."[71] For, unlike Binodini's self-constitution partly through indigenous dramaturgy, the nationalist instrumentalization of a constructed Sanskritic tradition was 'neo-Sanskritic'—deliberate, systematic, and political. Binodini's, on the other hand, was produced circumstantially, interpretationally, and personally through diffuse structures of feeling within a continuing though fragmented precolonial dramatic tradition. Binodini herself would likely not have been able to separate the conjoined genealogies of affective agency from

---

69. Ibid., 78.
70. Ibid., 80.
71. Dalmia, *Poetics, Plays and Performances,* 49.

liberal ideals of individual freedom; she was produced by, and drew on, all these influences according to whichever suited her project of demos expansion. This chapter traces an embedded genealogy of affective agency to show that the sole emphasis on colonial universalizing ideologies has made it difficult to recuperate the former and to fill in the resulting gap in the story of postcolonial demos expansion.

Binodini writes *Amar Katha* as a dramatic text through Sanskrit theory; she embodies the *bhavas* of sympathy, pity, sorrow, and self-pity (*shoka*) and anger (*krodha*) to incite the corresponding *rasas* of pathos (*karuna*) and fury (*raudra*) in her audience in response to the treatment she undergoes. In its use of these dramatic principles, her performative life-text blurs the distinction between acting and the autobiographical project of relating real life events. In fact, Binodini begins her autobiography with words proclaiming that her life is the stuff of drama: "And now, if you still have patience enough, listen to the dramatic story of my life."[72] The conflation of real life story and drama is a prominent *rasa-ic* (and Shakespearean) theme throughout the text. Describing a death, Binodini writes: "Such things happen regularly in the theater of our everyday life, the *natyashala* (theater) of *sansar* (society). Nothing stops for anybody, only he who is gone is gone. Those who have stayed on, perform their assigned roles and then leave."[73]

Such a blurring between acting a fictional role and real life was partly a result of a process of training in indigenous dramaturgy so complete that Binodini approached her own life as the practice of playing different roles and embodying particular *bhava* effectively. In other words, Binodini collapses her real life persona into characters she plays and her actress self into a writerly self. Her writing of her life thus becomes a performance dependent on self-conscious role-playing. Writing functioned as Binodini's substitute for acting, for she used prose to translate the embodiment of *bhava* into words. And, in both her real life/writerly and fictional/dramatic modes, she appears as a dramatic character, an inspirer of *bhava* and a transmitter of *rasa*.

How, then, does Binodini's autobiography itself function as a performative text in line with these *rasa-ic* dramatic principles? First, Binodini dwells on her training as an actress at length, explaining the requirements of embodying particular *bhava* and of splitting herself into the many selves of the characters she plays during her theatrical career.

> In order to experience as many *bhavas* as possible, I kept . . . living in the world of imagination. Perhaps that is why, whatever role I happened to play,

---

72. Dasi, "Amar Katha," 66.
73. Dasi, "Amar Abhinetrir Jibon," 150.

> I never lacked the *bhava* necessary to portray that character. I never felt that I was acting to dazzle others or simply because I was a salaried actress. I forgot my own self: the joys and sorrows of the character I played were mine and I was always surprised to find that I was only acting out these emotions.[74]

In line with Bharata Muni's injunctions in the *Natya Shastra,* this is a transformation so complete that it blurs the distinction between an actress performing the role of a character and her embodying of the character's emotions. How this happens in practice is more easily understood when one considers cognitive psychologist Elaine Hatfield's research into the ways that emotional experience is affected and produced through facial, vocal, postural, and movement mimicry in daily interactions. Individuals change their own emotional states on the basis of their expressive behavior, or 'acting,' in the course of their regular interactions with each other. The emotional experiences of subjects tend to be affected by the facial expressions they adopt.[75] This is a process that occurs unconsciously among nonactors during daily interactions but also one that a highly skilled actress is able to consciously perfect. Indeed, this process enables Binodini to effectively become the characters she performs so that for the duration of the performance she embodies different emotional states. Through this process, Binodini is able to transcend her commodification as a "salaried actress," for her identity is not exclusively determined by the ideological constraints that bound her as a working woman.

Secondly, Binodini mirrors this onstage dramatic procedure in her writing. Because her writing is itself a dramatic performance of her life, and because she collapses her autobiographical self into the characters/roles she plays, the readers of her life story come to take the place of a dramatic audience to whom she transmits the *rasas* of fury—*raudra*—and pathos—*karuna*. She thereby prompts the reader/audience to undergo what she experiences, so that they may understand her actions and successfully question and overturn the labels through which she was judged. As Abhinavagupta puts it, "*rasa* does not consist in the inference of someone else's mental state but is a personal experience—the spectator identifies himself with this mental state and lives it himself."[76] Theoretically there is, then, no distinction between the emotions felt by the characters in a drama and those felt by the actor and the audience—drama becomes reality, thereby suggesting that a character's response to particular emotions are aimed at producing adequate agentive actions in the character as in the actor and audience. In transferring her character's/her own

---

74. Dasi, "Amar Katha," 81.
75. Hatfield, "Emotional Contagion," 96–97.
76. Abhinavagupta, *The Aesthetic Experience*, 80.

pain to the audience, Binodini displaces interpretations of herself as a 'fallen woman' in need of repentance. The many selves of her autobiography become possessed of an affective agency that 'moves' both her and the reader/audience away from oppressive discursive frameworks of the fallen woman. In other words, just as in the precolonial *Sakuntala,* Binodini's text frames her own actions not as predetermined by dominant patriarchal discourses of the time but as arising in the body in response to particular instances of mistreatment. In the process, the character of Binodini personifies particular *bhavas,* thus transferring appropriate *rasas* to the audience and working to revise oppressive hierarchies in accordance with her will.

Two main episodes instrumentalize this affective agency. The first is the episode of the Star Theater when Binodini was denied the right to have the theater named after her because she was a 'fallen woman,' despite being central to its inception and construction. In 1883, a young Marwari businessman, smitten by Binodini, offered to build a theater for the company and give her shares in it if she became his mistress. This was an offer that would have enabled Binodini to escape poverty, please her colleagues, as well as acquire a theater of her own. In recognition of her decision, the new theater was to be called Binodini Theater. Binodini writes: "I had set my mind on acting and had resolved that on no account would I be bound to him if the theater was not made for me . . . it was at my insistence that land was leased on Beadon Street and [the Marwari businessman] began spending unlimited sums of his money."[77] However, when the time came, her colleagues registered it as the Star Theater since it was felt that naming a theater after a *patita* would not be good for business. Used and then abandoned, the character of Binodini within the autobiography reclaims her agency through an affective process:

> When they came back after the registration (everything was ready by then . . . the theater was to open within a few weeks) I asked them anxiously what name they had given the new theater. "The Star" Dasu Babu had said with some satisfaction. I was so affected by this news that I sat down and was incapable of speech for the next two minutes. A little later, controlling myself, I said "Alright."[78]

Just as in Kalidasa's *Sakuntala,* the female protagonist of Binodini's autobiography responds to situations through an affective lens; Binodini's body and mind do not function separately here; her cognition of the situation is a bodily one. Her affective response to the betrayal is one of grief, and it is so power-

---

77. Dasi, "Amar Katha," 88–89.
78. Ibid., 89.

ful that it 'moves' her to sit down, thereby transmitting the *karuna rasa*. We, as the reading/watching audience, see in our mind's eye a Binodini staggered by the depth of the betrayal and the casual way it is conveyed to her, thereby experiencing the pathos of the situation ourselves.

Moreover, this affective performance of the ill treatment she experiences is described as the direct precursor to an appropriate action that is derived from the affective texture of the betrayal; Binodini clarifies that it is this incident that directly leads to her quitting the stage:

> I wondered afterwards, was all their love and affection only a show of words to get some work out of me? I had never dreamt that they would deceive me and behave in such a dishonest manner. The grief that I had not felt in my refusal of such a huge sum of money I now felt intensely . . . eventually, it became virtually impossible to continue working in the theater because of various kinds of estrangements and betrayals. . . . I loved the theater very much. But I have not been able to forget the blows of deception. . . . Consequently, I had to take leave from the stage.[79]

Just as in Kalidasa's play and Sanskrit dramatic theory, Binodini describes the 'determinants' or situation leading to her decision as arising from affective anubhava or 'consequents.' She deploys affective descriptions of the blows of deception, grief, and hurt as direct dramatic precursors to her decision to leave the theater. These affects build up a sense of self that transcends and exceeds the compulsions of a commodified actress who can be exchanged for "a huge sum of money." This is a radical explanation for Binodini's reason to quit acting, given that it completely counteracts contemporary castings of Binodini as a woman who left the stage after receiving enlightenment about the errors of her ways at the hands of the holy Ramakrishna. Indeed, a rewriting of these mainstream perceptions of Binodini's blessing by Ramakrishna appears as the second pivotal moment in her autobiography.

The episode depicting Binodini's performance of the eponymous bhakti saint in *Sri Chaitanya* is a focal point in *Amar Katha*, for it led directly to her being blessed by the saint-guru Ramakrishna. Nevertheless, this was a role that must have turned Binodini inside out. As she tells us, the process of Ghosh's training her for the role of a *patit-paban*, or redeemer of the fallen, ironically also involved an acceptance of herself as a fallen woman in need of redemption:

---

79. Ibid., 90.

He advised a lowly woman such as I on how best to bring alive and in the most subtle manner, the character of that divine being. Chaitanya ... was *patit-paban* and His grace was boundless. I listened to him fearfully. My mind was tormented by doubts and I wondered how I was ever to find a way out of the abyss. I called out to Him at all times: O *Patit-paban!* Look kindly upon this lowly fallen woman!⁸⁰

Thus Binodini was forced to embody a seeming contradiction: both a *patit*, or fallen, and *patit-paban*, or redeemer of the fallen. Yet, rather than dwelling on her own unworthiness to play the role of a divine persona, Binodini uses the episode as an opportunity to establish herself as one deserving of grace. This redemption is not described as a charitable forgiveness of her past sins, however, but as a well-deserved recognition by Sri Ramakrishna of Binodini's own divinity, embodied in her acting. For the *Natya Shastra* and precolonial interpreters of the treatise such as Abhinavagupta describe true acting as akin to the process of achieving spiritual salvation (*moksha*)—a complete loss of the self through union with the divine.⁸¹ Within this schema, the dominant *rasa* of a successful work always resolves itself into *santas-rasa*, the *rasa* of peace, a temporary and partial version of the endless and perfect peace that accompanies *moksha* due to the self's separation from its individual ego:⁸²

> It was as though a powerful light filled my heart ... my body thrilled and all of me filled with a blossoming. Everything around me appeared obscured by a mist. When I argued with the teacher and said "Prabhu, what is one to another? All is Krishna!" I truly felt it ... in joy and exultation I cried. . . . There was no consciousness of the "I" within me.⁸³

Binodini portrays her acting of the role of Sri Chaitanya as a spiritual process of enlightenment in which her many selves—writer/actress/character in the autobiography or play—become one with God, losing any "consciousness of 'I.'" As she states: "It seemed as if my own spirit leapt out from within me and sought refuge at the lotus feet of Hari." This is an enactment of the universalizing bhakti notion that every being has a divine consciousness within her that can be realized through ethical work in the world, itself a form of spiritual practice. Once again, within the drama of her textual as well as onstage performance, it is Binodini's body that affectively embodies the recognition of her

---

80. Ibid., 92.
81. Abhinavagupta, *The Dhvanyaloka of Anandavardhana*, 226.
82. Abhinavagupta, *The Aesthetic Experience*, 86–87, 96–97.
83. Dasi, "Amar Katha," 93.

divinity through the "powerful light that filled my heart" and her body "thrilling" and "blossoming." Through these affective *anubhava*, Binodini embodies the *devbhava*, or *bhava* of divinity, that elevates her to a form of holiness in her own right. Binodini the writer/actress/character challenges the reader to contradict her own divine nature, despite it having been affectively embodied onstage and even recognized by Sri Ramakrishna: "my body that was dedicated to the theater had truly been blessed. If the world looks upon me with contempt, it does not matter to me, for I know that he who was the most worthy of worship, Ramakrishna, has been kind to me."[84] Such an account effectually rewrites the narrative of Binodini as having been "redeemed" by Ramakrishna, instead reinforcing a perception of Binodini as the affective agent of her own salvation.

Amar Katha stresses the power of Binodini the writer/actress/character's divinity and her embodiment of *devbhava* to transfer the mood of salvation, the *shanta-rasa,* to her audience within a process of dissensus:

> That I had indeed received His (God's) grace was confirmed by the response of the many wise and discerning members of the audience . . . some of the women in the audience would sob so loudly that my own heart trembled. The heart rending cries, my own excitement, and the enthusiasm of the spectators would affect me to a point where I would be completely overwhelmed by my own tears.[85]

Binodini's transfer of *shanta-rasa* to a shared space that can be inhabited by both her and her audience is carried out through her own affective embodiment of divinity, a process that orchestrates demos expansion. Through the embodiment of *bhava,* Binodini is able to keep her sense of self intact from the oppressive structures of colonial capitalism and nationalist patriarchy that constantly buffet her. These forms of power cannot overdetermine or surmount affective agency, even as they threaten and often do overpower Binodini.

III. *RASA* AND AFFECTIVE AGENCY IN POSTCOLONIAL BOLLYWOOD

While *Sakuntala* no longer remains a defining text of the era, the indigenous theatrics of freedom it contains continue to linger. This section returns to the text with which I started, *Kabhi Khushi Kabhie Gham* (*K3G*). The 2001

---

84. Ibid., 95–96.
85. Ibid., 96.

film was a superhit, grossing a worldwide total of $19 million and earning the status of the highest-grossing Indian film ever and the fifth-highest grosser in world history, with Box Office India calling it "one of the true worldwide blockbusters of Hindi cinema."[86] The film's director, Karan Johar, is a young Hindu descended from the Bollywood elite. He is one of the biggest names in Bollywood production, known for directing romantic family dramas centered on the Hindu joint family. The film itself is a hegemonic text marked by neoliberal ideals of individualism and self-development as they conspire with Hindu patriarchies. Yet I choose this hegemonic rather than subaltern text, a clear misfit when compared with my other primary texts, because its ideas of freedom pertaining to upper-caste Hindu women testify to the complexity of their position within colonial and postcolonial modernity. These women were not 'subaltern' figures in the sense that Guha describes when he speaks of an autonomous sphere of resistance that was wholly removed from elite domains. For upper-caste Hindu women were subjugated *within* the interstices of elite configurations of power as they were buttressed by caste, colonialism, and capitalism and could only resist their subjugation through these structures. *K3G* is a film that portrays and also issues from this elite nexus of colonial and postcolonial Hindu identity as it continues to register on the body of the Hindu woman. Its complex status as an elite patriarchal text that nevertheless deals with freeing that woman is compounded by the complexity of the *rasa* universalism through which it does so for, as we have seen, affective agency issued from an elite as well as more marginalized lineage from the time of Kalidasa onward.

The film concerns a wealthy Indian businessman, Yash Raichand, his wife Nandini, their adopted son Rahul, and their younger biological son, Rohan. Rahul falls in love with Anjali, a girl from a much lower social class, but Yash forbids Rahul to marry her. Rahul initially agrees to obey his father but then eventually weds Anjali after the death of her father leaves her helpless and alone. As a result, Yash disowns Rahul. He stresses the value of 'blood' ties over other relationships, stating that his biological son would never have committed such an action. Heartbroken, Rahul leaves for London with Anjali. Ten years later, Rohan, home from college, finally learns why his brother left and travels to London, eventually succeeding in bringing his brother back to the family.

The film's affirmation of personal freedom through this plot is a reflection of its universalizing message, for the film remains critical of Yash's rejection of Anjali as a daughter-in-law because of her inferior social standing and of Yash's disowning of Rahul. Rahul's decision to marry Anjali anyway, as Patrick

---

86. Box Office India, "Ten Years On: Kabhi Khushi Kabhie Gham," last modified 16 December 2011, http://www.planetsrk.com/community/threads/10-years-since-kabhi-khushi-kabhi-gham.25047/.

Colm Hogan affirms, thus becomes an illustration of one of the film's main themes: a "romantic affirmation of individual choice." The film offers a "general critique of identity categorization," and the discourses that buttress such categories. And it does so through a syncretic conceptual network pertaining to freedom grounded in embedded as well as post-Enlightenment principles.

Such syncretism is not self-evident, for the film itself simplistically sets up a binary between wholesome Indian—read Hindu—'tradition' and corrupting 'Western modernity.' Tradition is represented through fetishized Hindu rituals, *pativratadharma*, and family unity, and modernity through helicopters, degrees from London business schools, scantily clad blond women, and fancy cars.

Rahul functions as the symbolic embodiment of both tradition and modernity, showing that the advantages of 'Western modernity'—above all, individualism and self-development—must be restrained and transformed by Hindu 'tradition.' In London, Rahul and his small family are the lost children of Mother India and through them the film constantly implies that the traditional Indian identity is threatened in Western exile. In this context, the film's opening subtitle, "It's all about loving your parents," carries a reference not just to the community of the family but to an imagined community of conservative tradition represented by the Hindu nation-state, or *Hindutva*, that Rahul and his family still belong to.

Aside from reinforcing such stereotypical binaries, the film is awash with a celebration of consumerism, with emotional reunion scenes that take place in shopping malls as well as the glorification of Euro-American brand-name clothes and fancy cars. These instances suggest that the film forgets the link between consumerism and the oppressive notions of social class it also critiques and even buys into the conflation of democratic universalisms with capitalism. However, one of the film's major subtexts also testifies to the productive harnessing of truly syncretic conjoined genealogies of autonomy and self-determination, which exceed and resist the ideological schisms and social divisions that global capitalism produces.

An important element of this syncretic conceptual network is a post-Enlightenment conception of individual freedom derived from Kantian notions of free actions as rooted in reason. Kant refers to the exercise of such 'practical reason' as "the power to overcome the impressions on our faculty of sensuous desire."[87] Yet this notion of individual freedom exists with, and is fundamentally altered by, the contextual universalism of affective agency. For the latter depicts and harnesses an embodied cognition by demonstrating the ways that rational choices and actions are themselves produced by affective

---

87. *The Critique of Pure Reason*, 633.

FIGURE 4. Nandini worships Yash at a family *puja*. Source: Still from *Kabhi Khushi Kabhie Gham*.

bonds, which include but are not limited to "sensuous desire." These affective bonds can lead to a self-realization that exceeds the value of individuals as sellers or consumers within global capitalism.

K3G's syncretic affective rationality is one in which rational motives cohere with dominant affective moods such as the *sringara rasa* of romantic love or the *vatsalya rasa* of love between a parent and child. Indeed, many Bollywood films such as *K3G* involve the prevalent use of *rasa* as a structuring principle. This means that the main aim of a film, whatever the genre, commonly remains the transfer of emotional moods to the audience. As Matthew Jones explains, "before a film is made the writer, director, actors, etc. determine the emotion that is to be elicited. This is *rasic* in nature, even if the final performance is not dictated by the theory of *rasa*. . . . *Rasa* theory mandates that performers become the living embodiment of the *rasa* they are depicting. Character development, story progression and realism are put aside in order for the performer to convey completely the grief, anger, fear or whichever *rasa* they desire for the performance."[88] The dominant *bhava* and *rasa* that configures the film is not *sringara* or *vira* as in *Sakuntala*, nor *karuna* or *raudra* as in *Amar Katha* but *vatsalya*, the mood pertaining to the love between a parent and child.

---

88. See Jones, "Bollywood, Rasa and Indian Cinema," 33–43.

Kabhi Khushi Kabhie Gham declares that *vatsalya* is the central *rasa* in its opening titles with the declarative heading, "It's all about loving your parents." And taking a cue from the *kavya nataka*, Johar employs affective *anubhava* to do with *vatsalya* in service of his humanist message of exercising one's free will against authoritarian and chauvinist identity categories. Nandini remains a symbolic evocation of *vatsalya rasa*. She offers unconditional love to her son even when he elopes, acting as a counterpoint to her husband's discriminatory views. At the beginning of the film, Nandini states that there is no answer to the question of how much a mother loves her son for that love is an *ehsaas*, an Urdu word synonymous with a sensation/feeling. In other words, *vatsalya* is affective, with a reach beyond what can be articulated through words or the worldly, material laws that discriminate against people based on their social backgrounds. To convey this point, Johar glorifies the affect between Rahul and his mother through strategically invoked *anubhava* that alert the audience to the mother's bodily cognition of her son's presence even before she has laid eyes on him. For instance, a breeze that ruffles his mother's sari symbolizes Rahul's affective connection to her even when he is absent, prompting Nandini to run down the stairs and throw open the front doors in anticipation of him.

The affective *vatsalya rasa* alters the post-Enlightenment Kantian concept of individual freedom because instead of precluding rational judgment, Nandini's embodiment of *vatsalya* produces rational evaluations of her situation, rendering rationality the product of affective sensuous impulses. Such a rational affective agency is depicted in the exchange between Nandini and Yash I quote in Story One at the beginning of this chapter. Nandini denigrates Yash's behavior and suggests that it was irrational for her to worship him as a god:

> Mother always told me that a husband is a god. No matter what he says—no matter what he thinks—he is always right. Whatever he does is right. You brought Rahul home one day. Right. But then one day Rahul left. Wrong. You let him go. Wrong. You separated a mother from her child. Wrong. Our family shattered to pieces. Wrong. Then how does a husband become god? My husband is just a husband, just a husband, not god. Not god.[89]

Here, Nandini challenges her mother's *pativrata* conviction that a husband is a god by subjecting it to Kantian rational testing, evaluating "its coherence with the criteria of [her] actual experience," which, for Nandini, is above all the *vatsalya rasa* pertaining to her love for her son. Listing Yash's violations of these affective familial bonds, Nandini concludes that empirical evidence flies

---

89. Johar, *Kabhi Khushi Kabhi Gham*. Translation mine.

in the face of her worship of him, for Yash has behaved like a petty, fallible being rather than as a god. Truly rational choices are in fact those that cohere with the evidence of affective ties.

In contrast to the elevation of Nandini, the film consistently denigrates Yash for acting in a way that privileges an instrumental reason over affect.

> YASH: I cannot tolerate that an ordinary girl from a commonplace locality live in this house. You didn't even once think about the appropriateness of that girl, her background, status or breeding. How did you even dare to think that she can be a part of our family? That she can be a part of *my* family? How did you think . . . ?
> RAHUL: When did I think papa? I didn't think at all. I just loved . . . love.[90]

Yash is so opposed to his son's choice of wife because she is the daughter of a sweet shop owner from a "down market" bazaar area, a judgment that relies on a capitalist rationality that evaluates the girl through her social status, precluding affective ties. Rahul, on the other hand, casts his falling in love as a form of affective agency, responding that he did not "think" in this manner at all. Thus he suggests that the affect of romantic love takes precedent over the criteria upheld by Yash, who, as Meheli Sen comments, "gathers much of his political and emotional charge from his ability to speak from positions that are emphatically those aligned to the new India being envisaged by the bourgeoisie at this time. This Father is aligned to the world of big business—ranging from heavy industry to corporate finance."[91] Indeed, Yash represents corporate competence working alongside a heavyweight patriarchal 'tradition' in an era of economic liberalization, and his home is awash with Hindu rituals and husband worship as well as consumable wealth. In fact, Yash's 'traditional' patriarchal power comes from his control of capital. This nexus of patriarchal capitalist rationality is demonstrated in the speech through which Yash names Rahul as his business heir:

> YASH: This is for you my son. From today, the Raichand empire belongs to you. Follow the steps of your grandfather. He said life always offers you many paths to choose from. Never take a step in life that will bring shame to your family name or prestige. Anyone can make money but earning respect is not as easy. Promise me that you will follow the tradi-

---

90. Ibid. Translation mine.
91. Sen, "'It's All About Loving Your Parents:' Liberalization, Hindutva and Bollywood's New Fathers," 156.

tions of this family. Promise me that you'll never compromise the self-respect of this family.

RAHUL: I promise that I will always keep the family name flying high. I promise you that I will always keep you happy papa.[92]

Yash in effect asks Rahul to make sure that capitalist rationality represented by his business 'empire' guides all of Rahul's choices and produces his 'free' will. The family name here is both a patriarchal slogan of tradition and the brand of the "Raichand empire"—which has to do with "prestige" and "making money." The "right path" that Rahul must follow, then, is one that collapses the universalizing logic of capital as it spreads into new markets, into the path that preserves the "traditions of this family." Yash relates self to other solely through the lens of capital so that personal freedom here is reduced to consumer choice. Indeed, his choice of daughter-in-law is a girl from the same social class and business background as himself. Within this matrix, the individual's right to free 'choice' refers to a broader cultural logic of a free-market economy so that the system that determines subjects' right to choose between multiple commodities also governs other aspects of existence. In effect, the father and the capitalist discourses that he embodies end up reducing 'choices,' rendering the idea of free will obsolete.

The opposition between the truly democratic universalism of affective agency and the universalizing force of capitalism is constantly referenced in the film. Even Anjali, for instance, first mistakes Rahul's unlikely romantic interest in her as evidence that he wants to buy out her father's small sweet shop. In response, Rahul rejects his father's instrumental capitalist rationality as the only way to see the world:

RAHUL: Shut up! There are other bonds besides those. There are relationships that we cannot understand rationally (*samaj*), that we do not want to understand rationally. These relationships don't have a name. They are only feelings (*ehsaas*). Such bonds have no walls, no borders (*sarhad*). Such bonds are of the heart, of love, of passion.[93]

Rahul's response privileges affect over any other type of quality, thus challenging and exceeding other frameworks that seek to define and produce free actions. Affective bonds must take precedence as cognitive processes given that they are truly universalizing, having "no walls, no borders." The word for border that Rahul uses is *sarhad*, the same word used for national borders.

---

92. Johar, *K3G*. Translation mine.
93. Johar, *K3G*. Translation mine.

This is a significant choice because it explicitly opposes the truly universalizing power of affective bonds to the falsely universalizing logic of capital, which spreads itself across national boundaries even as it aids in the categorization of people within divisive borders of identity. Rahul's speech suggests that the 'walls' or 'borders' that these categories represent are to be toppled when they come in the way of the affective relationships between a parent and a child, a lover and his beloved, and between one sibling and another.[94]

As in the other texts examined in this chapter, affective relationships spur the main events of the plot and characters' agentive actions through *bhavas* and their corresponding *rasas*. These affective moods constitute an embodied agency because they produce the acts of resistance exercised by both male and female protagonists who suffer on account of Hindu patriarchies or caste/class division. In line with this structuring principle, Johar depicts the film's main plot turns as produced by the upholding or violation of *vatsalya*, just as affective *anubhava* tied to particular *bhavas* and *rasas* shape the plot in *Sakuntala* and *Amar Katha*. In *K3G*, these plot turns include Rahul's adoption, his initial decision not to marry Anjali (to uphold his father's wishes), his later choice to marry Anjali (on the death of her father), his move to London, Nandini's path-breaking anger toward Yash, and Rahul's eventual return.

First, Johar depicts Rahul's initial decision to capitulate to his father's wishes and leave Anjali as an affective action brought about by *vatsalya*. When Yash learns of Rahul's wish to marry Anjali, he states that Rahul has disappointed him and hurt him badly. He sits down with his head in his hands and wipes away a single tear. There is a flash of white and the scene changes to a black and white montage of Rahul as a little boy. He has just found out he is adopted and is standing before his father, his hands folded in respect and tears streaming down his cheeks. His father comforts him and tells him that Rahul will always be his son, and the adoption is not to be spoken of ever again. The scene switches back to the present day where Rahul, unable to believe he has brought the man who offered him a place in his family to tears, lays his head in his father's lap and asks for forgiveness. "I will do whatever you tell me to," he states, sobbing. His choice to obey his father here is clearly an action matching the affective texture of the *vatsalya bhava* that pervades this scene. *Vatsalya* here eclipses *sringara rasa*, or the mood of romantic love that suffuses the film in earlier scenes. *Vatsalya* produces Rahul's actions even when they support Yash's chauvinist beliefs about social hierarchy. And the scene ends with yet another evocation of *vatsalya* when Yash, satisfied with Rahul's capitulation to his wishes, lays his hand on his son's head as a gesture

---

94. Hogan, *Understanding Indian Movies*, 160–90.

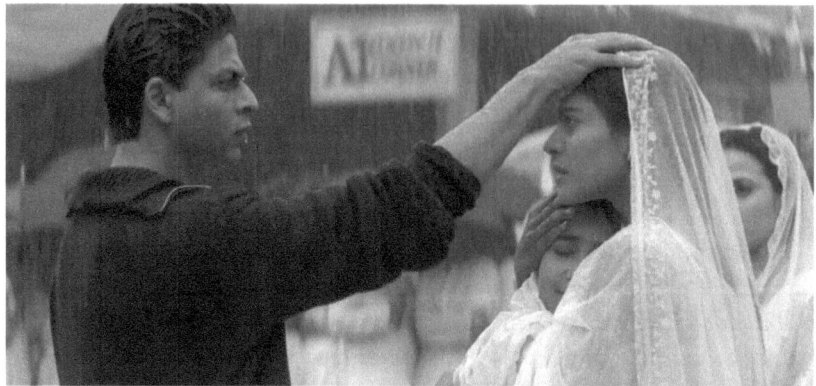

FIGURE 5. Rahul makes a vow. Source: Still from *Kabhi Khushi Kabhie Gham*.

of parental affection and forgiveness for Rahul's supposed transgression. *Vatsalya* undoubtedly produces and affirms Rahul's decision to leave Anjali.

However, Johar also depicts Rahul's eventual and more ethical decision to marry Anjali as an affective action produced by *vatsalya*. The scene switches to Anjali's neighborhood. Rahul is making his way there to let Anjali know of his decision to leave her. But as he draws close he realizes that he is in the midst of a funeral for Anjali's father. The camera zooms in to capture Anjali's devastated expression. In a heartrending scene, she embraces her father's corpse and cries for him not to leave her, for she and her school-age sister will be left alone in the world without him. The scene cuts to Rahul walking purposefully toward Anjali as she gazes at him with a desperate, grief-stricken expression. Then he raises his hand and lays it on her head—a version of the same gesture of loving protection embodying *vatsalya* that his father conditionally granted Rahul when he promised not to marry Anjali.

Johar uses these parallel images to make a clear point; once more *vatsalya* produces Rahul's action, but this time it is not an action made in the service of class hierarchies. Instead, the affective texture of Anjali's plight as it registers in Rahul's being evokes *vatsalya* in service of other discourses that, while carried out within a patriarchal social structure that evokes Anjali's need of male protection, also stresses ethical actions and personal responsibility toward others.

Vatsalya also structures and produces other major plot turns. It is worth returning to the way that *vatsalya bhava* finally leads to Nandini's decision to challenge her husband's godlike status when at the end of the film he once again refuses to accept Rahul into his home: "My husband is just a husband, just a husband, not god. Not god."

FIGURE 6. Nandini rejects *pativratadharma*. Source: Still from *Kabhi Khushi Kabhie Gham*.

These words are strengthened through the staging of the scene. Nandini is seated beside Yash on a swing as she speaks her mind, but her body language here is cold and withdrawn, her expression forlorn. Even more significantly, she is wearing a white sari—the recognizable mourning costume worn by widowed women. Symbolically, the scene suggests that Nandini has forsaken *sringara rasa* and her role as his wife, instead stressing the primacy of *vatsalya rasa* and her role as Rahul's mother. Yash's desecration of the affective ties of motherhood demand the liberating action of standing up to Yash so that Rahul can reenter his parent's home. When he crosses the threshold, the scene flashes back to sentimental black and white footage of his childhood with his parents. It is clear that, in terms of plot, *vatsalya* not only spurred him to leave but has brought him home again. *Vatsalya* structures the plot, including Rahul's adoption, his transgression and subsequent departure, and his return.

These three very different texts, *Sakuntala*, *Amar Katha*, and *Kabhi Khushi Kabhie Gham*, each rethink freedom as a contextual universalism, a universalizing idea of autonomous action that emerges from within locally situated epistemes and syncretic conceptual networks. Dramatic theorizations of an affective agency collude with but also challenge and exceed the workings of capitalism. My reading of *Sakuntala* showcases an important precolonial repository of *rasa*-based affective agency that influences future theatrical and cinematic texts, schooling the audience in less oppressive ways to think about the female subject. *Amar Katha* harnesses the same precolonial dramatic techniques in conjunction with European liberal ideals of individual freedom to critique constricting models of upper-caste womanhood as they worked with colonial capitalism to leave out whole swathes of the female population. *K3G,* meanwhile, uses *rasa* and affective agency to reflect an alternative route into modern ideals of personal freedom and self-determination that simultaneously resists and exceeds globalization's reduction of freedom to neoliberal individualism. Together, these texts suggest that the universalizing roots/routes of representative change and of democratic world making are various and dispersed. Moreover, they lie at least partly within indigenous and embedded epistemologies and ontologies, including affective agencies, which posit the self in relation to the other through a dissensual mode of demos expansion.

While the last two chapters have explored how South Asian contextual universalisms work with post-Enlightenment universalisms to challenge local hierarchies, colonialism, and capitalism, the next chapters turn to South Africa, where contextual universalisms also buttressed corresponding institutional arrangements. Such a difference between the two contexts may be explained partly through the differential status of subaltern subjects in each of these regions. Indian subalterns, including lower castes, tribals, and women, were minorities who functioned as symbolic and literal capital for hegemonic forms of indigenous and colonial organization, thereby living *within* the interstices of these forms of institutional power. The black subjects of colonial and apartheid modernity, meanwhile, constituted a large and segregated majority of disenfranchised and dispossessed subalterns, who had been spatially segregated within hegemonic forms of settler colonialism for much longer periods of time. Consequently, their bids for freedom could draw on surviving and relatively autonomous noncapitalist institutions of exchange and popular sovereignty, thereby building democracy up anew in the face of a despotic modernity they could never hope to belong to. In the analyses that follow, I ask: What does it look like when literary contextual universalisms are institutional rather than only ontological? What part did these universalisms play in the run up to democracy in South Africa? What remains of these universalisms now that a neoliberal postapartheid state has largely destroyed any meaningful bid for equality and freedom?

CHAPTER 3

Redefining Economic Exchange from Precolonial Proverbs to the Colonial and Postcolonial African Novel

STORY ONE: In a recent popular interview, Nelson Mandela (1918–2013), hailed by the interviewer as a "personification of *ubuntu*," was asked: "What does *ubuntu* mean to you?" The interviewer was referring to the popular South African universalizing ideal of humaneness, "a person is a person through other people." Mandela responded unhesitatingly: "A traveller through a country would stop at a village and he didn't have to ask for food or for water. Once he stopped, the people gave him food, entertained him. That is one aspect of *ubuntu*, but it will have various aspects. *Ubuntu* does not mean that people should not enrich themselves. The question therefore is: are you going to do so in order to enable the community around you to be able to improve?"[1]

Story two: It is 1890 and the Austrian Catholic missionary, Franz Mayr, has just arrived in Natal to work among the Zulus. Mayr is a short, awkward man who, for much of his life, has suffered from a spine disorder that has resulted in progressive deformities. His back is bent, and he has restricted lung capacity so that he is always short of breath. Yet, when it comes to 'civilizing' the Zulus, Mayr is a man of strength, speaking with passion and conviction. It does not take him long to learn English and Zulu, and he is quickly entrusted with founding and running the Zulu mission in Pietermaritzburg. In 1912,

---

1. Mandela, Nelson, "The Ubuntu Experience," last modified 1 November 2006, http://www.youtube.com/watch?v=ODQ4WiDsEBQ.

just two years before his death, Mayr expresses his sense of his parishioners: "these are savages, hunting in the wilds of Africa, herding their flocks of cattle, indulging licentiously their craving for plenty of meat, beer and wives, or in war and troubled fear of all kinds. Yet . . . we find good qualities as well, especially a sense of justice and noble pride."[2] Mayr is intrigued by these "good qualities." How is it that these "savages" could have a sense of morality in regard to each other, involving the generous giving and taking of agricultural products, food, and cattle? In his quest to arrive at the answer, he decides to document the Zulu proverbs and folktales he comes across, including those that deal with this phenomenon.

And, finally, an origin riddle: Describing the layout of a Zulu village through the metaphor of a pumpkin plant, a staple crop in Zulu farming, a precolonial riddler narrates:

> Guess a pumpkin-plant; it is single, and has many branches; it may be hundreds; it bears many thousand pumpkins on its branches; if you follow the branches, you will find a pumpkin everywhere; you will find pumpkins every where. You cannot count the pumpkins of one branch; you can never die of famine; you can go plucking and eating; and you will not carry food for your journey through being afraid that you will find no food where you are going. No; you can eat and leave, knowing that by following the branches you will continually find another pumpkin in front; and so it comes to pass. Its branches spread out over the whole country, but the plant is one, from which springs many branches. And each man pursues his own branch, and all pluck pumpkins from the branches.[3]

The riddle depicts the pumpkin plant as a village and the pumpkins as its individual homesteads to echo "a person is a person through other people." The parallelism of the phrase, "you will find a pumpkin everywhere; you will find pumpkins everywhere," with the repetition only distinguished by the pluralization of "pumpkin" to "pumpkins," asserts that a single pumpkin found "everywhere" is the same as, or connected to, the many pumpkins found everywhere. One pumpkin is linked to many; therefore one is many. The singular is only possible through the existence of the plural, and vice versa. In representing the village as a unified whole made up of many homesteads just as a pumpkin plant is "one from which springs many branches," the riddle negates the idea of individual ownership. The individual is inextricable from the community, and so his branch and pumpkin are inseparable from the

---

2. Mayr, "Zulu Proverbs," 957.
3. Anonymous in Callaway, *Nursery Tales, Traditions, and Histories*, 364.

branches and pumpkins of the rest of the village. Since the pumpkins belong to everybody, the traveler does not have to carry his own food, for "all pluck pumpkins from the branches." When "a person is a person through other people," food must exist as a communal resource rather than an individual possession. The pumpkin plant ends up being not only a metaphor for a sprawling village made up of many homesteads but also a metonym for a communal system of food sharing that realizes "a person is a person through other people."

These particular stories each reflect changing manifestations of *ubuntu*, a South African and pan-African popular cultural discourse present in many languages, including Zulu, Xhosa, and SeSotho. *Ubuntu* concerns itself with morality and interhuman relationships, signifying a symbolically African quality to aspire to and embody. In the Zulu sources that this chapter reads, *ubuntu* is generally understood as a unifying worldview enshrined in the popular maxims *umuntu ngumuntu ngabantu*, or, "a person is a person through other persons," and *Bonk'abantu bayadingana*, "everyone needs other people," which are part of a long cultural tradition that emphasizes interdependence. These proverbs define the individual in terms of her relationship with others so that both the self and others find themselves in a whole wherein they are already related. Within this understanding of the "human," one becomes oneself through other people, for the self is conceptualized as an extension of the other and the other as an extension of the self.

While all three of these stories have something to do with *Ubuntu*, they also show that the discourse is itself made up of conflicting strands that continuously evolve according to changing socioeconomic contexts. For instance, Story One arguably has more to do with the power of global capital than with precolonial discourses of "a person is a person through other people." Mandela's 'trickle down' idea that one should "enrich themselves" as a way of helping the community elides the gross inequalities still suffered by the majority of South Africa's population. Mandela's statement also sits strangely beside the kinds of interpersonal relationships idealized in Zakes Mda's 1995 postcolonial African novel in English, *Ways of Dying*. In the novel, the poor "rabble" share food and provisions with others while the richer characters depicted as striving for wealth usually do so in bad faith and at the expense of others. In contrast to Mandela, Mda's understanding of ethical interpersonal relationships seems to be derived from a lineage closer to that traced by the other two stories, which refer to moments of precapitalism in tribal Zululand. In both, general ideas of "justice" and "noble pride" are conveyed through references to the generous reciprocal exchange of food and cattle. The riddle in the third story is the most explicit, negating the idea of individual possession highlighted by Mandela and referring instead to communal agricultural and property systems. Nevertheless, despite their differences, all three divergent texts take the sharing and ethical exchange of food and resources as central to their ideas of moral interpersonal relationships.

When read alongside each other, the texts from which these stories are taken capture how South Africa's route to democratic change was worked out around issues such as material nourishment and economic empowerment, which affected a vast and general population of colonized blacks. This was quite different from the central nodes of India's nineteenth-century debate on development, which included issues affecting narrower populations such as the caste, tribal, and Hindu-woman question formulated by and through elite native groups in response to colonial discourse. One reason for South African literature's attention to issues that affected the general black population was that, unlike Indian exploitation colonialism, apartheid settler colonialism after 1948 created a relatively uniform subjugation by deliberately mis-educating blacks into subalternity; the Bantu Education Act of 1953 and the subsequent National Educational Policy Act of 1967 prepared Africans for their 'rightful' place in society by limiting them to education in the mother tongue, thereby preparing them for menial labor while restricting their use of English. The implementation of mother-tongue programs made a mockery of using native languages because Afrikaans and English were the languages of employment. Since Afrikaans was closely associated with the racism of the oppressive government, black writers either rejected vernaculars altogether or began to use a combination of English and the mother tongue as a mode of resistance. The source texts in this chapter, which are in Zulu as well as English, reflect these historical changes, with both languages used to espouse the similar worldview of a subaltern *ubuntu* universalism.

This chapter traces an *ubuntu* universalism from the precolonial past into the postcolonial present. I read multiple sources, including precolonial proverbs, folktales, and riddles, that ground ethical behavior in forms of reciprocal and continuing exchange, particularly the giving and receiving of food, land, and cattle to others. And I also trace how the colonial capitalist system that encroached on the rural agricultural and cattle economy of Zululand challenged such a contextual universalism due to its very different perception of the self and other as well as of objects of exchange. The first section of this chapter explores the concept's bloatings into hegemonic contemporary manifestations. The second traces a precolonial ontology of *ubuntu* that sustained and reflected systems of equitable agricultural exchange within precolonial rural cattle economies. This is apparent in precolonial Zulu oralities as collected and explored by the Zulu writer C. S. Nyembezi (1919–2000) and the colonial missionaries Reverend Henry Callaway (1817–90) and Franz Mayr (1865–1914). The section also turns to Nyembezi's 1961 Zulu novel *The Rich Man of Pietermaritzburg*, translated by Sandile Ngidi, to argue that versions of "a person is a person through other people" existed as puissances that continued to buttress reciprocal systems of ethical exchange well into the mid-twentieth century despite the epistemic and material violence posed by colonial capitalism. Finally, the third section of this chapter traces these contextual universalisms into the postcolonial African novel in English, where they work to resist apartheid dehumanization. Zakes Mda's *Ways of Dying* depicts communal rituals of food consumption and sharing as correctives to apartheid violence. *Ways of Dying*, like *The Rich Man of Pietermaritzburg*, cultivates a locally derived experimental aesthetics through vernacular oralities that redefine the novel form. In doing so, these texts demonstrate that a locally born universalism remains partly constitutive of postcolonial modernity's democratic universalisms and literatures.

As we will see, these texts reinforce "a person is a person through other people" by emphasizing and harnessing those cognitive processes within which the self is understood through mental representations that imagine one's own actions and thoughts in terms of an other's. The texts transmit this cognitive framework in which the self is quite literally an extension of the other—as well as its associated universalizing concepts of exchange—through literary devices that perform "a person is a person through other people," including communal narrative voices, reader-narrator co-constitution, and the projection and communication of collective emotional states.

I. THE MANY USES AND ABUSES OF *UBUNTU* IN THE POSTAPARTHEID PRESENT

Current notions of *ubuntu* carry a whole range of meanings that go beyond "a person is a person through other people" as it existed in precolonial and colonial South Africa. The concept appears repeatedly on television, radio, and in official messages in the postapartheid present, serving as a vehicle through which religious and political leaders such as Nelson Mandela and Archbishop Desmond Tutu have constructed a postcolonial, modern African identity.[4] In this capacity, *ubuntu* has served as a discourse of racial reconciliation, a narrative that highlights the community over the individual by promoting generosity, one that conversely emphasizes personal enrichment, and one that signifies an authentic African identity. The term was also co-opted by the sports economy and by multinational conglomerations such as Coca-Cola in

---

4. Shutte, *Philosophy for Africa*, 46.

the run-up to the 2010 FIFA World Cup. *Ubuntu* is now being used as a moneymaking device—a cultural commodity in the transnational economic circuit of globalized sport. Given these various iterations of the concept, it is not surprising that *ubuntu* has been critiqued for being too generalized and not historically grounded enough. Irma J. Kroeze has argued that *ubuntu* has become a "bloated concept" that "tries to do too much" and as such has no transformative potential.[5] It has also been critiqued for being essentializing and homogenizing of South African culture and as reinstating tribal hierarchies.

The postapartheid "bloating" of "a person is a person through other people" is apparent in my findings from a month's fieldwork in Johannesburg and Cape Town in July 2010, just after the World Cup had ended. During my visit to Johannesburg, I interviewed about twenty native speakers of Bantu languages, including Xhosa and Zulu. My interviewees were from a variety of socioeconomic backgrounds, ranging from gardeners, taxi drivers, tour group operators, waiters, and receptionists to graduate students in African literature departments. I asked basic questions about when they had heard the word used last and in what context as well as what values they associated with the word.

What became increasingly clear during the course of my fieldwork was that the notion of "a person is a person through other people" has undergone much transformation in its journey into the postapartheid present. The majority of the people I interviewed tied "a person is a person through other people" to ideas of multiracial and multicultural unity within nationalist discourses of reconciliation. About a third of my interviewees remembered it used in the context of overcoming the May 2008 xenophobic attacks on African immigrants in South Africa, which left sixty-two dead. These usages of the word make more sense once one considers official discourses of *ubuntu*. In 2008, archbishop Desmond Tutu described a person with *ubuntu* as "open and available to others, affirming of others, does not feel threatened that others are able and good, for he or she has a proper assurance that comes from knowing that he or she belongs in a greater whole and is diminished when others are humiliated or diminished, when others are tortured or oppressed."[6] This clearly refers to the way blacks were treated during apartheid and calls for a new society in which all races live together constructively and humanely.

This marriage of *ubuntu* with racial reconciliation is also reflected in the context of the Truth and Reconciliation Commission (TRC). Antjie Krog's *Country of My Skull*, a fictional yet journalistic memoir interested in *ubuntu*'s

---

5. See Kroeze, "Doing Things with Values," 340.
6. Tutu, *No Future Without Forgiveness*, 31.

FIGURE 7. Logo of Ubuntu Sports Outreach.
Source: http://ubuntusports.blogspot.com/.

role within the TRC, interprets *ubuntu* almost completely through the lens of interracial harmony. Krog draws on contemporary South African thinkers such as Jabu Sindane and Willie van der Merwe to declare that we should encounter the difference of people's humanness so as to inform and enrich our own.[7] Respect for the particularities of the beliefs and practices of others is especially emphasized by a striking yet lesser-known translation of *umuntu ngumuntu ngabantu*: "a human being is a human being through (the otherness of) other human beings."[8] Such an emphasis on "otherness" is a far cry from the precolonial ontology explored later in the chapter, which posits the self as an extension of the other.

Ubuntu also appears repeatedly in the media surrounding the growing South African sports economy, for it is continually appropriated by state-sanctioned nationalist discourses of racial reconciliation as well as by the very different universalizing force of capitalism. Within the latter, *ubuntu* works as a marketing tool that drives capital's self-expansion into new markets, relating the self to the other predominantly as sellers and consumers. This materialist universalizing force is apparent in the advertising of organizations such as the Ubuntu Sports Outreach Program in Cape Town, which aims to find professional employment in soccer for disadvantaged unemployed youth. The organization's logo features black and white hands clasped in a symbol of victory, with heavenly rays of light emanating from such a union (see figure 7).[9]

---

7. Sindane, *Ubuntu and Nation Building*, 8–9; Van der Merwe, "Philosophy and the Multi-Cultural Context," 1.

8. Van der Merwe, "Philosophy and the Multi-Cultural Context," 1–3.

9. Ubuntu Sports Outreach, "Ubuntu Sports Outreach blog," accessed July 2010, http://ubuntusports.blogspot.com/.

Soccer, here, is uplifted as a divinely sanctioned vehicle for a humanity that does not differentiate according to race or social standing. However, while this discourse of *ubuntu* has done valuable work toward reconciliation in the postapartheid context, it has also diluted the concept. The Ubuntu Sports Outreach Program's website states:

> Ubuntu (oo-boon-too) is an African expression of togetherness. It means that what I am is intrinsically linked to and part of what we are. Nowhere is this idea of human synergy more perfectly expressed than on a sports field where a group of individuals together rise or fall depending on the presence or absence of that intangible alchemy, melding individuals into one seamless unit. Ubuntu.[10]

The sports field emerges as a place where racial and social tensions become inconsequential and where the individual's rise and fall is linked to that of the community. Such a symbolic transcendence of social difference is, in fact, a common strategy used to sell global sports to disadvantaged South African youth, who, as Jean Comaroff specifies, are marginalized racial minorities who live at the borders of respectable society in cities all over the world. Their idleness and unemployment is caused by the "inability of governments to subject the workings of international capital to their own rules and regulations."[11] The discourse of *Ubuntu* in this context is a cathartic vent for negative energy; crying "*ubuntu*" channels rage and idle energy into the emotion of 'being in it together' and conquering odds. The game serves as a wishful metaphor for the game of their life, assuring youth that they will not be left behind. By promoting their own "unique mission" to "open remarkable doors for education and employment in the professional game," the organization presents urban black youth with a way into the global workforce by producing the myth that they matter, that there is not only a place in the national community for them but an opportunity for privilege and status.

A similarly questionable appropriation of *Ubuntu* was especially evident in the popular culture surrounding the 2010 FIFA World Cup. The majority of the people I interviewed in Johannesburg had been told, on radio shows, television, advertisements, and in official announcements, to treat foreign tourists with *ubuntu* in the run-up to the 2010 FIFA World Cup. During this time, *ubuntu* was used to remind South Africans not to turn foreign visitors into targets of crime since they were bringing global capital to the local economy.

---

10. Ibid.
11. Comaroff, "Beyond Bare Life," 210.

FIGURE 8. *Ubuntu* in Coca-Cola advertisements on buses in Johannesburg. Source: Author's photograph taken in July 2010.

The conflation of discourses of racial reconciliation and global capital was also apparent from the images I spotted on the backs and sides of buses all over Johannesburg.

Coca-Cola, one of the major official sponsors of the FIFA World Cup, suggests that drinking Coca-Cola is to "open happiness" by embracing the spirit of a commodified *ubuntu*. The *ubuntu* logo in the image depicts people of all colors of the rainbow holding hands while standing around a soccer ball, thereby symbolizing Mandela's concept of the rainbow nation. Here, opening a Coke bottle while watching the World Cup unites people of all races by imbuing them with the spirit of *ubuntu*. The problems with such a message were raised by a prominent newspaper, which pointed out, "this World Cup is not for the poor—it is the soccer elites of FIFA, the elites of domestic and international corporate capital and the political elites who are making billions and who will be benefiting at the expense of the poor."[12] This appro-

---

12. Zirin, Dave, "South African Violence and the 2010 World Cup," *Liberator Magazine*, accessed July 2010, http://weblog.liberatormagazine.com/2008/06/south-african-violence-and-2010-world.html.

priation of *Ubuntu* works to privilege the nation's economic relationship with the international community at the expense of the disadvantaged consumers of multinational products like Coca-Cola. The Eurocentric tendency to not recognize contextual universalisms as complex working modes of democratic self-definition in the postcolonial present encourages their commodification, for it leaves them open to being interpreted as static cultural essences and signifiers of tradition that can be easily packaged toward antidemocratic ends. Such hegemonic transformations of *ubuntu* are very different from the ethics of being expressed by the preapartheid oralities explored in the next section.

II. *UBUNTU* EXCHANGE IN PREAPARTHEID ORALITIES AND THE ZULU NOVEL

The term '*ubuntu*' has clearly meant different things within the varying contexts in which it has been instrumentalized. It is no wonder, then, that many cultural commentators have concluded that the term should not be divorced from the context in which it had meaning—"a mainly feudal socioeconomic system in which the chief, the chiefdom, clan, and the extended family were crucial providers of wealth and values."[13] Maluleke asks: "given the fact that the global village is nothing like a 16th century African village consisting of a network of extended families, what is the effect and wisdom of recommending Ubuntu to blacks in the present?"[14] Yet, others have countered that *ubuntu* remains meaningful to young South Africans and that such ethical ideals may be "integrally tied to struggles for social and economic transformation."[15]

The rest of this chapter confirms this view of *ubuntu*'s transformative universalizing potential in the South African present. But it does so in response to Maluleke's question above, which takes for granted the absolute disjuncture between precolonial African villages, where *ubuntu* was first conceptualized and instrumentalized, and the postapartheid present. Contradicting Maluleke's interpretation of such a disjuncture, the chapter shows that *ubuntu* remains useful and relevant because an embedded lineage of the concept, undergirded by practices of reciprocal and communal exchange central to precolonial cultures, remains partly constitutive of postcolonial processes of demos expansion, though it diverges significantly from capitalist exchange.

In order to trace such an embedded lineage of *ubuntu*, it first becomes imperative to ask: What has ethical treatment of the other looked like within

---

13. Maluleke, "The Misuse of Ubuntu," 12–13.
14. Ibid.
15. Cornell, *Law and Revolution in South Africa*, 147.

the ontological schema of "a person is a person through other people" in precolonial cultural texts? And what implications has such an ontology had for the understanding of one's selfhood, for the individual's place within a community, and for the social and economic structures within which one lives? This section considers these questions through various precolonial proverbs and folk sayings as well as through the writings of C. S. Nyembezi, Reverend Henry Callaway, and Reverend Franz Mayr, among others.

Nyembezi was the author of three novels, *Inkinsela yase Mgungundlovu*, or *The Rich Man of Pietermaritzburg* (1961); *Mntanami! Mntanami!*, or *My Child My Child!* (1950); and *Ubudoda abukhulelwa*, or *One Does Not Have To Be Old To Do Manly Deeds* (1953) as well as an abridged translation of Alan Paton's *Cry, The Beloved Country—Lafa elihle kakhulu* (1957). His father was a minister of the Methodist Church, admired for his setting up of Christianity and school education among the Zulu. Nyembezi's parentage ensured him a place among the mission-educated elite so that he obtained a degree from the well-known Native College at Fort Hare and the University of Witwatersrand (Wits), where he later became faculty. It was here that he did his pioneering work on Zulu proverbs, remaining at Wits until 1954, when he was appointed to the chair of Bantu languages at Fort Hare University College. In 1959, he became the first Zulu to be appointed to a professorship there. Nyembezi was one of the major figures in twentieth-century Zulu letters and wrote primarily for a Zulu audience. He was perhaps best known among nonnative speakers for his important manuals, *Learn Zulu* (1957), *Learn More Zulu* (1970), and his coauthored *English-Zulu, Zulu-English* dictionary. His *Zulu Proverbs* (1963) contains an entire section on proverbs that constitute a discourse of *ubuntu*.

Nyembezi was born in the decade following the Act of Union of 1910, which united the former British colonies of the Cape and Natal with the Boer republics and, in the process, excluded Africans from full citizenship. Union served to consolidate a white settler colonial state, leading to an African national convention and the founding, in 1912, of what became the African National Congress. These political events acted as a catalyst for black writers, especially after 1948, when the draconian legislation associated with apartheid curtailed African land ownership, regulated African labor and movement between towns and cities, and restricted the franchise. Nyembezi's Zulu writing in response to these sweeping changes can be set alongside that of his black contemporaries writing in indigenous languages, including authors like Thomas Mofolo, Sol Plaatje, John Dube, and later A. C. Jordan. Yet, Nyembezi's writing was thematically very different from these writers who largely exhibited ambiguous and paradoxical relations with Christianity, the 'civilizing mission,' the 'Enlightenment,' and colonial modernity; unlike Nyembezi's works, their novels often turn back to the great nineteenth-century African empires with a mixture of nativist idealizing of their histories and disgust with their 'uncivilized' cultural backgrounds. Nyembezi's Zulu writing about life in rural areas was also very different from urban writers associated with the transnational modernism of the Johannesburg *Drum* magazine. For these writers reacted to the reduced teaching of English enforced by the Bantu Education Act by rejecting African languages in favor of an African English inflected with *tsotsi taal*. By contrast, Nyembezi was steeped in the local vernacular episteme of *ubuntu*, using it to challenge and exceed the modernity brought about by colonial rule.

Yet Nyembezi, along with the other writers I consider, cannot be regarded as transparent, definitive transmitters of a contextual universalism related to *ubuntu*. In documenting these oralities, Nyembezi is himself tracing a history of a concept that has undergone multiple mediations. As Christian B. N. Gade has shown, the term has frequently appeared in printed colonial texts since at least 1846, yet carries very different valences in different historical periods. Gade documents that prior to 1950, *ubuntu* was defined broadly in multiple written sources as a positive quality related to being human, as an optimal state of ethical being, and as synonymous with humaneness. Then, at different stages during the second half of the 1900s, *ubuntu* began to enter the national vocabulary and to cohere as a recognizable discourse, especially when the Zulu writer Jordan Kush Ngubane wrote about it in the popular *African Drum* magazine. In 1960, the term made another leap in popularity when it was used at the South African Institute for Race Relations conference, thereby beginning its consolidation as an African humanism, a philosophy, an ethic, and multicultural harmonious worldview.[16] And it was only in the period from 1993 to 1995, when the drafting of a new South African constitution made the recovery of a positive definition of black South African culture imperative, that the philosopher Augustine Shutte explicitly connected the diffuse discourse now called *ubuntu* to the Nguni proverb *umuntu ngumuntu ngabantu*,[17] although, as this chapter argues, "a person is a person through other people" captures the gist of *ubuntu* contextual universalisms in a way that precedes Shutte's connection. It is not surprising, then, that most authors today refer to the proverb when describing *ubuntu*, irrespective of whether they consider *ubuntu* to be a human quality, African humanism, a philosophy, an ethic, or a worldview.[18]

---

16. Metz, "Toward an African Moral Theory," 321–41; Van der Merwe, "Philosophy and the Multi-Cultural Context," 1.

17. Shutte, *Philosophy for Africa*, 46. See also Shutte, *Ubuntu: An Ethic for the New South Africa*.

18. Gade, "What Is Ubuntu?" 303–29.

I focus mainly on Nyembezi's iteration of *ubuntu* because he excavates elements of a precolonial discourse in the 1960s, before it had cohered into a recognizable capitalist- and nationalist-inflected narrative within the nation-state. Nyembezi's references are not, therefore, overdetermined by any later instrumental articulation of "a person is a person through other people." Indeed, he does not even mention the word '*ubuntu*' explicitly in *The Rich Man of Pietermaritzburg*, only using it as a general heading in his 1963 book *Zulu Proverbs* and in his evaluation of ethical modes of behavior and how they related to economic and social systems. In doing so, he seems far more interested in the evolution of a fluid and as yet undefined worldview under strain from threatening outside forces, suggesting that *ubuntu* as a cultural system exists as a diffuse contextual universalism that only becomes crystallized as resistance in the face of colonial and postcolonial challenges to it. I support my readings of Nyembezi by bringing in corresponding discursive elements from other writers who refer to the same proverbs and oralities prior to Nyembezi, including the missionaries Franz Mayr, who arrived in Natal in 1890 and lived there until his death in 1914, and Reverend Henry Callaway, who served in South Africa from 1854 to 1886.

What is at stake in using precolonial and colonial sources as historical evidence of indigenous economic systems given that any sources of early Southern African history owe their capture in written form to colonial recording practices? We must consider that the sources I quote by missionaries are examples of colonial bias and clearly display a sense of racial superiority. Mayr's article "Zulu Proverbs," quoted at the beginning of this chapter in Story Two, reads:

> These proverbs clearly show how sentient the wisdom of the Zulus is and how shrewd their thoughts are ... but more tell us at once that these are savages, hunting in the wilds of Africa, herding their flocks of cattle, indulging licentiously their craving for plenty of meat, beer and wives, or in war and troubled fear of all kinds. Yet ... we find good qualities as well, especially a sense of justice and noble pride; so much so that it can well be said of a Zulu that he loves only those whom he fears. If a Zulu was in the wrong and knows it, he will like the master the more for having given him a good thrashing.[19]

Mayr conceptualizes the Zulus as an inferior 'other,' referring to them as "savages" who respond only to force as animals supposedly would, even as he disconcertingly notices nodes of comparison between these animals and 'civilized' Europeans. Mayr's writings, along with those of other colonialists

---

19. Mayr, "Zulu Proverbs," 957.

such as James Stuart, testify to the truth of Ranajit Guha's assertion that any attempt to describe the consciousness of the subaltern involves a mediation that results in distortions and biases. Yet, while such sources are clearly compromised by their origins in the colonial encounter, their contents cannot be dismissed wholesale. For, as Caroline Hamilton notes, it is also true that the origins of many of the components of colonial discourse about Africa lie in indigenous African discourses. "The identity and desires of the colonizers were not simply projected or inscribed on Africa, nor was Africa drawn from the imagination."[20] Following Hamilton, I suggest that while it is not possible to recover indigenous discourses intact, it is possible to identify their traces in colonial and Africanist discourses and to reconstruct more of the process of their incorporation into the present. Taking a similar stance, Guha acknowledges the impossibility of fully grasping or reconstituting an insurgent subaltern subjectivity, while simultaneously testifying to the presence of such a subaltern consciousness within colonial recordings of these events.[21] In the case of *ubuntu*, acknowledging and attempting to partially reconstruct such a subaltern consciousness is particularly viable because recordings of the same, or very similar, proverbs and understandings are found in multiple sources distinct in origin and ideology, including in Mayr, Callaway, and Nyembezi. As the following analysis shows, to dismiss precolonial sources as colonial discourse is to close off the possibilities of recovering material about Africa's precolonial past and ultimately to revert to a denial of that history.

In his collection, *Zulu Proverbs*, Nyembezi identifies the ethical discourse of *ubuntu* as regulating six broad ways of being: *ukuphatha kahle abanye,* hospitality; *ukuwiphatha okubi,* bad manners; *ukuziqhenya,* pride; *ukungabi nambongo,* ingratitude; *inkani,* obstinacy; and *ukungabi nabuntu,* lack of humanness and good moral nature.[22] These areas provide guidelines of how to manage and enact ethical relationships. What became increasingly clear as I researched the use of these precolonial proverbs was that multiple sources ground ethical behavior in forms of communal and reciprocal exchange, particularly the giving and receiving of food to strangers and others within the community.

Ubuntu within Nyembezi, Callaway, and Mayr outline a particular system of ethics built on the giving and receiving of food gifts and favors from other people. Within this ethical system, a willingness to receive emerges as just as important as giving. As Marcel Mauss elaborates, a true gift always expects reciprocation, creating community, and solidarity. A gift that expects nothing

20. Hamilton, *Terrific Majesty,* 28.
21. Guha, "The Prose of Counter-Insurgency," 78–82.
22. Nyembezi, *Zulu Proverbs,* 48.

in return is not a true gift for it does nothing to cement relationships.[23] In contradiction, Derrida argues that the gift is impossible since, from the moment one even recognizes a transaction as a gift, it becomes weighted with obligations and therefore no longer qualifies as a pure present.[24] *Ubuntu* epistemology as it appears in the writings I consider differs from Derrida's position, for within "a person is a person through other people" one *expects* reciprocation, for the other is not an absolute other; instead the proverbs contain an uneasy tension between aspirationally conceptualizing the other as an extension of the self as well as simultaneously thinking of the other as a whole separate entity. When one conceptualizes the other as an other who is also an extension of the self, one's act of gifting is also an act of receiving; giving a gift to another is the same as giving to the self. This is metaphorically true—for gift giving to an extension of the self constitutes giving to oneself. And it is also literally true—for a gift carries the real expectation of reciprocation within it. Such a contextual universalism thus locates ethical behavior, and therefore a true "gift," precisely in obligation to the self and by extension to the other. Pleasing the self is built into the condition of the gift so that altruism does not constitute ethical behavior.

Giving and receiving food within this ontology did not just represent an ethical philosophy but also a socioeconomic system. The Zulus defined the basic values of humanity through the sharing of food and cattle because historically they were agriculturists. Cattle and food represented wealth, valuable as providers of meat and milk, which, in the form of curdled milk (*amasi*), was the mainstay of the diet, together with maize (*ummbila*) and millet (*amabele*) and the nutritious tshwala beer (*utshwala*). Cattle also formed the bride wealth or *lobola* that legalizes marriage. They were the food offered to ancestors, with all family ceremonies being performed in the cattle fold. References to cattle pervade Zulu oralities, with the language containing literally hundreds of terms for cattle, distinguishing them minutely as to horns, colorings, and markings. Cattle were considered so central to the cultural life of the Zulu nation that they even had praise names, and the owner of a favorite or beautiful beast would compose and recite praises in its honor. As South African literary scholar Michael Chapman points out, in binding the living to the ancestral dead, land and the cattle and crops it produced provided both physical and sacred roots of existence.[25] The sharing of the fruits of the land therefore served as the basis of the economy but was also an ethical imperative, without which the ancestors could not be happy. As a result, there are count-

---

23. Mauss, *The Gift*, 3.
24. Derrida, *Given Time*, 7–13.
25. Chapman, *Southern African Literatures*, 51.

less customs related to the giving and taking of food that Nyembezi records under the heading "UBuntu." For instance, the word '*ukuthekela*' referred to the sharing of one's crops, '*ukunana*' referred to the sharing of one's household items, and '*ukusisa*' referred to the lending of one's female livestock to a neighbor till it gave birth to calves, which the neighbor would keep, only returning the cow. These customs functioned for the mutual benefit of the owner and the recipient. Within *ukusisa,* for instance, the owner could amass larger herds than his family could ordinarily care for by using the labor of other, less wealthy families.[26] The caretakers, meanwhile, benefited from milk while the cattle was under their care, and usually received an *isiSinga* (literally a rope for tying up cattle but known as a gift of cattle) beast from the cattle's reproduction.[27] From this natural increase, a poorer family could build up a herd of its own. Ownership of the original cattle remained with the lender, but long-term arrangements gave some security to the recipients. The custom also served as a safeguard against localized outbreaks of disease or drought by spreading the cattle over a number of different geographical zones.

Such institutions of sharing operated on principles different from capitalism in relation to the status of the objects being exchanged, the aim of the exchange, and the status of people doing the exchanging. First, cattle, land, and agricultural products as objects of *ubuntu* exchange did not function as commodities, for they were defined in terms of their usefulness rather than their exchange value in relation to other objects. Moreover, this usefulness was measured not only in terms of concrete physical properties but from their symbolic and metonymic value in consolidating sacred connections between people, chiefs, and the ancestors. Because these objects stood for connections between people, they could not be seen as private property owned by one individual. Rather, they were always already communal resources. Third, these customs established the 'self' and 'other' as mutually related equivalents but, unlike in capitalism, such an equivalence was not limited only to a finite act of exchange, for customs like *ukusisa* bound people together indefinitely through the continuing life, productivity, and spiritual significance of the entities being exchanged. A family whose calf was obtained from a cow belonging to another family would continue to consume milk and meat and rear more cattle descended from the initial animal and were expected to reciprocate when the need arose.

These systematic institutions of reciprocal sharing were expressed through Zulu proverbs, *izagu,* which expressed and amplified cognitive processes in

---

26. Beinart, *The Political Economy of Pondoland,* 82–84.
27. Krige, *The Social System of the Zulus,* 187.

which the self mentally represents one's actions in terms of an other's. During the observation of actions produced by other individuals, the same neural structures are recruited that would normally be involved in the actual generation of the same actions. These results suggest that we understand the actions of others in terms of our own motor system, and that one's sense of self is impossible without imagining the other as the self.[28] *Izagu* harness such a cognitive process to activate "a person is a person through other people." For instance, the proverb *imikhomb' ayiphambane,* or "let the meat gifts cross one another," represents one's own actions of giving in terms of internal mental representations depicting the same action being done by the other. Nyembezi writes of the custom that "a person who receives a gift of meat is expected to reciprocate the act by giving a gift of meat when he, too, slaughters a beast. Therefore when a gift is made it is regarded as going to fetch a gift from the other person."[29] These words capture the essence of perceiving the self as an extension of the other, serving as a mental representation that structures real material practices within the social sphere. Reflecting these cognitive processes, the wording of the proverb implies giving and receiving but the syntax simultaneously undermines such a formulation as an interaction between an absolute self and other. The meat gifts are described as "crossing each other," which suggests that the giving and receiving is happening simultaneously—for if the self is an extension of the other, then when the self is giving or receiving so is the other. A comparable notion is expressed in the proverb *Ukuph'ukuziphakela,* or "giving is to dish out for oneself."[30] Mayr records the same proverb, though he spells the Zulu words differently, referring to *Ukapa kuzibekela* and translating the proverb as "to give is to provide for one self."[31] Similarly, *adla ngandoda,* or "they eat through other men," refers to the practice of helping a man to slaughter and skin his beast and then sharing the meat with him. Another prominent proverb is *isandla sigez'esinge,* or "the hand washes the other."[32] In all these examples, a literal practice is undergirded by a metaphor, enforcing the idea that the sustenance of another directly translates into the sustenance of the self.[33]

What was the ethical imperative of the receiver in such a schema? Multiple *izagu* point out that recognizing the giver as an extension of the receiving self carries certain behavioral obligations. Proverbs repeatedly stress an ethical

---

28. See Decety and Sommerville, "Shared Representations."
29. Nyembezi, *Zulu Proverbs,* 52.
30. Ibid., 54.
31. Mayr, "Zulu Proverbs," 961.
32. Nyembezi, *Zulu Proverbs,* 52.
33. Ibid., 67–68.

willingness to receive whatever was given. For instance, Nyembezi collects phrases such as "the stomach of a stranger is small"; "the stomach of a traveler does not finish anything"; "the mouth does not despise"; and "a beast that is passing finishes no grass," which were usually recited by strangers at one's door asking for a bite to eat, with the custom being to ply such strangers with food.[34] The obligation of the receiver also extended to always showing gratitude, for ingratitude undoes the sense of "obligation" built into the receiving of a gift. A true gift is one that expects recognition followed by reciprocity should the need for it arise. Another proverb, *uyaw'alunampumulo*, or "the foot has no nose," conveys this particularly well. It refers to the needs of a traveler whose feet carry him forward without being able to "smell" the path that will lead one to the most hospitable environs.[35] Strangers must not be ill treated because one day one may find oneself in the position of having to ask that someone for hospitality. Unlike commodity exchange, then, *ubuntu* posits obligation as an indefinite mode of connection between the 'self' and 'other,' functioning as an ethical imperative.

Since ethical behavior has the obligation of continuity and reciprocity built into it, one who receives but does not give is heartily criticized. Multiple *izagu* collected by Nyembezi and Mayr therefore speak of people who do not share food as displaying *ubuqili*, or cunning, as in the proverb "he is the crafty one whose locusts are roasted last."[36] Nyembezi adds: "a person who never gives others assistance should not expect to be helped."[37] Mayr records other proverbs that express the same point: *ikot' eyikotayo*, or "the cow licks the one that licks her. Said of people who help one another," and *kuhlonitshwana kabilli*, or "it is respected twice (on both sides). If you want others to respect you, you also must respect them."[38] Such similar references by writers living in such different contexts testify that this was a coherent cultural system and one in which reciprocity and obligation formed the basis of an ethical ontology.

These explorations of ethical ways of being related to "a person is a person through other people" do not mean that Zulus always embodied such a discourse. Rather, I suggest that this was a prominent aspirational discourse articulated alongside other discourses that captured the difficulties of living up to such ideals. Mayr, for instance, records numerous other proverbs that contradict "a person is a person through other people," indicating a complex cultural system that captured multiple ways of being human in practice. The

---

34. Ibid., 52–53.
35. Ibid., 53.
36. Mayr, "Zulu Proverbs," 957.
37. Nyembezi, *Zulu Proverbs*, 70.
38. Mayr, "Zulu Proverbs," 958.

proverb "*Aku 'nkwaliepandela enye,*" or "there is no partridge that scratches for another," suggests that "everyone looks after his own interest."³⁹ And the proverb "*kudhla umndeni kwotamele izibankwa,*" or "the family circle eats and the lizards bask in the sun (look on)," suggests, contrary to *ubuntu*'s emphasis on the recognition of the linked humanity of even a stranger, that "strangers cannot expect the attention given to one of the family."⁴⁰ Nevertheless, alongside these contradictions remains a very prominent embedded universalism that successfully buttressed multiple reciprocal practices within a larger community of 'persons.'

The Rich Man of Pietermaritzburg *and* Ubuntu *in Colonial South Africa*

C. S. Nyembezi's novel *The Rich Man of Pietermaritzburg* (1961) depicts this holistic domain only to delineate the effects of an encroaching capitalist modernity. The novel charts how two different temporal registers, one linked to *ubuntu* and the other to the colonialist modernity of preapartheid capitalism, exist simultaneously. Both temporalities convey universalizing stories about the self. Within the world of *ubuntu*, a person is connected to the other through reciprocal exchange of food and cattle so that social value is derived not from previously determined identity categories but from one's ethical managing of relationships with others. Within the capitalist republic, meanwhile, one's value is produced solely within the act of exchange of one's commodities, an act that posits equivalences in material value between the goods being exchanged as well as between commodities and the people exchanging them. However, as Nyembezi demonstrates, this is a false universalism because it sets up new hierarchies, with a person's value continuing to be determined through divisive categories such as class or racial status. The novel challenges this colonial modernity through a carefully crafted indigenous experimentalism that combines the 'traditional' narrative of the Zulu trickster figure, Chakijana, with a critical realism of a kind described by Satya Mohanty as "seeking to analyze and explain social reality instead of merely holding up a mirror to it."⁴¹ Within this process of representational critique, the novel reveals that rural economic systems of equitable exchange, buttressed by discourses of "a person is a person through other people," coexisted

---

39. Ibid.
40. Ibid.
41. Mohanty, "Introduction," 2.

with but also challenged a rapidly encroaching capitalist system enforced by the colonial state.

The novel was written in the late 1950s and published in 1961, a moment when the infiltration of the colonial government and the capitalist system into rural areas was bringing about changes in the entire social and economic order described above. Indeed, 1961 was also the year in which the white South African government declared the country a republic, ending the country's status as a British dominion and consolidating Afrikaner racism. Historians such as Aran S. MacKinnon have shown that the reciprocal functions of customs like *ukusisa* were undermined. Under the encroaching capitalist order, recipients of loaned cattle were judged through prejudicial notions of charity and stattus. They were seen as impoverished and had to pay a cash sum to retain any natural increase in cattle. This was a far cry from the *ubuntu* view of giving as always already reciprocal and unaltruistic.[42] Chiefs with massive herds, previously the centers of economic distribution and exchange within a kingdom, now jealously guarded the productive and reproductive capacities of their cattle, severing the link between economic and political infrastructures. MacKinnon notes that Chief Mtubatuba reportedly owned fifteen thousand cattle, which were spread out among his people. However, he retracted the customary chiefly duties he owed his people, claiming that commoners could not use the oxen because they would be overworked; that only he could slaughter the cattle for meat for himself; and that while his people could drink the milk, they could not retain hides or natural increase.[43] In other words, cattle exchange was transformed from a form of barter to a saleable commodity. As the Setswana put it: "money eat cattle."[44] The introduction of direct cash costs to cattle keeping and the manipulation of social institutions surrounding cattle changed the value of stock in the capitalist context. It was not just the economic system that had changed, however, it was also an entire worldview in which the self had been an extension of the other. The concept of differentiated ownership introduced by colonial capital disrupted the ontology of "a person is a person through other people" as well as the holistic economic, social, and political system that it underpinned.

Yet, despite the infiltration of the capitalist system, Aran S. MacKinnon has shown how practices such as *ukusisa* and the cattle economy linked to *ubuntu* persisted through adaptation and resistance,[45] a process also reflected

---

42. Vilikazi, *Zulu Transformations*, 115.
43. MacKinnon, "The Persistence of the Cattle Economy," 113.
44. Comaroff and Comaroff, *Ethnography and the Historical Imagination*, 151.
45. MacKinnon, "The Persistence of the Cattle Economy," 98.

in *The Rich Man of Pietermaritzburg*. Thus the novel explores the widening gap between the theory and practice of indigenous ethical systems as colonial, capitalist structures of rule encroached on a rural communal cattle economy but also stresses that, in the face of attack, embedded systems of equitable exchange were reflected and sustained by local literary forms. The novel incorporates Zulu proverbs and elements of communally recited folktales to convey its universalizing message of ethical reciprocity.

The story concerns a relatively well-off villager, Mkhwanazi, his wife, maNtuli, his college-educated son, Themba, and daughter. One day Mkhwanazi receives a letter from the provincial capital, Pietermaritzburg, signed by a man who calls himself Ndebenkulu. Ndebenkulu, who is unknown to Mkhwanazi, professes to be a helper of his people and announces that he will be arriving by train at the station closest to Nyanyadu in a matter of days. Ndebenkulu's use of the title "Esq." has a formidable effect on Mkhwanazi and he extends his hospitality to Ndebenkulu despite the latter's self-aggrandizing arrogance. Ndebenkulu soon reveals that he has a capitalist plan involving selling off the village cattle for much higher prices than the villagers had ever thought it possible to obtain. However, Themba becomes convinced that Ndebenkulu is nothing but a trickster and consults his local friend, a detective, about Ndebenkulu. At the end of the story, just as Ndebenkulu is driving the cattle to the station in preparation to steal them, he is caught by the local police.

Ndebenkulu represents the Zulu trickster figure, Chakijana, a name derived from *ichakide*, the slender mongoose known for being small, swift, and tricky. This trickster either appears in Zulu folktales as Chakijana the mongoose or Nogwaja the hare and is characterized as self-centered, egotistical, and devoid of any real emotion.[46] Ndebenkulu exhibits all of these qualities, embodying the emptying out of relationships under the encroaching rule of capital so that people and their relationships with each other begin to be reduced to the material things they own. As a counterpoint to the malignant trickster of the new republic represented by Ndebenkulu, the novel employs the ironic narrative voice of the anticolonial Zulu trickster of indigenous storytelling. This narrative voice consolidates "a person is a person through other people" in opposition to Ndebenkulu's capitalist logic and is modeled after the real historical Chakijana who appeared during the colonial era. The historical Chakijana was a clever, crafty rebel involved in Zulu guerilla wars against both the Boers and the English in the Anglo-Boer war, acting as a double agent. This Chakijana is celebrated in Zulu historiography and storytelling as

---

46. Canonici, "The Trickster in Zulu Folktales," accessed November 2014, http://alternation.ukzn.ac.za/docs/01.2/05%20Can.pdf, 44.

one who was always eager for combat in multiple forms to protect his people. Nyembezi uses the historical anticolonial Chakijana to rework the indigenous narrative trope of the unscrupulous trickster. The traditional Chakijana, here symbolically working toward the ends of the colonial government in the form of Ndebenkulu, is outdone by a new Chakijana working in the tradition of the anticolonial trickster of the nineteenth century.

Nyembezi's ethical vision is embodied in this anticolonial trickster narrative style, which orchestrates a critical realism by leading the reader into treating the narrative voice as a real person—a constitutor of the self as active reader—who must be continually interrogated and whose opinions thereby become crucial to the formulation of the reader's own ethical stance. The narrative voice continually tricks us into being dynamic interpreters who can figure out Ndebenkulu's orchestrated fraud. For instance, when describing Mkhwanazi's admiration of Ndebenkulu, the narrative voice declares that "he was in awe of him, his social status, knowledge and even, perhaps, his shadow."[47] Social status and knowledge are both, at first glance, qualities that it makes sense to admire. However, the addition of the word "shadow" creates an active reader who is an extension of the narrative voice by suggesting that in fact Ndebenkulu's "social status" and "knowledge" are not what they seem and that the narrator does not in fact respect them. This leads the reader to the possibility that these qualities do not deserve to be respected, for Ndebenkulu's "knowledge" of English and social status as an urban, educated "gentleman" are in fact implicated, directly and indirectly, in the oppression of the rural community of Nyanyadu. Through this process of reader–narrator co-constitution, the novel actively generates our suspicion of the capitalist ontologies represented by Ndebenkulu.

Another key way that the narrator constitutes the reader as an active interrogator is through irony. Statements made by the narrator as well as the characters are tinged with double meaning, insinuating that titles, designations, and marks of social status cannot be taken as straightforward markers of character, for people and social structures are not in reality what they appear when depicted through the language of the powerful. This subtle irony, moreover, often veers into an irreverent sarcasm, thus encouraging readerly critique and evaluation. For instance, when describing Ndebenkulu's meeting with the villagers to convince them to sell their cattle, the narrative voice declares: "when it was time for the congregation to sit down, he would take much longer to sit, as if he expected applause. There are men, and then there

---

47. Nyembezi, *The Rich Man of Pietermaritzburg*, 76.

is Ndebenkulu."[48] The last sentence can be taken at face value, accepting Ndebenkulu for who he says he is—someone who is greater than other "men." However, interpreted sarcastically, the narrative voice suggests that in fact Ndebenkulu does not even deserve the status of "man." This use of sarcasm pits an *ubuntu* ontology in which a man is a man through his relationships with others against a capitalist evaluation of people as defined by their social status. In these ways, the narrative voice prods the reader into an interrogation of the social reality of the novel. At first, like the historical anticolonial Chakijana, the narrative voice seems too close to the powerful, acting on their behalf. But in fact he is engaged in critiquing the world of power that has eroded existing communal systems and produced Ndebenkulu. The critical experimentation of the trickster narrative voice thus creates a world of humor, satire, and social criticism to reinstate the ethical vision embodied in "a person is a person through other people."

In line with the aim of discrediting Ndebenkulu's worldview, Nyembezi establishes the importance of ethical discourses related to "a person is a person through other people" from the start of his novel, thus laying the groundwork to convincingly depict their erosion and the necessity of their preservation. He constantly references practices of hospitality premised on customs of giving and receiving. When his characters visit neighbors, they almost always declare: "Sakubona!" continuing with dialogues such as: "what more can a visitor ask of his host than to be grateful for whatever is provided?"[49] 'Sakubona' translates as "I see you," and inherent in this greeting and response is the sense that one's existence depends on being "seen" by another. This greeting encapsulates the understanding of self and other in "a person is a person through other people."

However, Nyembezi also conveys that this is by no means an idealized context in which everyone practices or is constituted by *ubuntu*. Instead, he seeks to communicate that such discourses clearly still serve as moral touchstones and represent extant cognitive frameworks even as they seem to be losing force; although Mkhwanazi and his wife do not always practice these injunctions, they are familiar with these precepts and know they are important. This is made clear when Ndebenkulu comes to stay and irritates maNtuli with his demanding arrogance. When maNtuli refuses to serve him, her friend maShezi admonishes her:

---

48. Ibid., 78.
49. Nyembezi, *The Rich Man of Pietermaritzburg*, 129.

> maNtuli, you're at fault. You must learn to manage your emotions maturely. You know quite well that in our culture one isn't allowed to be discourteous to a guest. As we say, there's no telling where your itchy foot will take you tomorrow.
>
> Well that expression of our elders was definitely not coined for the kind of guests who insult their hosts and create disharmony in a family on their arrival.... Do you think it's my problem if he's hungry?
>
> Please don't act like a child maNtuli, and stop being heartless. Even if this man has angered you, he's still your guest and you owe it to yourself to do the right thing.[50]

This passage conveys the tensions implicit in the practice of ethical discourses of giving and receiving. On one hand, it is clear that a guest is to be treated well predominantly because of the expectation of reciprocity. MaNtuli "owes it to herself" to serve Ndebenkulu, for "as we say, there's no telling where your itchy foot will take you tomorrow." This is a reference to a slew of metaphorical proverbs, "the foot has no nose," "the foot has no rest," and "the foot has no eyes," that Nyembezi references in *Zulu Proverbs*, adding "giving strangers, or any other people food is not to waste food but merely to provide for oneself."[51] However, the universal essence posited by *ubuntu* is also contingent on who the "other people" of "a person is a person through other people" are; maNtuli is also completely justified in refusing this guest good treatment because his lack of courtesy makes him unlikely to reciprocate should the need arise: "well that expression of our elders was definitely not coined for the kind of guests who insult their hosts and create disharmony in a family on their arrival." Nyembezi's emphasis on "proper behavior," "right thing," and "duty," shows that these are aspirational ideals rather than social mechanisms that are always already in place. Furthermore, they are discourses that come with their own contradictions and tensions.

Nevertheless, these contradictory discourses are pervasive because they undergird material structures of ethical exchange very different from capitalist principles of social differentiation. At one point, Mkhwanazi references *ubuntu*, reminding maNtuli that a stranger must be treated hospitably even though at this time other people would "wash their hands of him," for being inhospitable would violate *ubuntu* understandings of the self–other. Mkhwanazi further alludes to other discursive elements of *ubuntu*: "he must realize

---

50. Ibid., 62.
51. Nyembezi, *Zula Proverbs*, 53–54.

that he's far from home. When one is far away from home even mud may be offered as food. He's bound to know that hard reality quite well."[52] This is reminiscent of the proverbs "the stomach of a stranger is small" and "the beast that is passing finishes no grass," also referenced in *Zulu Proverbs*, which emphasize the duty of the stranger to receive with gratitude whatever he or she is given.[53] Yet maNtuli is concerned because she has "nothing befitting his status,"[54] thus signaling a new order in which people are not evaluated through a universalizing discourse of co-constitution and reciprocity but through their class position.

Indeed, it is clear in the novel's context that things have changed. The novel contains two parallel registers of temporality, one belonging to the modern republic of South Africa with its falsely universalizing capitalist system and divisive racial policies and one of the Zulu village's local discourses of mutual reciprocity and embedded systems of exchange. The disjuncture between these two temporalities is signposted from the first passage of the novel, which refers to a time when the village was unconnected to central areas and differentiates it from the present when "one is able to travel all the way to Nyanyadu by bus."[55] Ndebenkulu, who is constantly associated with the whites and urban bourgeoisie, represents the consequences of the accessibility of previously distant rural lands to the colonial bourgeoisie. As such, Ndebenkulu is a personification of the erosion of the rural cattle economy because of the policies of colonial capitalism. Indeed, in colonial Zululand, agriculture declined in the first half of the twentieth century because the colonial government gave a lot of the land to whites. Cattle thus came to be a fragile barrier for the rural poor between penury and having to leave home to join the migrant labor system within the money economy. Simultaneously, however, the Native Affairs Department (NAD) began holding auctions to buy up Zulu cattle to limit what it viewed as overstocking in the cattle reserves. This was, of course, a judgment that was itself the result of a capitalist mode of evaluation for, within *Ubuntu*, cattle were not 'stock' but stores of use value as well as representations of political bonds between a chief and his subjects, reciprocal bonds between family and friends, and sacred bonds between people and the ancestors. The colonial republic's attempt to alleviate 'overstocking' only added to rural Zulu misery. Zulus resisted these encroachments into their communal economies, especially after the Second World War when suspicions about the motives of the government grew with the rise of African-nationalist politics.

---

52. Nyembezi, *The Rich Man of Pietermaritzburg*, 18.
53. Nyembezi, *Zulu Proverbs*, 53–54.
54. Nyembezi, *The Rich Man of Pietermaritzburg*, 18.
55. Ibid., 8.

Nevertheless, finding themselves in increasingly dire circumstances, Zulus finally had no choice but to turn to private cattle speculators to sell what the state was calling 'surplus' cattle.[56]

Ndebenkulu pretends he has connections to white cattle buyers, professing to be working on the side of the Zulu peasants even as he implements the policies of colonial capitalism. He takes advantage of the villagers' fears, claiming to have the ability to obtain fantastically high prices of £40–60 per head of cattle, even though the going rate in 1947 was £4–5 per head.[57] Ndebenkulu reminds the men that "It is unusual that a black person's cattle fetch twenty pounds per head."[58] The statement reveals the lie behind colonial capitalism's supposedly universalizing logic. For the system posits equivalences between people and the commodities they own but does not translate this equivalence into universalizing ideals of 'equality' in the social sphere. Rather, the act of exchange undoes these ethical ideals, for a black person's cattle is valued as less than that of a white person. Rather than beginning from an abstract premise of human equality as contextual universalisms attempt, capitalism is always already contextualized by social divisions such as race. This gives Ndebenkulu, who professes to know white buyers personally, the justification for selling villagers' cattle off on their behalf.

In doing so, Ndebenkulu evaluates the villagers' cattle solely according to capitalist logic:

> People like us who live in the city do not care much about a cow with four legs, hair and horns. Our kind of cow stays in the bank. This kind of cow doesn't get cold and sick. This cow doesn't need to be taken to the dipping tank, it doesn't wreak havoc in other people's fields and cause unnecessary legal troubles, doesn't become a problem that requires one's kraal to be increased, because in our kraal there is no overcrowding. In short, I just want to tell those who still believe that a cow with hair is everything, to think again. They must also consider the cow that is mined down under the ground."[59]

For Ndebenkulu, cows are nothing but commodities, equivalent to gold or the money form, and stripped of their sacred, political, and economic functions. Their material and symbolic use values are transubstantiated into nothing more than exchange value, thus alienating them from other social relation-

---

56. MacKinnon, "The Persistence of the Cattle Economy," 119–25.

57. Nyembezi, *The Rich Man of Pietermaritzburg*, 95; MacKinnon, "The Persistence of the Cattle Economy," 108.

58. Nyembezi, *The Rich Man of Pietermaritzburg*, 96.

59. Ibid., 88.

ships and meanings. Ndebenkulu's metaphor of the "cow that is mined," then, delineates an entire capitalist cognitive framework that disregards the spiritual significance of cattle as sacred entities involved in binding the living to the ancestral dead and in buttressing ethical economic, social, and political systems. It is not surprising that Ndebenkulu's words are greeted with repugnance: "the disappointment of the men was overpowering. Some uttered audible sounds of disgust. Some even concluded that perhaps the man was an agent of the state."[60]

Yet, Nyembezi shows that people are eventually taken in by Ndebenkulu's words because of the disjuncture that now exists between discourses of ethical exchange that define people through their relationships with others and the systematic rule of capital that empties out these bonds, reducing people to nothing more than possessors of capital. This disjuncture is best demonstrated by Mkhwanazi's awe of Ndebenkulu's title "Esq." As Mark Sanders points out, the title "esquire" carries two completely different meanings depending on the worldview one brings to it. If one confines oneself to English, the language of capital, as Themba does, then 'esquire' is only a convention relating to one's social status.[61] As Themba tells his father, "the fact that he calls himself an Esquire doesn't mean much, father."[62] However, the *ubuntu* system of reciprocal exchange treats titles very differently—as being synonymous with one's functions, relationships, and duties to the society within which one lives. Nyembezi signals this different understanding of a title by Zulu-izing the word 'esquire' into *ubukwaya,* or esquire-ness,[63] thus conveying Mkhwanazi's equation of a noble social status with nobility in personality and comportment. Nevertheless, the anticolonial trickster narrative voice simultaneously alerts the reader that such social designations should not be taken at face value by narrating a scene in which Mkhwanazi discovers Ndebenkulu eavesdropping on their conversation: "Mkhwanazi was stunned. He wondered for how long Ndebenkulu had been eavesdropping. . . . This annoyed him—how could a man of Ndebenkulu's stature do such a low thing?" As if reading Mkhwanazi's mind, Ndebenkulu responds to Mkhwanazi's shocked silence with, "how can a man of my stature be caught tip-toeing in another man's house? The reality is that I wouldn't be seen dead doing such a low thing. Such deeds are the deeds of low class people." Since the reader knows Ndebenkulu has been eavesdropping, his equation of social stature with moral behavior is also called into

---

60. Ibid., 88–89.
61. Sanders, "Undone by Laughter," 352.
62. Nyembezi, *The Rich Man of Pietermaritzburg,* 56.
63. Ibid., 104; Sanders, "Undone by Laughter," 353.

question, leading the reader to trust Themba's skepticism about labels such as "esquire" more than Mkhwanazi's willingness to buy into them.

In contrast, the chief of the village embodies his title in a way that is inextricable from his responsibilities toward other people. Nyembezi writes that he "had been to school, and whenever he had guests he believed in attending to them without delay, not letting them suffer under the scorching sun. When he entered the traditional Zulu hut where Diliza and Mpungose were waiting for him, he politely shook their hands and welcomed them warmly."[64] In recognition of these qualities, the chief is described as the one who oversees important processes such as the selling off of cattle, leading some villagers to protest Ndebenkulu's attempts to usurp that role:

> If "this man" is here to discuss such important matters as reducing our livestock who else but the chief should take charge of an issue as serious as this? So Mkhwanazi you must explain to all of us who made you the chief? When was Sisolengwe removed from the chieftancy? Who did it and at which imbizo? What are you trying to say Mkhwanazi when you invite visitors to our tribal authority to discuss issues that are so important that only the chief should preside over them?[65]

The chief, the traditional guardian of all the cattle in the village, is deliberately left out of these discussions because in this new world produced by the injunctions of capital, a title does not have to be earned and need not remain a signifier of the self's relationships with others. This disjuncture between "*isikwaya*" and "esquire" is signposted repeatedly throughout the text as Nyembezi continually highlights "esquire" as a floating, empty signifier when used by Ndebenkulu: "I'm highly respected where I come from and there is not even a single white person who writes to me without addressing me as an Esquire. Perhaps most of you have no idea what the word Esquire means. What I can tell you is that the title is only reserved for very important white people and no insignificant white person uses that title. That is why when a sillyboy does what even whites don't do when I talk to them at very important gatherings, I am really annoyed."[66] Ndebenkulu uses the word "esquire" to signify his participation in whiteness, thereby consolidating the villagers' impression of his supremacy over them. He confirms this difference at another moment in the novel, declaring that he cannot travel on the villagers' wagons, for "people were never equal madam. There are people who can be transported on makeshift

---

64. Nyembezi, *The Rich Man of Pietermaritzburg*, 135.
65. Ibid., 94.
66. Ibid., 82.

carts. I am not one of them."[67] This refusal is in direct contradiction to the view that the other is an extension of the self, for it implies that the villagers' kind yet impoverished treatment of him does not befit Ndebenkulu's status.

Far from being an '*isikwaya*' whose title signifies meaningful relationships with other people, the text hints that if "a person is a person through other people," Ndebenkulu is clearly not a person—an entity constituted by obligations to give and receive. Ndebenkulu constantly talks about giving, but his real intentions are betrayed as unethical because he does not talk about receiving. Instead he constantly points out that he does not need anything from the villagers because he is already a rich man.

> I would like to emphasize that I'm a man of means, Mr. Mkhwanazi. I've got enough money for my family and me. I've got properties I bought through my own sweat. I have my own livestock. I have two cars, one for me and another for my wife. I'm not trying to show off about my material possessions, no, it's not the case. I'm merely showing you that for someone who is as successful and self-sufficient as I am, it's truly disappointing when people doubt your good intentions. It's truly disappointing.[68]

Ndebenkulu evaluates himself as a human being of "good intentions" solely in terms of the capital he owns. In fact, he even attributes his interest in selling the village land and cattle purely to benevolence. The text suggests that this unlikely equation between good intentions and one's social status in itself should have alerted the villagers to his lack of honesty, for an altruistic gift is both impossible and immoral—it is a way of stepping out of a discourse of common humanity that relies on reciprocity.

As the novel proceeds, Ndebenkulu's title, and finally Ndebenkulu himself, is revealed as nothing but a floating signifier, a title without substance or duties. In fact, Ndebenkulu's alias, Mlomo, means "mouth," signaling that he is just words that don't translate into action.[69] He is "all mouth and little else."[70] His own name points to his lack of anchoring in fixed, stable relationships with others. As characters repeatedly point out when they hear his name, no Ndebenkulu clan exists among Zulus,[71] and "Ndebeningi" (many-lip), maNtuli's parody,[72] does not yield one either. The man is clearly not who he says he

---

67. Ibid., 39.
68. Ibid., 67.
69. Sanders, "Undone By Laughter," 355.
70. Kunene, *The Zulu Novels of C. L. S. Nyembezi*, 196.
71. Nyembezi, *The Rich Man of Pietermaritzburg*, 12.
72. Ibid., 41.

is for, in Zulu and as a Zulu, Ndebenkulu is impossible.[73] Thus, in constantly foregrounding Ndebenkulu's ridiculous name, the anticolonial trickster narrative voice foreshadows that Ndebenkulu is made up, while also signaling that his most prominent features are nothing but false costumes and props. Ndebenkulu is insubstantial as a person, nothing more than a questionable intruder, and will sooner or later disappear. Thus, Nyembezi constantly highlights his material objects, suggesting that Ndebenkulu has no other substance apart from his ten-pound portmanteau, five-pound hat, and "my clothes [. . .] Do you have any idea how much I paid for these clothes?"[74] Ndebenkulu's selfhood is constituted by material objects that symbolize an empty capitalist modernity rather than being made up of substantial interpersonal relationships within the universalizing worldview of *ubuntu*.

III. TRACING *UBUNTU* INTO THE POSTCOLONIAL AFRICAN NOVEL

Despite the hegemonic iterations of *ubuntu* described in the first section of this chapter, novels like *The Rich Man of Pietermaritzburg* show that in the twentieth century some iterations of "a person is a person through other people" remained tied to ethical practices of exchange in response to the excesses of colonial capitalism. In this section, I trace these universalizing ontologies into a popular postcolonial South African novel in English, Zakes Mda's *Ways of Dying* (1996). The novel demonstrates Mda's interest in the ways that precolonial cultural forms such as "a person is a person through other people" live on within postcolonial modernity. In an interview in which Mda was asked what he thought about the term 'African Renaissance,' he responded:

> Renaissance involves both "development" and "rediscovery." I would have a problem with "revival." It implies "going back" to the archive to reinvent culture and reclaim a pre-colonial authenticity that is lost. All these, in my view, are conservative and reactionary notions. . . . We cannot hope to revive the great civilizations that existed in many parts of Africa. But we can rediscover them—their literature, their philosophy.[75]

Ways of Dying reflects how communal oral traditions linked to prior forms of social organization ground and enact "a person is a person through other

---

73. Sanders, "Undone By Laughter," 353.
74. Nyembezi, *The Rich Man of Pietermaritzburg*, 34, 41.
75. Mda in Robins, "City Sites," 117.

people" in the present but does not do so in a nativist attempt to revive a lost, precolonial past. Instead, Mda suggests acknowledging the ways that the past, its sensibilities and its aesthetic forms, lives on in the present. As Liz Gunner elaborates, instead of seeking a "purist orality that is beyond the grasp of the modern," one must recognize the ways in which "orality has been extended into various configurations of modernity."[76]

Mda's text traces the contextual universalism of "a person is a person through other people" into a troubled, violent South Africa during the interregnum period, right before the apartheid government gave way to the democratic state. The text depicts this era through the unusual relationship between a "professional mourner," Toloki, paid to publicly grieve at funerals, and his bereaved friend Noria, once a notoriously wild young girl in their common home village whose young son has been murdered in factional violence. Mda describes their experiences of political violence via extended flashbacks to their shared childhoods through a vernacular poetics; using a communal narrative voice adapted from indigenous storytelling practices ("we live our lives as one"), Mda conveys the central insight that has shaped Toloki's life—that violent lives lead to violent deaths: "Death lives with us every day. Indeed our ways of dying are our ways of living."[77]

Ways of Dying portrays the need for "a person is a person through other people" through the harsh backdrop of Toloki and Noria's story. The residents of the settlement are subject to ethnic clashes, but tribal affiliation represents little but a "hunger for power," a transparent rationalization for sponsoring and fueling intra-black-community violence. The antiapartheid resistance group the "Young Tigers," for instance, teaches the children of the settlement about apartheid oppression and the imperatives of the liberation movement but eventually "necklace" and murder Noria's six-year-old son for being a "sell out." This violence is compounded by white racism. Early on in the novel a white manager douses one of his employees in petrol and burns him alive. Rather than focusing on mass resistance movements or defined ideological standpoints to counter these atrocities, Mda eschews an explicit position vis. a vis. the radical, often violent, politics he depicts, leading critics such as Rita Barnard to categorize the novel as post-antiapartheid in its form and content.[78] Grant Farred is troubled by the novel's retreat from radical politics, arguing that it "represents an unacknowledged, poorly disguised, and disturbing political neutrality."[79] However, building on Rita Barnard's reading of the

---

76. Gunner, "Africa and Orality," 1–5, 12–13.
77. Mda, *Ways of Dying*, 98.
78. Barnard, "On Laughter," 280.
79. Farred, "Mourning the Postapartheid State," 186.

novel, I suggest that one can also see the text as a call for a new kind of politics.[80] This involves what the writer Njabulo Ndebele has called a "rediscovery of the ordinary"; political action for Mda takes the form of humane everyday modes of living and dying grounded in small interpersonal gestures related to "a person is a person through other people."

Ways of Dying foregrounds the ways that reciprocal practices of exchange continue to produce valuable modes of being within postcolonial modernity, even when they are no longer bolstered by systematic institutions of agricultural distribution. The concept of "a person is a person through other people" buttresses these practices within a larger conceptual network, which also includes Christian notions of redemption and healing and a post-Enlightenment notion of the commons pertaining to "the greatest happiness for the greatest number." The prevalence of this conceptual network in the interregnum era makes sense when one considers that apartheid capital had not just abstracted blacks from their labor but reduced them to objects to be used themselves; perhaps this is why as racialized capital encroached into all areas of life, subaltern resistance was expressed by clinging to universalizing ontologies that resisted the commodification of the self. If "a person is a person through other people," the products of one's labor always already belong to everyone else, existing as a communal resource to be exchanged and given freely, as needed.

It is not surprising, then, that an *ubuntu* universalism involving sharing food is prevalent within the novel. Nelson Mandela refers to these practices in Story One at the beginning of this chapter,[81] and Archbishop Desmond Tutu also hints at them, defining *ubuntu* so:

> When we want to give high praise to someone we say, "*Yu, u nobuntu*"; "Hey, so-and-so has *ubuntu*." Then you are generous, you are hospitable, you are friendly and caring and compassionate. You share what you have. It is to say, "My humanity is caught up, is inextricably bound up in yours."[82]

Mda also describes rituals of sharing food among funeral mourners to convey that local universalisms, and the practices that they buttressed, still survive, albeit in altered, fragmented forms. However, the text first shows that impediments to such practices exist, for if "our ways of dying are our ways of living," then death does not do away with capitalist and social stratifications such as class and race, and "a person is a person through other people" too

---

80. Barnard, "On Laughter," 279.
81. Mandela, "The Ubuntu Experience."
82. Tutu, *No Future Without Forgiveness*, 31.

often remains an empty proverb in a context where only the rich are "people" worthy of being given food.

> At some funerals, especially in the townships where there are better off people, the system of dispensing food is different. The most important people ... are served food inside the house at the table. The food that is served there will include not only the usual funeral fare of samp and beef, but rice, and some salads, and jelly and custard. The second stratum is made up of those people who are fairly important, but not well known enough to sit inside at the table. They form a line outside, and women at a table dish samp, beef, and sometimes cabbage onto their individual paper or plastic plates. The final stratum is that of the rabble. They are fed samp and beef in communal basins, as is done at this funeral in the settlement. No one ever has to stand there and separate people according to their strata. People know who they are and where they belong. These things always work themselves out.[83]

The food served to the upper classes, called "people," is different from everyone else's, who are called the "rabble," with methods of consumption symbolically enacting class differentiations. The passage conveys that the personhood and inclusion of some too often depends on the exclusion of others based on their lack of property and social status.

After depicting the erosion of contextual universalisms like "a person is a person through other people" by social hierarchies, Mda seeks to reinstate the proverb's aspirational philosophy through a depiction of the poor "rabble" at another funeral. These people are the only ones who come close to recognizing each other as people, for in the settlement there is no differentiation; "everyone eats like this." The poor funeral goers share food out of the same containers and engage in a ritual of communal consumption. Moreover, unlike the previous description of a stratified funeral, the food here is depicted positively, for it has been painstakingly prepared despite the limited facilities available: "Toloki is impressed by the care taken with the food. The meat is so soft ... that even old grandmothers and grandfathers can chew it with their gums. It is well salted. The samp is also soft and tender. Often the samp at funerals is hard and undercooked."[84] Rather than treating eating as an empty ritual related to the consumption of commodities, the providers have engaged in the sharing and gifting of food as recognition of the humanity of the other, for its preparation reflects care towards the elderly and otherwise vulnerable.

---

83. Mda, *Ways of Dying*, 162.
84. Ibid.

The food, appealingly described through alliterative adjectives, itself takes on representative qualities symbolic of ethical social relationships.

Mda repeatedly conveys the symbolic importance of giving and receiving food, suggesting that the act of receiving food from others is not worth undertaking if it does not also involve the giver's recognition that the receiver is human. "Hungry as he is, he will not partake of their food . . . when he used to join the men's basin they would make snide remarks. Blunt ones would even tell him rudely that he was not welcome at their dish."[85] Toloki's refusal to eat here is a refusal of a context where he is not recognized as a fellow human being. Similarly, when another wealthy character, Nefolovhodwe, insults him, Toloki vows to pay the man back for the food he has eaten there.

> Toloki was surprised that the great man remembered him, since on the previous occasion he had proved to have such a short memory. He told him that he did not want a job. He had come to pay for all the food he had eaten in his house. At first Nefolovhodwe felt insulted, but then decided that Toloki must be mad. Perhaps poverty had gone to his head and loosened a few screws. . . . Toloki walked to his desk and dumped some bank notes on it. He had already determined how much the food he had eaten in that house had cost. Then he walked out with all the dignity he could muster.[86]

In this passage, which I mention briefly in Story One, Toloki recognizes that he must pay Nefolovhodwe back because the food he has eaten is not given to him in recognition of his common humanity but as a form of pity toward an inferior in a commodified field of human relationships. In this moment, the text juxtaposes a capitalist modernity with another world of reciprocal, communal exchange, demonstrating their conflict. However, it also shows that within the embedded ontology of *ubuntu*, Toloki's insistence on paying Nefolovhodwe back is a weapon; by not accepting the food as a gift, Toloki infers that Nefolovhodwe is not a "person," thereby justifying Nefolovhodwe's initial feeling of being insulted.

Mda's novel seeks to recognize the ontological *puissance* of "a person is a person through other people" in resistance to the *pouvoir* of apartheid capitalism that pervades the interregnum era. At the end of the novel, Toloki and Noria refuse to sell Toloki's dead father's art figurines as commodities:

> On examining the work, the art dealer said that the figurines looked quite kitschy, but added that kitsch was the "in" thing for collectors with taste this

---

85. Ibid., 10.
86. Ibid., 165.

season. It was likely that this trend would continue for the next two years or so. The museum man disagreed. He said that the work was folksy rather than kitsch. And folksy works were always in demand with trendy collectors. Although the two men disagreed on how to define Jwara's work, they both agreed that it had some value. The problem, of course, was that because there were so many works, they would not fetch a high price.[87]

Mda points out that capitalist notions of exchange value have nothing to do with the intrinsic properties of an object, relying instead on completely subjective modes of valuation to do with seemingly random and fleeting market forces. Thus the art dealers have contrary notions of what the supposedly intrinsic properties of the figurines are, disagreeing on whether they are "kitsch" or "folksy" but agreeing that they are exchangeable for money. Toloki refuses this offer to commodify his father's artwork in line with a completely different cognitive framework pertaining to *ubuntu* exchange, for not only does he refuse to sell the figurines for profit, he also decides to acknowledge his dead father's wishes that he keep them, heeding Noria's advice that "our elders say that we should build a kraal around the word of the deceased, because it is precious like cattle used to be. When your father says you must have the figurines, then you must have the figurines." Mda's comparison of an ancestor's injunction to cattle recognizes that both transcend valuation in terms of exchange value, instead deriving their value as consolidations of the social and spiritual relationships between people and between people and their ancestors. It is not surprising, then, that Mda depicts the children of the settlement as more "fascinated by the figurines" than by the impressive commodity before them—that of Nefelovhodwe's limousine. This recognition of the true value of the figurines is derived from the enchanted way in which they, like sacred cattle, cement bonds between people, uniting the initially divided children into a dissensual space in which the only thing that matters is their shared humanity.

This contextual universalism works with a post-Enlightenment concept of the greatest happiness for the greatest number of people to exceed capitalist ontologies of exchange. Through Toloki's decision to share the figurines as a communal resource, they come to symbolize an idea of the commons within which the greatest number can be happy. Mda explains that Toloki refuses to sell the figurines because they have a magical capacity to bring about joy, causing the children to "fall into such paroxysms of laughter that they roll around on the ground."[88] The children's inexplicable experience of utter joy in

---

87. Ibid., 209.
88. Ibid., 210.

the presence of the figurines coincides with the beginning of the new year, prompting the "settlement people to burst into a cacophony: beating pots and pans and other utensils together, while shouting "Happe-e-e-e! New Year!"[89] Mda repeats the word "Happe-e-e-e!" throughout the passage to signify that the happiness produced by the communal figurines seems to be contagious, affecting the entire settlement. In the last paragraph of the novel, the narrative voice therefore shifts to the perspective of the communal all-seeing 'We' and relates: "Two hours after midnight, we are still shouting 'Happe-e-e-e!' We do not touch [the figurines]. We just look and marvel. Our children have told us about the monsters that make people happy . . . it seems that we can see them through the boxes, shimmering like fool's gold. Not even the most habitual thieves among us lift a finger toward the boxes."[90] The "monsters" are "fool's gold" because they cannot be reduced to the universal equivalent of the money form but also because only fools would sell these enchanted generators of happiness as commodities. Even the "habitual thieves" realize that the figurines represent something akin to "the greatest happiness for the greatest number of people" and refuse to appropriate their value for individual profit.[91]

The syncretic conceptual network pertaining to ethical exchange also includes Christian notions of redemption and healing, which are put to work alongside "a person is a person through other people." Mda repeatedly alludes to the *ubuntu* proverbs recorded by Nyembezi and mentioned in the previous chapter, including *isandla sigez'esinye,* or "the hand washes the other."[92] Noria's neighbors, for instance, bring her provisions after the brutal murder of her son, stating: "We want to lend you these things, Noria. You can use them until your situation has changed for the better, when you have found yourself. . . . We are like two hands that wash each other."[93] "The hand washes the other" or *isandla sigez'esinye* is one of the proverbs recorded by Mayr in his portrayal of an 'authentic' Africa but also by Nyembezi in his Zulu collection, suggesting the inextricable interdependence of people, for one hand cannot wash itself; it needs another. In another significant passage, the proverb is enacted between Toloki and Noria in conjunction with Christian notions of reciprocity:

> They both kneel over the basin, and with their washing rags, bathe each other with the aloed water. They dazedly rub each other's backs, and slowly move down to other parts of their bodies. It is as though they are responding to rhythms that are silent for the rest of the world, and can only be heard

---

89. Ibid., 211.
90. Ibid., 212.
91. Ibid., 204–6.
92. Nyembezi, *Zulu Proverbs,* 52.
93. Mda, *Ways of Dying,* 69.

or felt by them. They take turns to stand in the basin, and splash water on each other's bodies. All this they do in absolute silence, and their movements are slow and deliberate. They are in a dream like state, their thoughts concentrated only on what they are doing to each other. Nothing else matters. Nothing else exists.[94]

Mda describes the water as "aloed water," an echo of holy or "hallowed" water. The ritual of "the hand washes the other" is, then, a contextual universalism that connects selves to others but does so through a Christian discourse of healing and redemption. "The hand washes the other" is a means of cleansing one's self and one another of violence and reminding each other how to live.

Mda activates and transmits "a person is a person through other people" and the syncretic conceptual network within which it exists through the same vernacular aesthetic practices and narrative forms that previously buttressed "a person is a person through other people," including proverbs (*izagu*) and folk storytelling (*indaba*). Both Mda's figures of the nurse and the professional mourner exemplify such reinvented precolonial narrative forms and oral cultural practices adapted to fit the needs of the present. The job of the person designated a nurse is to speak at funerals, telling the story of the events surrounding the death of the deceased. The job of the mourner is to punctuate this telling with mournful sounds that evoke grief in the participants, using the performance to initiate a cognitive process whereby people simulate grief and mourning in their own motor system in order to recognize and understand another's. The characterization of Toloki as a professional mourner who initiates collective processes of grieving thus builds on a process described by cognitive neurologists whereby simulation is key to generating ethical empathy, for simulating our own pain causes us to feel someone else's.[95] Moreover, as in the *rasa* universalism explored in chapter 2, an other watching this simulation comes to feel versions of the simulated emotional states through the activation of his own motor neuron system, thereby leading to a process of emotional contagion.[96] The text suggests that these practices are part of a continuing embedded tradition of orality and public performance, for they "add an aura of sorrow and dignity that we last saw in the olden days when people knew how to mourn their dead."[97]

---

94. Mda, *Ways of Dying*, 192.

95. This is because to recognize and understand another agent's action, one simulates the perceived action in one's own motor system. More generally, social neuroscientists propose that such 'mirror circuits' provide a general mechanism for understanding diverse mental states in others See Rizzolatti and Craighero, "The Mirror-Neuron System," 169–92; and Gallese and Rizzolatti, "A Unifying View," 396–403.

96. Dimberg et al., "Unconscious Facial Reactions," 86–89.

97. Mda, *Ways of Dying*, 109.

Both the professions of the nurse and professional mourner enact and transmit "a person is a person through other people" in the minds of audiences by seeking to dignify the lives that have been lost; they recognize the deceased as belonging to networks of interpersonal relationships that exceed political, tribal, and regional factions. In doing so, they orchestrate a kind of dissensus during these troubled times, bringing self and other into the same space in a way that expands the demos. In their public modes of grieving and storytelling, they turn one person's grief, one person's story of suffering, into everyone else's, thereby uniting them on a dissensual stage. Such an interpretation contests Grant Farred's contrasting of Toloki with antiapartheid praise poets who "provide a focus of communal identity and solidarity,"[98] for Mda depicts Toloki's public mourning as clearly providing a community service: "Shadrack wants to know why, if his services are to the benefit of humankind, the people did not want him yesterday. . . . [Toloki responds] 'those were people who wanted to hoard all the mourning to themselves. We do come across such greed sometimes'" (54). In the *ubuntu* worldview, mourning on one's own is selfish, for if "a person is a person through other people," one person's grief must necessarily be everyone else's. The understanding that another's grief is also one's own is an ethical vision for the future, for if everyone felt the pain of another person's grief, they would not harm others in the first place.

An enacting of "a person is a person through other people" is similarly apparent in Mda's description of the nurse, whose embodied storytelling and political commentary produces a visceral experience of shared agitation at injustice. The nurse incorporates the oral performances of praise poets (*imbongi*) in tribal Zululand to generate this common affective experience.

> The Nurse is a toothless old man who has seen many winters. He holds a flywhisk made of the tail of a horse, and as he talks he uses it to whisk invisible flies from one side to another. He sways to the rhythm of his speech, working himself into an almost dance like frenzy that leaves us panting with excitement.[99]

This is very similar to how Trevor Cope describes the communal performative mode of *imbongi*: the praiser wore a fantastic costume of furs, feathers, and animal tails, reciting the praises at the top of his voice and as fast as possible. The high pitch, loudness, and fastness, aimed to create an emotional excitement in the audience as well as in the praiser himself, whose move-

---

98. Chapman, "From Shaka's Court," 35; and Farred, "Mourning the Post-Apartheid State," 192.

99. Mda, *Ways of Dying*, 153.

ment became increasingly exaggerated. Cope notes that it was a dramatic performance of suiting actions to words, producing an effect of seriousness and occasion.[100] Mda's lines convey that this mode of oral poetry is very effective in getting the audience to share in the nurse's own sentiments about the deaths he is relating: "he sways to the rhythm of his speech, working himself into an almost dance like frenzy that leaves us panting with excitement." While it is the nurse who is frenzied, the spectators and listeners affectively embody the nurse's agitation so that they become one with the nurse, the other grievers, as well as the person being grieved. Such an enacting of "a person is a person through other people" within communal practices of grieving becomes a way of assuaging political ills and human rights abuses by affirming the humanity of the wronged.

It is not only the nurse's bodily performance of shared agitation but his words too that enact "a person is a person through other people" through dissensus. The nurse's stories are personal, subjective narratives that nevertheless represent and shape everyone's experiences because they incorporate multiple opposing voices of the self and other within their fold. One such episode is presented early on in the novel, when the nurse explains at a funeral why someone died:

> "There are many ways of dying!" The Nurse shouts at us. Pain is etched in his voice, and rage has mapped his face . . . "It is not the first time that we bury little children. We bury them every day. But they are killed by the enemy . . . those we are fighting against. This our little brother was killed by those who are fighting to free us!" We mumble. It is not for the Nurse to make such statements. His duty is to tell how this child saw his death, not to give ammunition to the enemy. Is he perhaps trying to push his own political agenda? But others feel that there is no way the Nurse can explain to the funeral crowd how we killed the little brother without parading our shame to the world. That the enemy will seize hold of this, and use it against us, is certainly not the Nurse's fault. Like all good Nurses, he is going to be faithful to the facts. Tolokí belongs to the section of the crowd that believes strongly in the freedom of the Nurse to say it as he sees it. He has been to so many funerals, and has developed admiration for those who are designated Nurse at these rituals. . . . Usually they are a fountain of fascinating information about ways of dying.[101]

---

100. Stuart, *Izibongo*, 28–29.
101. Mda, *Ways of Dying*, 7.

Here, Mda suggests that the only way to come close to any objective version of the truth is to acknowledge the multiple perspectives inherent within any telling. Like the *imbongi*'s praise poems (*izibongo*) that critiqued chiefly despotism, the nurse's orality recognizes that letting various opinions exist together in discordant unity is the only way to undo hegemonic narratives of political violence. Indeed, as I demonstrate in chapter 4, the effectiveness of the *imbongi* in critiquing political power was primarily due to the communal nature of his performances. Thus, even though "people were not thrilled at the Nurse's constant editorializing," he continues to indulge in deliberate digressions that unmask the workings of power. To destabilize hegemonic political agendas is not to avoid mentioning them but to make sure that multiple voices, including the Nurse's, make clear their own subject positions in relation to power.

In line with this political realization, the structure of the above passage itself refuses to present a singular version of any event, orchestrating dissensus by presenting multiple opinions that coexist in the same space. As readers/listeners, we are simultaneously individual yet multiple—"we" are part of the communal narrative voice, "we" are listening to the nurse as spectators within the novel among Toloki and other discordant voices at the funeral. And, as readers "we" are also reading the narrative voice telling us what the nurse is saying. In presenting these multiple narrative perspectives at the level of the reader of the text, of the narrative voice recounting the text's stories, and also at the level of the characters within the text, the passage presents a perspective that is simultaneously one yet many; it consists of one voice—the narrator/storyteller's—that is composed of the perspectives of many: of a community of readers, of the nurse, of Toloki, and of the other spectators. The tensions between these multiple tellings are deliberately left unresolved, resulting in a sense of discordant unity that underlines how events can only be understood when they have been filtered through multiple lenses that inform one's own telling. Indeed, the passage suggests that stories of individual experiences are validated "by being placed side by side . . . and by being linked to the storehouse of collective wisdom."[102] This orchestration of "a person is a person through other people" suggests that one person's voice only matters when it is heard by others, giving way to the expression of a collective vision that is necessarily discordant in its unity.

In addition to the characters of the professional mourner and nurse, the novel's narrative voice also reminds the reader that it is itself the voice of unstable and subjective "gossip":

---

102. Obiechina, "Narrative Proverbs," 123–40.

It is not different, really, here in the city. Just like back in the village, we live our lives together as one. We know everything about everybody. We even know things that happen when we are not there; things that happen behind people's closed doors deep in the middle of the night. We are the all seeing eye of the village gossip. When in our orature the storyteller begins the story, "They say it once happened . . ." we are the "they."[103]

The narrative voice insists that every story is part of a living oral tradition that is jointly retold, elaborating that "no individual owns any story. The community is the owner of the story, and it can tell it the way it deems fit. We would not be needing to justify the communal voice that tells this story if you had not wondered how we became so omniscient in the affairs of Toloki and Noria."[104] The last statement forcefully affirms the authority of such a joint retelling of the story by stressing its omniscience. If everyone tells the story, everyone necessarily partakes in, and even creates, the knowledge it contains. Thus, the story will always belong to the community, a community that continues to grow with each invocation of the storyteller. Such a perspective enacts "a person is a person through other people" because if one person's story is necessarily everyone else's, one person's experiences are necessarily and spontaneously felt by everyone else in the village: "we live our lives together as one . . . we even know things that happen when we are not there; things that happen behind people's closed doors deep in the middle of the night."

Mda's textual performance of communal storytelling in the service of "a person is a person through other people" is a revitalization of the indigenous *indaba* tradition. As Ingrid Byerly explains, "*indaba* is a Zulu word meaning both an update on topical matters and a conference, symposium or meeting-place at which members of a group contribute equally towards the solution of a problem. It represents a process in which combined efforts are made by opposing parties towards achieving consensus through discussion of matters concerning the group as a whole."[105] In invoking the *indaba* tradition through its characters and narrative voice, the text suggests that Mda's storytelling, as well as the stories within his story, function as a way to work through disturbing social realities. The multivocal narrative in the passages quoted above performs just such a symposium, depicting various opinions, stories, and versions of experiences in order to come up with a collective solution to the political ills that haunt the characters.

---

103. Mda, *Ways of Dying*, 12.
104. Ibid.
105. Byerly, "Mirror, Mediator, and Prophet," 1.

If, as Joseph Slaughter has argued, the linear *bildungsroman* form naturalizes the dictates of international law and liberal humanism in the cultural consciousness of colonizing and colonized subjects, Mda's nonlinear, circular narrative and performance of communal multivocality can be seen as doing the opposite; Mda challenges the official single-voiced histories of what Rancière would label the 'ethnos'—of the apartheid government and of falsely universalizing nationalist groups wreaking violence within the settlement.[106] Instead, the novel invites the community to inhabit multiple perspectives at once as a way of understanding political injustices, thereby possibly participating in a solution. Through "a person is a person through other people," Mda's creative vernacular narrative recognizes numerous subjectivities as constitutive of one's own personhood.

This chapter has traced a rich history of linguistic, cultural, and political exchanges grounded in ethical systems of exchange linked to "a person is a person through other people." While *ubuntu* has been appropriated by the *pouvoir* of global capital for questionable ends, colonial and postcolonial literatures, including Nyembezi's *Rich Man of Pietermaritzburg* and Mda's *Ways of Dying*, reveal that precolonial versions of the concept extend into the present to exceed and challenge exclusionary capitalist principles of exchange. The next chapter elaborates on the way that *ubuntu*'s resistance to exploitative principles of commodity exchange was expanded to critique apartheid's commodification of black labor power. In the run-up to the end of apartheid, black workers harnessed the contextual universalism of "a chief is a chief through other people" in support of intertwined goals of economic and political justice.

---

106. Slaughter, *Human Rights Inc.*, 107.

CHAPTER 4

Electing the Demos from Tribal Praise Poetry to Twentieth-Century Trade Union Protest Poetry

STORY ONE: In July 2010, I was visiting the University of Witwatersrand to interview students, workers, and young professionals on the shifting meanings of *ubuntu*. When I asked one of my interviewees, a Xhosa man in his forties originally from a village in the eastern cape, about what *ubuntu* meant to him, he inexplicably began talking about a system of electing an *inkosi*, or "chief," in his village:

> Back home, the people choose someone with *ubuntu*. Who is not selfish. If he changes his behavior, we remove him and choose someone else unless he apologizes. You can criticize him if you don't like something he does; you can sit down with him. He is not allowed to work since his primary work is to serve his people, so we pool our money and our cows and goats and bring them to him. But if you cannot afford to give him anything, that is okay too. A chief with *ubuntu* should never ask for anything. He should just take what he is given. We say to him, "don't treat people badly just because you are a chief, don't sell land to them. Because we make you responsible for the whole village, you are just supposed to distribute it fairly to those in need. Don't take money from people who cannot afford to give you anything." If our boys are fighting we take him to the chief, not to the police, and he decides whether they have to go to the police or not. This small chief is our real government, not the local government. They have nothing to do with us."

I was fascinated. As I asked increasingly probing questions, it became apparent that in some cases "a person is a person through other people" also translated into another popular proverb, *Inkosi yinkosi ngabantu,* or "a chief is a chief through other people." That is, in some rural areas, the formation of cultures of 'rule by the people' had a lot to do with the sharing of material resources between a chief and his subjects in a way that positioned the *inkosi,* or chief, as an extension of, rather than the authority over, them. Such an ontology was linked to the production of communal agricultural economies that represented a relationship of mutual responsibility between a 'chief' and his subjects.

Another story: It was 1985 and two worker-poets stood atop a stage in the King's Park Stadium in Durban. It was the occasion of the launch of the Congress of South African Trade Unions (COSATU), the joint trade union formed to protect the interests of the hundreds of thousands of workers across apartheid South Africa. The poets Alfred Temba Qabula (1942–2002) and Mi S'dumo Hlathswayo (1951–) sang verses composed in the precolonial genre of the 'praise poem,' or *izibongo,* which was historically performed in criticism of the ruling chief, or *inkosi.* However, at this occasion they addressed the trade union and not a tribal chief as their *inkosi,* singing to a vast audience of gathered workers:

COSATU
Here we are!

We say:
Let your hands deliver us from exploitation
Let our freedom be born
Let our democracy be born
Let our new nation be born[1]

The crowd rose up in excitement with each line, cheering wildly. In another praise poem, or *izibongo,* to the trade union, Qabula and Hlatshwayo incited workers to rise above their oppression and fight for democracy, noting that:

Your labor
Has turned you
Into prize game
For the hunters of surplus

---

1. Qabula and Hlatshwayo, "Tears of the Creator," 289–90.

Within worker imaginations, the trade union was meant to safeguard workers in the way a chief would have. COSATU needed to replace an apartheid state that refused to reward workers' labor with material resources and sustenance. In positing a link between just government and equitable economic distribution, these poets drew on the precolonial discourse of "a chief is a chief through other people," within which the fulfillment of good government necessarily involved the constitution of a fair economic order in which citizens were adequately materially compensated.

And an origin story: In early nineteenth-century Zululand, in colonial South Africa, praise poets, or *imbongi*, sang about the terrorized subjects of Shaka (1785–1828), the dictatorial warrior chief. They protested that when Shaka went on rampages to neighboring territories

> women who were with child gave birth easily;
> The newly planted crops they left still short,
> The seed they left amongst the maize-stalks.
> The roots of the trees looked up at the sky.[2]

This *izibongo* was a searing critique of Shaka's authoritarian power; far from providing for his subjects, Shaka's military rages ripped the "seeds" of future generations from wombs, leaving the "seeds" of crops unplanted, saplings abandoned, and fully grown trees uprooted.

These seemingly disparate stories all make a point about good or bad government through metaphors of food sharing, food destruction, or food production, using imagery related to rearing livestock, hunting, gathering animal products, or harvesting crops. This chapter explores how within some South African political systems equitable practices of food distribution and usage were connected to ideals of democratic government. These aspirational principles referred to the belief that "a chief is a chief through other people," for the authority of the ruling party or ruler is created and sustained by the consent of its people, who are the source of all political power. Such an idea of 'rule by the people' supported a form of political organization that aimed at subjects' control over matters that affected their own interests. Moreover, within the Zulu public sphere examined here, 'rule by the people' referred not just to a political system where people had a right to decide who ruled over them and the laws that governed them but also to an institutionalized *culture* that involved being able to freely speak criticism of those chiefs or governors who did not share power with their subjects or rule ethically.[3]

---

2. Stuart, *Izibongo*, 90.
3. Chapman, *Southern African Literatures*, 49–53.

The contextual universalism of 'a chief is a chief through other people' is universalizing because it relates the self to the chiefly other as an equal. The chief, or the governing power, only acquires authority from the people and has to consistently earn the right to keep it. This is a contingent universalism because it is born of local, culturally specific ontologies such as "a person is a person through other people" and because it is dependent on the varied practices employed by the chief/government to economically sustain the people based on differing historical situations. In tribal South Africa, the achievement of economic sustenance depended on the just distribution of food, cattle, and agricultural resources to the people. In apartheid and postapartheid South Africa, economic sustenance was to be achieved by treating the trade unions as temporary 'chiefs' in a bid to desegregate a racist, exploitative state as well as the hierarchical multinational corporations that supported it.

The contextual and Enlightenment universalisms at work within the antiapartheid worker struggle were universalizing in a very different way than the universalizing force of capitalism as it was realized through multinational corporations. Like capitalism elsewhere, apartheid capitalism's universalizing force was not based on abstract premises of human equality that structured practices of wealth and food distribution accordingly; it was universalizing only within material practices related to capitalist systems of exchange as they expanded into new markets. But apartheid capitalism was unique in that it was explicitly and unambiguously racialized, for it only equated black workers working for multinational corporations with each other as producers of surplus value. And it did so through spatial segregation of black workers to tribal and linguistic enclaves called 'homelands,' where they were confined to the very periphery of economic activity until they were tapped as cheap labor by white corporation heads and brought to live without their families in urban areas, their existence limited to that of a worker. Apartheid capitalism also attempted to create an exploitable black working class by undereducating an entire black population into menial laborers alienated from the languages of industry. Apartheid capitalism, in other words, could relate the white self to the black other only in terms of the economic relationship of black commodified labor power with white racist owners of the means of production. And, as I show later, apartheid capitalism buttressed these exploitative principles by generating management discourse in line with profit-oriented goals. As a result, the segregated hierarchical environments of multinational corporations ensured that opposing raced classes could never come together on a dissensual stage. Demos expansion could only happen by achieving a dissensual unity between other black selves within trade unions, which used contextual and post-Enlightenment universalisms to create working-class solidarities, overthrow a deeply racist state, and build postcolonial modernity up anew.

The first and second parts of this chapter excavate cultures of 'rule by the people' in nineteenth-century Zulu oralities, including in *izibongo* that were chanted ritually by poets to capture the strengths or excesses of chiefs such as the infamous Shaka. Despite their uneven transmission, these texts testify to democratic political cultures tethered to communal practices of food sharing. The proverb "a chief is a chief through other people" referred to an intertwined political and economic system within which the sharing of political power was metonymically conceptualized in terms of the just distribution of milk and cattle. Finally, this section demonstrates how such a universalizing worldview was buttressed by the performative literary forms of praise poetry, particularly the *izibongo* of Shaka. These poems enacted a repetitive parallelism and universalizing multivocality that activated and transmitted a conceptual network concerning consensus-based political decision-making.

The third section of this chapter explores how the local literary and political cultures expressed by *izibongo* continued to be used by trade union workers to build mass resistance to oppressive social conditions well into the antiapartheid era. The poems of worker-poets such as Qabula and Hlathswayo were embedded in the tribal custom of publically chanting political praises to chiefs; the trade union was similarly conceptualized as a leader sanctioned by the ancestors to sustain the people by sharing power as well as material resources. The chiefly position granted to trade unions within these poems was due to the ways that black workers in the 1970s and 1980s imagined democratic government; the latter was to perform a role equivalent to that of a good chief, ensuring the political subject material sustenance in exchange for her labor. By this logic, a fight for equal citizenship within a democratic nation-state needed to achieve what the trade union also set as its ultimate goal: the emancipation of the workers. The contextual universalism of "a chief is a chief through other people" thus worked with post-Enlightenment ideals of majoritarian democracy in support of the African National Congress (ANC) as well as with notions of Marxist working-class revolution. Moreover, just as in nineteenth-century praise poems, *imbongi* used the vernacular poetic devices of multivocality and parallelism to harness these universalizing messages.

I. *INKOSI* UNIVERSALISM IN THE PRECOLONIAL AND COLONIAL PAST

Precolonial and colonial sources pertaining to aspirational ideals of 'rule by the people' convincingly testify to the communal behavior of food sharing that enacted "a person is a person through other people" and extend this behavioral reciprocity into the exchange of food and agricultural products between a chief and his subjects. The chief had a symbolic as well as functional role within the agricultural economy. Symbolically, he was considered a link to the ancestors and therefore partook in rituals such as the First Fruit Ceremony that infused the harvest with ancestral blessings. Only after he had done so was the harvest filtered down to the people. This was a ceremonial action that buttressed a functional role; as the guardian of the ancestor's wishes, a chief carried the ethical imperative of ensuring the material prosperity and well-being of his subjects through the collection and subsequent distribution of cattle, milk, and harvest from and to his subjects. Paul J. Bjerk, a historian of the Zulu kingdom, argues that because the chief's cattle were collected from every homestead in the realm, the chief "bound the strength of the entire kingdom unto himself, centralizing and controlling its power."[4] He then distributed this concentration of power by sharing land and cattle among his subjects, literally letting his warriors drink from the udders of the collected cows.[5] This was done without the chief formally 'owning' any of the items he collected, thereby negating any individualist conceptions of private property. In depending on the goods the chief received from his people, the organization of the communal food economy effectively literalized the maxim "a chief is a chief through other people."

This system of food distribution buttressed a political understanding of 'rule by the people,' with subjects continually evaluating a chief's performance of his duties through economic metrics to do with food distribution within public gatherings and meetings. While only open to males, individuals of any rank could express criticism of the chief's behavior.[6] Oral texts that circulated within such a public sphere repeatedly approve of chiefs' rule through descriptions of their sharing of crops and cattle and critique authoritarian rulers by speaking of their destruction of communal food economies. Cattle, milk, and food functioned as metonyms of power, and in praising those chiefs who shared their food, Zulu texts were also referring to how well chiefs extended their power to their subjects. References to how readily a chief shared his milk and cattle, and therefore his power, with his subjects symbolically conveyed his fitness to rule. Bjerk draws on sources that discussed the eating habits of the chiefly rivals Zungu and Makoba to determine which one should accede to the throne. He notes that since Makoba ate up everything he was given, whereas Zungu would only take one mouthful and let the rest fall through his hands, Makoba was a glutton and would be mean, whereas Zungu would be

---

4. Bjerk, "They Poured Themselves into the Milk," 6.
5. Ibid., 9.
6. Chapman, *Southern African Literatures*, 53–63.

content with a little and leave some for others; hence it was right he should become the chief despite Makoba's seniority.[7]

Evidence of these alimentary metonyms for power remain in evidence through the African continent. Poetic metaphors regarding amounts of food eaten, distributed, or stolen still serve as a gauge for the quality of political rule. For instance, the political theorist Jean Francis Bayart demonstrates how the size of the politician's "belly" functions as a critical metaphor for a nepotistic, corrupt African state in which government and business elite use their influence to enrich themselves, their families, or ethnic kinsmen.[8] Use of such metaphors serve as a popular mechanism by which to sanction democratic rule and challenge the misuse of political power. As Achille Mbembe has written, the belly is the "principal locale of the idioms and fantasies used in depicting power . . . the obesity of men in power, their impressive physique or, more crudely, the flow of shit which results from such a physique—these appeal to a people who can enjoy themselves with mockery and laughter. . . . They thus become part of a system of signs that the commandement leaves, like tracks, as it passes on its way, and so make it possible for someone to follow the trail of violence and domination that is intrinsic to the commandement."[9] Such references gesture to an established and common vocabulary of critique used to denounce those who are unwilling to share power or rule ethically.

The precursors to these contemporary vocabularies of critique are evident in precolonial and colonial proverbs, or *izagu,* and riddles, which also connect the ideas of interdependence that produced a communal food economy to viewpoints about a chief's function as the sustainer of his tribe. One riddle collected by the missionary Reverend Henry Callaway (1817–90), for instance, records a metaphoric description of the chief as the eye of his tribe:

> Guess ye a man who makes himself a chief; who does not work but just sits still; his people work alone, but he does nothing; he shows them what they wish, but he does nothing; his people do not see, he sees for them, they are blind, the whole of his nation; he alone can see. They know that though they cannot see; they see by him; for they do not go without anything they want; he takes them by the hand, and leads them to where there is food, and they return with it to their homes; but he touches nothing, for he makes himself a chief; he remains a chief for ever [sic], for his people are supported by him. . . . At first there was a dispute, and his people said, "You cannot be our king and do nothing; we cannot see the power of your majesty." He answered them,

---

7. Bjerk. "They Poured Themselves into the Milk," 7.
8. Bayart, *The State in Africa.*
9. Mbembe, *On the Postcolony,* 107.

saying, "Since you say I am not a chief, I will just sit still, and look on the ground. Then you will see that I am truly a chief, for if I look on the ground the land will be desolate; you will fall over precipices and into pits; you will be eaten by wild beasts through not seeing them; and die through famine, being unable to find food; because you dispute with me, you are blind."[10]

The riddle begins by building up the uselessness of the chief, reflecting what may have been a popular complaint regarding a chief's power, that he "does nothing." Indeed, the riddle uses repetition to reinforce this notion, asserting that the chief "does not work." However, the riddle then goes on to note, without altering the structure of the sentence or the syntax and therefore effectively replacing the previous negative statements, that the chief "sees" for his subjects. This "seeing," furthermore, is directly linked to the chief making sure that "they do not go without anything they want; he takes them by the hand, and leads them to where there is food, and they return with it to their homes." Significantly, the riddle highlights that the chief "touches nothing" himself. Nothing belongs to him. Perhaps most importantly, the riddle stresses that the chief "makes himself the chief" through these actions. He "remains a chief for ever [sic], for his people are supported by him." The direct causality in this sentence makes a radical statement. The "chief is only a chief through other people"; he does not inherently own his power but earns it through the effective performance of his duty to support his people, and it is only these actions that make him truly a chief.

II. PRAISE POEMS AND POWER RELATIONS IN PRECOLONIAL AND COLONIAL SOUTH AFRICA

Verses of poignant, mournful, and angry praise poems created and sustained these ideas in South African tribal cultures. Praise poems, a social institution based on communal chanting led by a ritual poet, supported a culture of critique that was uniquely placed to propound the popular proverb "a chief is a chief through other people." Praises, or *izibongo,* are an oral genre of poetry primarily composed and spoken in Zulu, Ndebele, and Xhosa. Praises, unlike written literatures, are not fixed in form or content—they are living, changing bodies of knowledge, crossing genres with ease and existing in close relation to songs, for they are performed, chanted, and danced to in communal settings toward various ends, including comments on important figures, peers, or

---

10. Callaway, *Nursery Tales, Traditions, and Histories,* 366.

even pertinent issues such as love, war, and money. *Izibongo* generally outline the feats, character, and physical features of the person or thing about whom or which they are composed.[11] In its focus on political power, this chapter is mainly concerned with *izibongo zamakhosi*, the praises of kings and chiefs, which testify to local notions of 'rule by the people' in the nineteenth-century colonial period and function as valuable forms of history. These praise poems sustained cultures of 'rule by the people' by explicitly criticizing chiefly transgressions. As Liz Gunner and Mafika Pascal Gwala point out, praise poetry was "a broadly based poetic tradition widely practiced and widely circulating, not a tradition tied to the aristocratic and powerful."[12] Thus, although South African literary scholar Trevor Cope contends that "the purpose of the praise is to present the chief as an object of admiration, and there is consequently a tendency to maximize praise and minimize criticism," I argue that the content of the praise poems themselves do not always bear this out; praise poetry also functioned as a vehicle of regulative complaint, defining the chief in both positive and negative terms through the opinions of other people.

Recognizing the historical value of *izibongo* as subversive forces affirms Carolyn Hamilton's point that oral literatures, including proverbs and *izibongo*, cannot be dismissed out of hand despite owing their capture to colonial recording practices.[13] This complexity is apparent in James Stuart's recorded *izibongo*. Stuart was a white Englishman who collected various praise poems in the late nineteenth century. He was born of British parentage in Pietermaritzburg and served as a civil servant and magistrate in various districts of Zululand between 1888 and 1912, learning Zulu from Zulu children. As Chapman points out, these praise poems reach us through multiple mediations in several Zulu language versions recorded and collated by Stuart, subsequently edited by others and translated into English. While Stuart himself made an intensive study of Zulu customs, history, and oral tradition based on verbatim reports from elders within the Zulu tribe, he also helped establish a body of ideas that underpinned later discourses of segregation and domination, partly as a result of his immersion in Zulu affairs and his noted linguistic skill. However, Stuart was also a highly self-conscious cross-cultural broker, mediating between the African and European colonial worlds in which he moved, voicing criticism of European colonialism, and reforming imperial policies even as he implemented them. These ambiguities are perhaps best captured by proposed titles for his work, including "The White Man's Tyranny in Africa" and

---

11. Gunner and Gwala, *Musho! Zulu Popular Praises*, 2–3.
12. Ibid., 2
13. Hamilton, *Terrific Majesty*, 28.

"Civilization of Lower Races: A Tyranny."[14] These complex sources, in other words, cannot simply be dismissed for their 'interestedness,' despite being collected by white missionaries and diplomats.

Critiques of despotic chiefs are prevalent in the praise poems Stuart collected from the nineteenth-century Zulu kingdom. Praise poetry, and to a lesser extent *izagu* and riddles, safeguarded cultures of 'rule by the people' and exemplified "a chief is a chief through other people" in their cultural status, performance, form, and content. These oral texts held immense cultural capital that made them politically significant because they were considered sacred activities sanctioned by ancestral spirits, lying outside the purview of even the most powerful chief. This position enabled the praiser to censure with impunity certain aspects of the chief's personality or actions, either by overt criticism or covertly by the omission of praise.

These literatures also safeguarded and produced cultures of 'rule by the people' in their aesthetic form and performance. In being shouted out at communal gatherings in response to the audience's calls to "*Musho!*" or "Speak Him!" praises had the ethical responsibility of being expressions of public opinion, providing an effective means of social control and literally speaking the chief into being as embodying the character traits that were attributed to him. Performances therefore created a space of communal orality that depended on interactions between speakers and listeners; the praise poet did not only present the chief to the people in his recitation, he also represented the opinion of the people regarding what qualities were praiseworthy to the chief. Characteristics of the recital therefore aimed to make it an important occasion in which the entire community took part. The praiser, or *imbongi*, wore fantastic costumes replete with furs, feathers, and animal tails and recited praises loudly and quickly while dancing around energetically. In doing so, he aimed to draw an affective response from the audience, thereby making conscious use of the cognitive process of emotional contagion described in previous chapters, by which audience members would come to feel pale reflections of the feelings being performed. Daniel Malcolm and Trevor Cope note that such a dramatic performance produced an effect of seriousness and occasion. Moreover, in its elimination of any downdrift intonation, praise poetry gave the impression of never ending and of always being open to further additions so that the subject of the poem was always aware that criticisms could be added to his praises and that he would continually be held to account for his actions.[15]

---

14. Ibid., 165.
15. Stuart, *Izibongo*, 29.

While the *imbongi* crafted the praises, anyone could recite and add to them so that voices of criticism and praise were not limited to a select few.

Like other oral sources, many praise poems collected by Stuart publically judge a chief's democratic tendencies by commenting on his egalitarian management of the communal food economy. For instance, the *izibongo* describes the chief Senzangakhona as someone

> who chewed with his mouth without eating
> I returned with yellow corn and threshed and cooked.[16]

Through the metaphor of "chewing not eating," the *imbongi* suggests that the chief controlled his own intake so as to enable the nourishment of others. The next lines describe the result of this generosity—that the speaking subject is able to find yellow corn to thresh, cook, and eat. Another chief, Khondlo of the Qwabe Clan, meanwhile, was so concerned about the well-being of his subjects that he is praised as food himself:

> Black millet that is eaten raw,
> They ate it as it showed on the dry maize stalks.[17]

Black millet is nutritious and does not have to be processed before it can be eaten. In describing Khondlo in these terms, the *izibongo* notes that the chief nourished and sustained the tribe while also highlighting his willingness to sacrifice himself for the well-being of his subjects.

Metaphors and metonyms related to eating and drinking did not only serve as literal praises but as negative criticism as well. A Chief Dingane was described in his praise poem as "the milk bucket which overflows (*gaba*) without having given birth."[18] This was a vivid praise, as well as a criticism, of the king's authoritarian power because it suggested that milk, which served as a staple source of nourishment as well as a metonym for power, had not been distributed to subjects, impeding their livelihood and ability to rule themselves. Another chief was criticized as the "miserly one who ate up the *lobola* cattle,"[19] significant because *lobola* cattle were not meant to be eaten; they carried symbolic significance as the animals given by the bridegroom to the bride's family at the time of marriage and were to be returned if the marriage

---

16. Ibid., 80.
17. Ibid., 140.
18. Ibid.
19. Ibid.

was to fail for any reason. Chiefs were also criticized for living at the expense of subjects without providing anything in return. For instance, the poet quotes Chief Zihlando's words that "I can never be rich in crops and in cattle, And also be rich in people," thus highlighting the chief's wish to acquire as many crops and cattle as he could regardless of how much popular support he lost.[20] The nourishment of political subjects was clearly a key gauge of the success of chiefly rule.

The most consistently negative praises, however, were reserved for Shaka. This is not surprising; Shaka was the infamous ruler who, from the late eighteenth century to the early nineteenth, radically changed the political structure of Zululand from one of informal systems of largely consensual rule between a chief and his subjects to a tyrannical kingship with its own army.[21] From 1820 to 1828, Shaka ruled as a dictator, replacing reciprocity and diplomacy with dominance, forcefulness, fearlessness and martial power.[22]

Shaka was born circa 1785, the child of a chief. When his parents' union did not last, his mother, Nandi, returned to her tribe, the Zulus. In his twenties, Shaka became a warrior for the Mtetwa tribe, fighting with them for six years. Dingiswayo, the chief of the Mtetwas, saw Shaka's potential and decided to train him as a future chief of the Zulus, reasoning that Shaka and the Zulus would act as a buffer against invading forces. As chief, Shaka carefully and meticulously planned and formatted brilliant battle strategies, even optimizing the weapons used during battle and building up a mighty army of Zulu warriors. He demanded total loyalty and obedience, punishing those who did not comply with death. By 1820, Shaka had conquered all the territories in Natal and southeast Africa. When the white man arrived in Natal in 1824, they immediately sought out Shaka, treating his wounds when an enemy stabbed him and tricking him into signing over land for next to nothing. When Shaka's mother died, Shaka ordered seven thousand people to be executed in her memory. He also demanded that his tribe fast to commemorate Nandi and lifted the fast only after three months, when many were near death. On 22 September 1828, Shaka was murdered by two half brothers on his father's side. One half brother, Dingane, immediately claimed kingship.

The figure of Shaka has undergone much transformation during the colonial, apartheid, and postapartheid decades so that there are multiple versions of the above story in popular novels by white writers, travelers' reports, Black Consciousness poems, as well as various films and television series. As Chapman puts it: "seemingly too immense for any one account, Shaka emerges as

---

20. Ibid.
21. Ibid., 22.
22. Ibid.

both hero (the Africanist nation builder) and villain (the blood-thirsty savage of the colonial record): in other words, as the construct of various authors' own prejudices, preferences, and political agendas."[23] What have these agendas been? In the late nineteenth century, Shaka was shaped according to the interlinked interpretations of Cetshwayo and Shepstone. In the 1910s and 1920s, the Zulu royal family, rural traditionalists, and the educated and Christianized African elite in Natal drew on images of Shaka in an attempt to forge a united identity. Segregationist and later apartheid ideologues used his figure to distinguish the basis of a Zulu homeland. And as Carolyn Hamilton has shown, more recently, Shaka has become the center of an ideological campaign promoting Zulu nationalism. In the early 1970s, the Zulu cultural organization, Inkatha, succeeded in proclaiming September 24 as 'Shaka day.' Every year since, 'Shaka day' rallies celebrating Shaka's military achievements have been held across Kwa Zulu Natal and in the migrant workers' hostels in and around Johannesburg. In line with these politically motivated celebrations, throughout the 1980s and '90s, literary texts, television shows, and even academic accounts have participated in a self-conscious reversal of the image of Shaka from villain to hero.

The praises to Shaka have also been subject to these various appropriations, traveling "beyond the 1820s to play a potent role in an ongoing political process, whether at the Battle of Isandlwana where in 1879 Zulu military might crushed the British or, more recently in KwaZulu-Natal, within struggles for resources, political power, and Zulu 'authenticity.'"[24] Yet, despite these contemporary adaptations, these praises also present an alternative perspective, even a corrective, to these constructions. Stuart's recorded praise poems suggest that, in abusing his power, Shaka was seen by his own contemporaries as failing to fulfill his chiefly duty of providing for his subjects. The *imbongi* echoes these sentiments when he describes Shaka as a beast who does not let himself be milked, not only denying sustenance and nourishment to his subjects but also denying them the ritual sharing of power this represented. As Bjerk notes, the king's own unique royal status was maintained by collecting the best cattle and milk from homestead heads for royal consumption—they, as the distilled essence of the Zulu state, then nursed him. The state, in a ritual sense, was the king's mother—evoking an intimate relationship of mutual obligation between the king and the homestead heads, that is, the citizens of the Zulu state. In turn, once the king had collected heifers and redistributed milk

---

23. Chapman, "From Shaka's Court," 40.
24. Ibid., 34.

and meat, he "became mother to countless warriors and citizens who suckled at his teats."[25] A verse that refers to this system exclaims:

> Powerful limbs, calf of a beast,
> The kicking of this beast puzzled me,
> It kicked the milker and left the one holding it.[26]

The phrase "kicking the milker" describes Shaka as collecting subjects' cattle and enjoying the benefits of rule without sharing either food or power, callously disregarding the symbolic and material Zulu economy. The *imbongi* stresses this idea in other verses too:

> Help me Maphtitha and Ngqengelele,
> And give him a cow that he may learn to milk into the mouth,
> And give him a sharpened stick so that he may dig for himself.[27]

Milking into the mouth describes the ritual whereby the king's subjects drank directly from the king's udders (those of his prize heifers), thereby symbolizing their right to the king's cattle and subsequently a share in his power. In noting that Shaka needs to "learn to milk into the mouth," the *imbongi* strongly criticizes Shaka's authoritarian rule. As cognitive linguists Lakoff and Johnson note, such metonymic concepts structure not just our language but our thoughts, attitudes, and actions by forming mental pathways whereby one thing is conceptualized by means of its relation to another concrete something else. In this case, metonyms make the thinking of 'rule by the people' extremely unlikely without also thinking of the just distribution of milk and cattle among a population. The metonyms of milk and cattle for power thus become not only poetic language but internal to cognitive processing and one's corresponding action in the world.[28]

As in the criticisms of other chiefs, the *imbongi* also disparagingly notes that Shaka lives off his subjects, both literally in eating the food and goods they provide and metaphorically in not sharing the power they give him. The *imbongi* describes Shaka as the

> Lazy one that eats the corn of the diligent ones.
> He who clears the ground with spears where chiefs use hoes;

---

25. Bjerk, "They Poured Themselves into the Milk," 6.
26. Stuart, *Izibongo*, 98.
27. Ibid., 106.
28. Lakoff and Johnson, *Metaphors We Live By*, 37.

He summoned an army from Menwiza saying it should gather the corn
before it is ripe.[29]

This verse notes Shaka's destruction of the crop in combination with a description of him living off other people and not doing any work himself. His capacity for annihilation, then, is twofold and unique in its damage; the *imbongi* stresses that Shaka does not do his duty like other chiefs. Instead, Shaka is "he who clears the ground with spears where chiefs use hoes." Since Shaka does not "hoe" the ground to provide his people with sustenance, he is like "gruel made of inedible millet." Instead, Shaka "clears the ground with spears," a reference to his many military rampages. Much praise poetry devoted to Shaka, then, focuses on the havoc he wreaked in neighboring territories to highlight his destruction of local food economies and sustainable consumption.

The *imbongi* criticizes Shaka for his unwillingness to produce systems of sustainable consumption for the Zulu nation by stressing instead that Shaka was interested only in holding on to power, even at the expense of other people. Indeed, a great deal of Shaka's praises concentrate on his penchant for murder and destruction through repeated metaphors of voracious consumption: "He who while devouring some devoured others / And as he devoured others he devoured some more."[30] The verse repeats these lines four times, stressing Shaka's insatiable appetite for power through endless repetition that would have been recited breathlessly without pause. In doing so the *imbongi* gives the impression that Shaka eats, or kills, without stopping.

Praise poems also describe these violent expeditions through metaphors depicting Shaka's ravenous greed and his killing for the sheer enjoyment of it:

> He ate up Mantondo son of Tayi,
> He felt him tasteless and spat him out,
> He devoured Sihayo.[31]

These actions are so horrific that the *imbongi* highlights them through a narrative intervention in his own point of view, chanting,

> I criticized them, the evil-doers,
> The cattle of Sihayo returned
> And then there followed those of Mangosi
> That were milked by a hysterical person at Mavela's place.[32]

---

29. Stuart, *Izibongo*, 114.
30. Ibid., 96.
31. Ibid., 98.
32. Ibid., 112–14.

The verse describes Shaka's and Mepho's (a Mkhize chief who flourished as a favorite of Shaka) "evil" effect on the communal food economy through their murder of neighboring chiefs, Sihayo and Mangosi. The *imbongi* presents a dramatic visual scene of the cattle, the most prized possessions of the Zulu homestead, returning to the kraal without anyone guiding them. He further emphasizes the pathos of the event by noting that they were milked by a person made "hysterical" by Shaka's crimes. The word "hysterical" supplants any specific description of Shaka's doings, leaving these up to the listener's imagination and memories, and giving them even more terrible force. The verse simply suggests that Shaka's effects on people were so horrific that they were rendered incapable of providing for themselves.

So devastating were these military expeditions, that the *imbongi* includes a veiled threat in his verse. In doing so, he highlights the kinds of actions that his listeners, Shaka's own subjects, could take against him. Warning against the dangers of cattle raiding, the *imbongi* exclaims:

> The people's cattle, Shaka, leave them alone, they are a cause of disaster,
> they tie sharp knives on to their tails.[33]

The description of the cattle as "the people's" combined with "they tie sharp knives on to their tails" demonstrates how the cattle are seen as collective belongings because of their significance to the local food economy. Stealing them is risking death. Remarkably, then, this poem contains the seeds of a democratic revolution against Shaka if he continues his destruction of the communal food economy and the political process of 'rule by the people' it was meant to buttress.

A key claim of this book is that indigenous literary forms such as the *izibongo* helped to achieve the democratic cultures they expressed. Moreover, I claim that they did so by subversively performing and transmitting their universalizing ideas through literary devices that were continuous with these socially progressive ideas. For instance parallelist praise poetry uses participatory repetition, thereby instantiating a democratic public sphere within the space of its performance by cognitively activating relevant conceptual networks within people's minds and the cultures within which they are situated. These poems transmit universalizing messages through a cognitive process whereby parallel repetition promotes a heightened mental ability to process the sentence as a whole. Much praise poetry makes use of particular forms of repetition including meter (repeated rhythms), rhyme (repeated final syl-

---

33. Ibid., 62.

lables), alliteration (repeated consonant sounds), assonance (repeated vowel sounds), and parallelism (repeated statements of identical construction, with different words expressing the same idea). These literary devices harness cognitive mechanisms whereby repetition speeds up an individual's processing of concepts by decreasing the load of information needing to be processed by the reader in order to grasp meaning.[34] Parallelism—in which paired sentences, phrases, or clauses are created with the same structure and syllables—stimulates a process that leaves the reader already persuaded of the political messages being conveyed.[35]

Parallelist repetition within praise poems also produced a universalizing multivocality, resulting in a mingling of different vocal registers to present one unified meaning, just as a consensus-based democratic system allowed all voices to be heard before reaching a common decision. This was a contrapuntal quality achieved by channeling two or more voices independent in their specific nuances because of the different words used to express the same idea but harmonically interdependent because they carried a unified meaning expressed through identical sentence construction, a regularity of rhythm, alliteration, and assonance. The formal elements of praise poetry, then, echoed the democratic nature of the activity by vocalizing different voices that expressed the same praises in consensus. Rich description stirred the emotions and imagination, activating the statements of critique the *izibongo* was making within individual minds.

Praise poems enact a multivocal consensus on Shaka's character through repeated statements that vary in their emphasis while presenting one main idea relating to his historical deeds or character. For instance, one verse describes Shaka's angry, violent disposition through repeated metaphors to do with fire:

He who goes along making fires and leaving behind conflagrations,
Who when he was rubbed flared up like a fire[36]

Both lines strive to convey different aspects of Shaka's fierce nature through the metaphor of fire. The first evokes the burned-down villages Shaka left in his wake while the second comments on the cause of this ferocity, noting the ease with which Shaka was provoked.

Another verse uses parallelism to achieve a universalizing accord on the linked nature of Shaka's greed and unwillingness to share power. The *imbongi* sings:

---

34. Frazier et al., "Parallel structure," 421–30.
35. Fahnestock, "Verbal and Visual Parallelism," 128.
36. Stuart, *Izibongo*, 98.

> For he ate up the cattle that were murmuring,
> For he ate up the cattle at the Dlodlweni kraal.
> Overflowing one that disregards warning;[37]

The parallelism of the first two lines, through similar accounts of the event placed in conjunction with each other, lends force to the *imbongi*'s view of Shaka, making it a democratic, yet unified, voice of critique about Shaka's overindulgence in eating other people's cattle. Last, the *imbongi* characterizes him as "overflowing" with the cattle he has eaten, a word that also refers to one who is overflowing with milk. He points out, in other words, that Shaka is so miserly that he allows his power to overflow and be wasted rather than sharing it and ensuring the proper governing of his tribe. Such verses achieve their rhetorical force by giving the impression of different people filling in aspects of critical information that indict Shaka for his "wrongness." Descriptive repetitive addition creates the impression of different speakers responding to each other, adding to, and confirming each other's points, thereby emphasizing that the creation of history was a communal project. Everyone's different nuances and additions need to not only be considered but recorded to enable posterity's own judgment of the specific process through which this consensus was reached. Together, these instances of parallelism serve to cognitively reinforce the democratic point being made, both activating and transmitting notions of 'rule by the people' within individual minds.

On 24 September 1828, three assassins from Shaka's own tribe crept up to the royal kraal and murdered him, dumping his corpse into an empty grain pit and filling it with mud and stones. This was a fitting symbolic rejoinder to Shaka's withholding of grain from his subjects. By that time, Shaka had made enough enemies among his own people to hasten his demise, which came relatively quickly following the devastation Shaka wreaked after the death of his mother. According to the mythological histories surrounding this event, Shaka ordered that no crops should be planted during the following year, no milk was to be used, and any woman who became pregnant was to be killed along with her husband. At least seven thousand people who were deemed to be insufficiently grief stricken were executed, along with thousands of cows so that their calves would know what losing a mother felt like. In his final years, then, Shaka carried out a terrifying, single-minded assault on the communal system of food production and sharing that produced and buttressed Zulu democratic cultures and behaviors. It is not surprising that his half brothers,

---

37. Ibid., 114.

along with tribal co-conspirators, were to take political power into their own hands, bringing the *imbongi*'s poetic warnings to fruition.

III. CONTESTING CORPORATE APARTHEID THROUGH TRADE UNION PRAISE POETRY

This genealogy of popular critique that aspirationally allied economic and political forms of democratic behavior continued in a fragmented form during a very different historical moment. *Izibongo* played an important role during the culminating moment of a later fight for 'rule by the people'—the inception of a democratic South Africa following decades of apartheid rule. In May 1994 in Pretoria, at President Mandela's inauguration and then later that month at the opening of South Africa's first democratic parliament, an *imbongi* took center stage. On the latter occasion, when *imbongi* Tembile Mhlangeni entered the Houses of Parliament, he wore beaded garments and a fur hat rather than the prescribed suit and tie, marking the momentousness of the occasion with celebratory ritual and praise poems for Mandela. The newly appointed education and training minister for the Western Cape, Martha Olckers, was outraged at what she saw as a usurpation of cultural space: "In spite of good intentions one can hurt people. I mean a praise-singer in parliament, and dressed the way he is. And clapping and ululating. It used to be a very dignified place and this is a terrible cultural shock for us."[38] Olckers clearly saw the *imbongi*'s presence as a conflict between two incompatible cultures, one civilized and the other uncivilized. She thus went on to lament that "there are certain things that some people see as culture that I don't."[39] These comments reflected a general disrespect for tribal customs and a real sense that the democratic governance of the nation was somehow incongruous with what these members of the white community perceived as an uncivilized, unmodern indigineity. The following section argues to the contrary that *imbongi* and the *izibongo* they chanted were ritually and instrumentally central to the achievement of democracy in South Africa. These later praise poems followed the form's long tradition of coupling 'rule by the people' with ensured and sufficient material sustenance from the ruler. In the run-up to the end of apartheid, the *izibongo* form was taken up by the trade union struggle, linking the fight for democracy and citizenship with the fight for adequate compensation for workers by the government. Because trade unions fought

---

38. Olckers, *Cape Argus*, 14.
39. Ibid.

for the latter, many praise poems conceptualized the trade unions as a democratic chief who fairly distributed food and cattle to subjects. This contextual universalism, moreover, was harnessed alongside post-Enlightenment ideas of working-class revolution and majoritarian democratic processes, articulated within a syncretic conceptual network pertaining to 'rule by the people.'

This section elaborates on this argument by focusing on the trade union movement of the 1970s, '80s, and early '90s, when, as various critics including Liz Gunner, Ari Sitas, S. Kromberg, and Jeremy Cronin have noted, *izibongo* played a significant role in raising workers' participation in their trade unions and in achieving the democratic transition.[40] Trade union movements for workers' rights were integral to political struggles toward black citizenship within a democratic nation, and *imbongi* were central to the success of industrial strikes and actions. They were guided by the goals of achieving majoritarian democracy, aligning themselves with the African National Congress (ANC) and the Pan African Congress (PAC) following the nationalist government's decision to unban organizations striving for black majority rule in 1990. The *imbongi* Bongani Sitole, for example, saw "himself as a mediator between organizations with differing viewpoints and also as a conduit to the African National Congress of authentic popular sentiment."[41] So central was the indigenous aesthetic form of *izibongo* to a political labor struggle that, during the 1980s, some of the Transkei's former leaders actually arrested poets who criticized their actions and even went so far as to prohibit the performance of *izibongo*.[42] This half of the chapter focuses on the *izibongo* of two prominent worker-poets, Alfred Temba Qabula (1942–2002) and Mi S'dumo Hlathswayo (1951–). During these uncertain days, when the end of apartheid still seemed a far-away possibility, Qabula and Hlathswayo's praise poems catalyzed worker struggles, enacting and theorizing a universalizing 'rule by the people' in the process. Just like the praise poems from the Zulu kingdom, the communal literary form of trade union praise poetry theorizes 'rule by the people' through a performed multivocality. This experimentalism embodies and enacts the voices of the workers themselves, voices that are not usually represented in South African historiography. By using the praise poem to negotiate relations between the workers in factories and the management, as well as between the apartheid state and its black inhabitants, these poets theorized 'rule by the people' within a much-needed medium that was accessible to all, regardless of their literacy levels.

---

40. Gunner, "A Dying Tradition?" 35; Kromberg, "Worker Izibongo and Ethnic Identities," 57–74.
41. Kaschula, "Imbongi in Profile," 66.
42. Opland, *Xhosa Oral Poetry*, 266–67.

The rest of this chapter moves through four interlinked parts. The first explores the joint political and economic role that trade unions played in achieving the transition to a democratic nation-state, illuminating the post-Enlightenment concepts of majoritarian democracy and Marxist revolution that fuelled the transition. The second provides an additional explanation for the role of the trade unions that is rooted in contextual universalisms. I examine how democratic ideals within the *izibongo* of trade union poets perpetuated an ongoing and familiar *inkosi* universalism of poetic political mediation and critique for alienated workers. The third section suggests that poets like Qabula and Hlatshwayo partly derived their conceptualization of worker as emancipated citizen and vice versa from this contextual universalism. This latter path into democratic change was rooted in indigenous economic and political systems and buttressed by *izibongo,* which evaluated political authority through its capacity for just and equitable economic distribution. Both Qabula and Hlatshwayo's poems therefore conceptualize the trade unions as a democratic chief through descriptions of shared food and cattle. In conflating an emancipated political subjectivity with ensured and sufficient material sustenance, these contextual vocabularies—working with indigenous conceptions of consensus-based democracy, Marxist notions of working-class solidarity and revolution, and post-Enlightenment ideals of majoritarian democracy—launched the trade union struggle. The corollary was that in the run-up to the end of apartheid, the fight for democracy and citizenship also became inextricably linked to the fight for workers' rights. Finally, the fourth section argues that these protest poems continued to ground the political and economic struggle against apartheid through universalizing content as well as through an indigenous multivocal and parallelist literary form, thereby transmitting a message of consensus-based forms of 'rule by the people.'

Trade Unions and the Transition to Democracy: The Struggle on the Ground

The civil rights struggle during the 1970s to early 1990s that achieved the end of apartheid was fought as a struggle for worker's rights, allying the concept of 'rule by the people' with that of economic justice for all.[43] For trade unions, the struggle for workers' rights also translated into a fight for equal citizenship within a democratic nation. Trade unions realized that the interests of

---

43. This despite the fact that ultimately democracy as achieved by the ANC did not always end up being in the interests of the workers. See Emery, "Privatization, Neoliberal Development, and the Struggle," 6–19.

apartheid and capital had historically always been aligned. As Bob Fine points out, the apartheid state imposed a myriad of restrictions on the rights of black workers to associate, to take industrial action, to affiliate to political movements, and to espouse political causes.[44] Apartheid was a brutal system of class exploitation that used racial divisions in the working class to quickly suppress any serious challenge to its supremacy. Indeed, a major effect of racist state repression had been to very rapidly establish a large capitalist economy in favor of white interests. To break apartheid, one had to break the power of capital.

Such an assertion of working-class centrality to achieving the end of apartheid revises understandings of the trade unions as simply mobilizing or restraining its members according to the negotiations of key political players.[45] FOSATU, which later became COSATU (Congress of South African Trade Unions), was a key force in the struggle for democracy.[46] For one, during the late 1970s when FOSATU was formed, the unions were the only universalizing, democratic, and self-ruled popular organizations available to workers. And the democratic traditions established by early trade unions, including policies of nondiscrimination, nonhierarchical organization, and national and international linkages between bodies of workers and different trade unions, were integral to the drive for parliamentary democracy. This was evident in the fact that leading negotiators of the interregnum like Cyril Ramaphosa of the Convention for a Democratic South Africa were drawn from the trade union movement.

The working class also became central to the end of apartheid because, by the mid 1980s, COSATU deliberately set itself a dual economic and political role, aiming to secure social and economic justice for all through a policy of radical reform.[47] Its constitution pledged to create a "united South Africa free from oppression and economic exploitation." In a fiery speech to the congress, its first president, Elijah Barayi, condemned the bantustans, the government, and apartheid and called for an end to the state of emergency, the removal of the troops from the townships, and the scrapping of the pass laws.[48]

Such a unification of the concept of 'rule by the people' with that of economic justice for all was partly based on post-Enlightenment ideas of majoritarian democracy. COSATU's power arose from its single-minded struggle

---

44. Fine, "The Workers' Struggle," 95.
45. Adler and Webster, "Challenging Transition Theory," 75–106. See also Sisk, *Democratization in South Africa*.
46. See Van Niekerk, "The Trade Union Movement," 159, 161.
47. See Adler, Maller, and Webster, "Unions, Direct Action, and Transition," 306–43.
48. Barayi, quoted in Plaut, "The Political Significance of COSATU," 64.

against apartheid in support of outlawed political parties such as the ANC.[49] In 1990, COSATU claimed more than 1.2 million members distributed in fourteen industrial unions,[50] making it the fastest growing nonhierarchical labor movement in the world.[51] It used this mass of people toward organized strikes and boycotts against apartheid corporations, forcing the state's decision to reform apartheid in 1989. The state president, Frederik Willem de Klerk, released veteran leaders of the ANC who had been jailed since the early l960s, including Mandela, and unbanned the ANC, the Pan African Congress, and the South African Communist Party (SACP). COSATU took the opportunity to enter into a formalized pact with the ANC and the SACP, negotiating the ANC's adoption of COSATU's Reconstruction and Development Programme (RDP) for the socioeconomic redress of poor blacks. In exchange, COSATU contributed indispensable organizational capacity in devoting personnel and resources to the election campaign and conducted voter education programs for an ANC victory. Thus, COSATU managed to influence the agenda of the country's transition, becoming a key determinant in the overwhelming victory of the ANC. A large number of COSATU unionists also secured parliamentary seats and key positions in government departments.[52] They stipulated that the new constitution needed to highlight worker and trade union rights and facilitate worker participation in economic decision-making.[53] Largely because of COSATU, the ANC enshrined these central trade union principles into the laws of the postapartheid state.[54]

This civil rights struggle was not only harnessed through post-Enlightenment concepts of majoritarian democracy but also through Marxist visions of working-class revolution. The president of FOSATU, Joe Foster, highlighted that trade unions had a duty not only to think of their members but the entire working class, for an equal citizen within a democratic nation was necessarily also an emancipated worker. Foster thus advocated the founding of a "working

---

49. Visser, "White Labour Aristocracy and Black Proletariat," 241; Bendix, *Industrial Relations in South Africa*, 329, 335; and Finnemore and Van Rensburg, *Contemporary Labour Relations*, 31, 158.

50. See Baskin, *Striking Back*, 448.

51. Labor law reforms, introduced by the Wiehahn Commission of Enquiry between 1977 and 1979, formally recognized African trade unions, expanding FOSATU's membership to ninety-five thousand by 1981 and unifying emerging unions. It was the first nonracial trade union federation for unskilled workers since the decline of the South African Congress of Trade Unions (SACTU) in the early 1960s.

52. Visser, "A Racially Divided Class," 7.

53. Adler and Webster, "Challenging Transition Theory," 75–106.

54. The 1996 Labor Relations Act was nonracial and inclusive of public-sector workers, as well as farm and domestic workers. It entrenched collective bargaining practices and institutionalized the right to strike and joint decision-making at the shop-floor level.

class movement" that did not involve only "worker activities such as strikes and protests" but the formulation of "large-scale organizations with a clear social and political identity as the working class."[55] Such statements drew on Marxist theorizations of the working class as an entity with common economic interests that should consciously engage in collective action towards advancing those interests. The logic of opposing classes meant that it was in the laborer's best interest to maximize wages and benefits and in the capitalist's best interest to maximize profit and generate surplus value, leading to a contradiction within the capitalist system that could only be resolved through revolution.

In line with these Marxist understandings, the COSATU leadership realized that the achievement of equal citizenship and worker emancipation could only happen if the workers took charge instead of simply allowing themselves to be guided by political leaders from the ANC. Workers worried that "the specific needs and aspirations of black workers" would "become subordinated to a democratic movement which neglects or even curbs the expression of working class issues and the independent organization of the working class."[56] As Foster noted, directing the political energies of the oppressed masses and of international critics predominantly to the apartheid regime and its abhorrent racism would allow capital to hide behind apartheid, making the government and Afrikanerdom the sole focus of attack.[57] Trade union leaders therefore sought to conceptualize the struggle against apartheid primarily as a wider working-class movement with local as well as global parameters, ensuring that they would not be impeded by the "definite limitations" of popular political organizations such as the ANC. Foster described these limitations, elaborating that the party had to engage in "undirected opportunistic political activity. . . . To the major Western powers it has to appear as anti-racist but not as anti-capitalist."[58] Reflecting this awareness, the alignment of the trade unions with antiapartheid goals involved intensive debate between workerists and populists throughout the 1980s about how and when to fight for political rights without sacrificing internal democracy and working-class leadership.[59] Workerists such as Ramaphosa, the general secretary of the 180,000-strong National Union of Mineworkers, would argue rightly that the unions were more democratic than political movements such as the United Democratic

---

55. Foster, "The Workers' Struggle," 101.
56. Fine, "The Workers' Struggle," 96.
57. Foster, "The Workers' Struggle," 112.
58. Ibid., 106.
59. While the populists insisted that antiapartheid political leadership had to come from the United Democratic Front (UDF), and, by implication, from the ANC, the workerists argued that the unions should follow the political line dictated by their members via union leaders. Plaut, "Debates in a Shark Tank," 389–403.

Front because of their structure and accountability to members.[60] As the end of apartheid drew nearer, Ramaphosa reinforced the idea that the workers rather than the political parties alone would determine the agenda of resistance, to ensure that the struggle was "on terms favorable to us as workers."[61] Apartheid was itself to be conceptualized and overthrown as a system of class antagonism that used race to entrench social division and extract surplus value from workers. Worker responses to apartheid had to include the achievement of a wider class consciousness and then eventual revolution.

Worker-Poets and the Continuing Use of Izibongo

The interlinked nature of post-Enlightenment principles of 'rule by the people' and economic emancipation was expressed by worker-poets through the *izibongo* form. These popular orators adapted the *izibongo* to reflect and sustain an ongoing cultural system of democratic principles that was familiar to the black working class. A multitude of ordinary black workers with performing and rhetorical power began orating their poetry, rebelling against the principles of corporate apartheid. One of the most famous was Qabula, a migrant laborer from the Transkei, the son of a miner, who had experienced the horrors of the Pondoland rebellion against apartheid segregation firsthand as well as the bitter working conditions of black workers. Some of his poems were reportedly composed on top of a forklift. Referring to the process of composition, he noted that: "I would see something that hurts, that causes me pain, and then I would spend the working day making a poem about it."[62] Qabula performed his praise poem to FOSATU at the mass rally of the Dunlop Strike in Durban, expressing resistance and anger at the struggles of black workers and releasing a groundswell of popular energy throughout Natal. His eulogy to FOSATU, delivered in Xhosa and Zulu at worker rallies throughout the 1980s, addressed the trade-union movement as the protector (or chief) of its members (political subjects) and stirred up a chain of subversive symbols about workers fighting for their rights in "the moving black forest of Africa." One of the listeners at the Dunlop strike was a young worker called Mi S'dumo Hlatshwayo who was so mesmerized that he added his own poem, "Black

---

60. As Edward Ritchken noted, while worker-based organizations emphasized a transparent democratic culture centered around collective decision-making, community organizations worked in a clandestine manner without going through formal open procedures. Ritchken, "Trade Unions and Community Organizations," 41, 68.

61. Ibid., 69.

62. Qabula in Sitas, *Black Mamba Rising*, 3.

Mamba Rising," to the fiery atmosphere of the struggle. Hlatshwayo was also from a working-class background and grew up in the 1950s as an 'illegitimate' child. The family's poverty severed his education in standard 7, an event that thrust him at the age of fifteen into the machinery of the labor market. As he mentioned in *FOSATU Worker News*, he thought his dreams had ended: "I wanted to be a poet, control words, many words, that I may woo our multicultural South Africa into a single society. . . . After 34 years of hunger, suffering, struggles, learning to hope, I am only a driver for a rubber company."[63] However, Hlatshwayo did become a poet after a serious illness took him to eChibini (or St John's Apostolic church), which was famous for its healing rituals. It was here that Hlatshwayo was not only 'cured' but also introduced to the *izibongo* tradition, for lay preachers in the church integrated praises into their religious sermons. As the 1970s rolled on and his work at Dunlop Sports continued, Hlatshwayo began to compose his own protest praises as part of Metal Allied Worker Union's strike actions. Both poets' works were largely circulated orally, achieving fame and popularity among workers at mass rallies and strike actions. The poems were rendered in print only when COSATU sponsored the publication of the poetry collection *Black Mamba Rising* in 1976. Subtitled *South African Worker Poets in Struggle*, it featured three writers, including Qabula and Hlatshwayo. They became known by thousands of workers for their poetry performances, songs, plays, and their struggle to create a cultural movement among workers in Durban.

Qabula's and Hlatshwayo's poems represent a changing yet continuing aesthetic form that is popular, opportunistic, and syncretic. Both poets used composition strategies typical of the indigenous genre of *izibongo* but actively adapted the form to fit their contemporary political context, chanting at mass gatherings, rallies, strikes, and boycotts. For instance, both poets played with the formal boundaries between different types of *izibongo* devoted to kings and chiefs, ordinary people, animals and birds, and inanimate objects, blurring them all to produce a medley of all four. In Qabula's "Praise to FOSATU" and Hlatshwayo's "Black Mamba Rising," the working class made up of ordinary people is also an animal—a mole or hen and a black buffalo or black mamba, respectively; an inanimate object or trade union; and a chief. Both poets also make use of the usual six sections of a typical praise: an exclamatory statement of intention or a salutation; emphasis on the physical and moral qualities of the subject, on his or her achievements; genealogical information; reference to the social context; exhortation of the audience; and a concluding formula at the end of a performance. ('*Ncincilili*'—'I disappear'—or, 'the *imbongi* has spoken'). They also composed their praises in an aggregative

---

63. See Hlatshwayo, "We Workers Are A Worried Lot!," 8.

FIGURE 9. Qabula performs his praise poem to FOSATU at MAWU's Annual General Meeting in Durban. Source: Historical Papers Research Archive, University of the Witwatersrand, Johannesburg.

way in the manner of traditional *imbongi* while retaining customary literary devices such as repetitive parallelism. However, unlike tribal praisers such as that of Shaka, both poets made use of these composition strategies intermittently. For instance, in Qabula's and Hlatshwayo's praise poems, the totemic animal symbols of the black mamba, buffalo, and ants are freed from their usual symbolic meaning within clan histories and instead carry the associative bonds of the fight against national and capitalist oppression. Thus, while metaphors involving *inkunzi*, a bull or buffalo, have been used since precolonial times to refer to chiefs, the *imbongi* Sitole used its symbolism to refer to Mandela as "Yinkunziethi yakugquba kulale amaty," or "a bull, kicking up dust, displacing stones."[64]

---

64. Opland, *Xhosa Oral Poetry*, 246.

FIGURE 10. Hlatshwayo performs "Black Mamba Rising" at a rally in 1985. Source: Historical Papers Research Archive, University of the Witwatersrand, Johannesburg.

Like *imbongi* in precolonial South Africa, both poets also relied on the performance of the poems in mass community meetings for their effectiveness in garnering resistance and conveying messages of 'rule by the people.' To stimulate audience participation and response, they used established rhythms and intonation with carefully modulated facial expressions and gesture, including arm gestures, clapping, and head nodding, thereby prompting processes of emotional contagion and collective audience participation. Both consciously sought out customary methods of performer-audience communication to achieve an acoustic and polyphonic poetry echoing many voices, although they did so to invent new gestures that suited their own styles and purposes; Qabula developed a type of dancing (which strongly resembled the *toyi-toyi*) and a range of dramatic gestures to accompany his trade union poetry performances. And the poets also drew freely from available popular political gestures, using the clenched fist salute of people's power (*amandlangawethu*).

Another crucial customary element of both poets' performances that they adapted to suit contemporaneous ends was costume. In precolonial Zululand, the *imbongi* would have worn an animal skin robe and hat and carried a spear. In the 1980s, worker-poets often chose to sport remnants of traditional dress, such as an animal skin hat, while wearing a Western-style suit and adding their own eclectic signature styles.[65] Qabula often wore a pair of trousers and

---

65. Cronin, "'Even Under the Rine [sic] of Terror,'" 42.

a shirt that had been deliberately shredded, with the trouser legs torn into strips. At the same time he wore a tie. These 'designer rags' symbolized poverty, especially the pain and suffering that the working class endured. The tie, on the other hand, depicted the capitalist world with its bosses and overseers, thereby creating a powerful contrast and suggesting a subversive usurpation of an exclusive space. Costume, then, was symbolic of the poets' constitution by the exigencies of a contemporary political struggle rather than being anachronistic to it.

But why did Qabula, Hlatshwayo, and other black worker-poets, turn to the *izibongo* to convey their revolutionary messages at all? Why not use another form of contemporary postcolonial poetry that would require little or no adaptation? Like their contemporaries, Qabula and Hlatshwayo were the products of Bantu Education. This policy, under Dr. H. P. Verwoerd, the then minister of Native Affairs, was very different from the elite missionary education available to select African Christians during the previous century. The later Bantu Education Act was much more an effect of South African settler colonialism's desire to separate European settlers and their descendants from the natives whose lands they had claimed. In line with this segregationist ideology, Bantu education introduced so-called vernacular instruction for Africans up to and including the first year of high school so as to lower their proficiency in the official languages, English and Afrikaans. As Verwoerd stated to the Senate in 1954: "There is no place for [the Bantu] in the European community above the level of certain forms of labor."[66] As a result, poets developed an eloquence of the streets in opposition to the eloquence of what might be called 'pre-Bantu-education' black writing in English that had previously been nurtured by mission or church schools. They protested and publicized the limitations of Bantu education by composing in their native tongues (Xhosa and Zulu) and then translating their poems into an English form that was a hybridization of several unofficial vernaculars, including *tsotsi taal* and slang. For, while black poets like Qabula and Hlatshwayo were cognizant of the role of English as the vehicle of their oppression, they were equally wary of the apartheid-driven divisions that could arise from the singular employment of their own mother tongues. As Chapman writes, these linguistic features were "a stylistic and moral imperative."[67] This poetry was militant, urging resistance and involvement in political struggle rather than mere protest. To be a black poet was to be involved firsthand in a people's struggle.

The turn to *izibongo* was part of this people's struggle partly because it involved the rejection of the alienating cultural baggage of Western literature

---

66. Clark and Worger, *South Africa*, 48–52.
67. Chapman, *Soweto Poetry*, 13.

and the white gatekeeping of literary publishers. Moreover, the *izibongo* form prioritized and affirmed the African cultural traditions most appropriate to a political context of intense repression and covert organization.[68] The performance of poetry in these syncretic forms provided an opportunity to actualize the communal values of the black consciousness movement through its requirement of audience participation. The use of these forms kept alive an African cultural past that colonialism and apartheid had sought to suppress. The poets themselves became suspicious of those among them who published because oral performance came to be viewed as 'authentic witness.' It was also one way of avoiding censorship and confiscation of materials by the state.

Yet the use of the *izibongo* form was not simply a form of postcolonial revenge, nor a nativist return to a supposedly unchanging tradition, nor solely a strategic use of an exclusive cultural vocabulary within a politicized context. It was also evidence of a fractured yet continuing custom of critique that was used because of its effectiveness in activating and transmitting universalizing principles linked to ideals of 'rule by the people.' Various critics, including Liz Gunner and Michael Chapman, have attested to the *izibongo* as a crucial part of a continuing process of political brokerage, mediation, and promotion of democratic ideals from precolonial and colonial Southern Africa to the present.[69] As Chapman notes, in the 1920s when Lesotho found itself wracked by disputes among an ever-increasing number of petty chieftains, the *imbongi* sang:

> I shall study the history of fallen kings
> And seek the cause of their downfall.
> I shall think of administrative ways of various governments,
> And end up by saying,
> "People are superior to their ruler."[70]

The verse attests to the idea that the authority of the government is created and sustained only by the consent of its people. It also testifies to the truth of Gunner, Gwala, Groenewald, and Opland's research into how *izibongo* remain available and used in much political discourse within an emergent and contested national "popular democratic" culture, whether as tools of power or critique.[71] The continuing effectiveness of these *imbongi* in directing public opinion and 'speaking truth to power' is apparent in the documenting of several cases of *imbongi* who were either harassed or arrested in the late 1980s

---

68. Brown, *Voicing the Text*, 182.
69. See Gunner, "Remaking the Warrior?"; and Groenewald, "The Praises," 73–78.
70. Chapman, "From Shaka's Court," 34–43.
71. Gunner and Gwala, *Musho!* 12.

and early 1990s because of criticism they expressed of certain political leaders and contentious political issues while reciting oral praises.

The use of praise poetry as a political tool is, then, evidence of a public culture of 'rule by the people' that did not simply die out with the onset of colonial rule. As Kromberg explains, the use of praises resulted from the audience's intimacy with this form of popular oral poetry, for it represented a narrative custom with which they and the audience were familiar and with which they felt an affinity.[72] As one poet noted:

> we . . . join the past to the present and to the future. Our poetry in the traditional form was done in the *imbongi* style. And once the person stood there and paced the stage, raised his voice, lowered his voice, screeched, pounded the air, immediately people recognized it—hey, this is poetry, let us listen![73]

Based on situations where workers enthusiastically received this form of poetry, Kromberg argues that the demand for praise poetry as political mediator has come from below and reflects an ongoing partiality for such forms among the broad membership of the labor and political organizations. As Chapman writes, "in reaching beyond its own attachments and updating itself in changing conditions, praising places the critic under an obligation to interpret oral tradition as retaining a contentious capacity: that of a usable past."[74]

Equating Economic and Political Justice via "A Chief Is a Chief through Other People"

Despite these strengths of the *izibongo* form in meeting the needs of the democratic struggle, apartheid-era *izibongo* had to grapple with a vastly changed ideal of personhood than the one explored in the context of "a person is a person through other people." In the latter, the 'people' were defined as members of a united whole rather than primarily as occupants within a social hierarchy. During the struggle against apartheid, however, the unitary popular deployment of 'people' central to *ubuntu* as an aspirational ideal was replaced by a reality closer to Agamben's conception of 'people' as "a dialectical oscillation between two opposite poles: on the one hand, the People as a whole as an integral body politic and, on the other hand, the people as a subset and

---

72. Kromberg, "Worker Izibongo and Ethnic Identities," 61.
73. Ibid., 67.
74. Chapman, "From Shaka's Court," 34.

a fragmentary multiplicity of the needy and excluded bodies."[75] During the run-up to the end of apartheid, *imbongi* and the trade unions they supported recognized this double nature of the concept of 'people' as that which already is and that which has yet to be realized—the citizen and the poor, underprivileged, and excluded black worker aspiring to become a citizen. Praise poems therefore sought to collapse the divide between the citizen and the underprivileged subject through a dissensual process by which both could occupy an expanded demos. *Imbongi* did so by unifying political justice with economic justice, conceptualizing the enfranchised citizen as an emancipated worker and the democratic state as an equitable employer.

Such a universalizing unification of political and economic justice was a very different kind of universalizing force from that of multinational corporations, which involved globalizing their modes of production and expanding the number of lands and workers through which they extracted surplus value, all while discursively supporting their practices through the ideology of 'free trade.' Chase Manhattan, for example, justified its loans to the South African government as a Cold War necessity, arguing that "it would endanger the free world if every large American bank deprived developing countries of the opportunity for economic growth . . . we can't be responsible for the social affairs of a country. Where there's commerce and trade, we feel we should be part of it." [76] This illogical statement was, of course, extremely ironic, for it conflated and yet contrasted the idea of 'free trade' and 'individual freedom' in the same breath. As a whole, from the early 1960s corporate leaders rejected the idea that they could or should use their economic clout to push for democratic freedom, in South Africa or anywhere else, all while universalizing the clearly very different 'freedom' of capitalist multinational trade; by 1972, nearly three hundred American corporations had established themselves in South Africa with a combined investment greater than $900 million. Meanwhile, even corporate responsibility movements like the Sullivan principles remained within apartheid's legal framework. Companies were not asked to ignore South Africa's job reservation rules (which "reserved" more skilled or higher paid jobs for white workers only) or to recognize unions for black employees—much less to challenge apartheid's migrant labor system or its pass laws.[77]

On the other hand, the *izibongo*'s posited continuity between emancipated worker and enfranchised citizen and between equitable employer and

---

75. Agamben, *Means Without End*, 30.
76. Quoted in Sampson, *Black and Gold*, 87.
77. Seidman, "Monitoring Multinationals," 10.

democratic government sought to connect economic and political freedom in more genuinely emancipatory terms. "The Tears of a Creator," for instance, was the praise poem in Story Two, which Qabula and Hlatshwayo wrote and performed together at the launch of COSATU in 1985:

> COSATU
> Here we are!
>
> We say:
> Let your hands deliver us from exploitation
> Let our freedom be born
> Let our democracy be born
> Let our new nation be born[78]
>
> COSATU
> Stop now
> Listen to our sound
>
> You'll hear us sing
> That the rulers
> And employers
> Are sorcerers![79]

The poem syntactically urges COSATU to merge freedom from economic "exploitation" with the political freedom of "democracy" and the "birth of a new nation." "Rulers" and "employers" are conceptualized as occupying the same subject position, conjoined to one another within the same verse. Thus, when asked in an interview: "Do you see your work as having a specifically working class character? How does this contribute to or conflict with the wider tradition of black cultural resistance and protest?" the poets responded, "Our work has to draw a line against any exploiter in the factory or townships; against *impimpis*; against white and black politicians who betray us; against divisions."[80] In other words, the exploitation and division of the working class in the factory is figured as continuous with exploitation and division in the townships. For Qabula and Hlatshwayo, economic and political exploitation

---

78. Qabula and Hlatshwayo, "Tears of the Creator," 289–90.
79. Ibid., 292.
80. South African Labour Bulletin Staff, "Interview with FOSATU Cultural Group," accessed February 2016, disa.ukzn.ac.za/sites/default/files/pdf.../LaJul85.0377.5429.010.008.Jul1985.25.pdf.

are conflated within a universalizing worldview that contests different kinds of division so that economic emancipation becomes continuous with political enfranchisement.

Such a conceptual unification of economic and political emancipation drew on contextual universalisms in the praise poems, proverbs, and folktales explored in the first section of this chapter. In the context of the 1980s and 1990s, cultural vocabulary linking consensus-based decision-making and power sharing with the equitable distribution of material resources had not disappeared. Just as power sharing by a chief translated into the fair distribution and consumption of agricultural wealth within 'a chief is a chief through other people,' democratic organization of a postcolonial nation-state had to be translated into the realization of workers' rights. Thus, both Qabula's and Hlatshwayo's *izibongo*, like nineteenth-century chiefly praises, use descriptions of the alimentary nourishing or devouring of subjects as metaphors for the sharing or abuse of political power. Within the despotic apartheid regime, workers are being literally and metaphorically "consumed" by their lack of rights:

> Your labor
> Has Turned you
> Into prize game
> For the hunters of surplus
>
> You are the raw meat
> The prey
> For Vultures
> Are you not the backbone
> Of trade?
>
> Now
> You are a nameless breed of animals
> A stock of many numbers
> And your suppressor's lust
> To suck you dry
> Recognizes neither day
> Nor night.[81]

Here, Qabula and Hlatshwayo describe the capitalist apartheid regime as feasting on the workers, who, significantly, are represented as the cattle that formed the "backbone" of tribal political and social systems of exchange. In Qabula and Hlatshwayo's transferred metaphors, however, the capitalist republic has

---

81. Qabula and Hlatshwayo, "Tears of the Creator," 286–88.

reduced these sacred "cattle," or the "workers," to commodities, to nothing more than "surplus": "You are a nameless breed of animals / A stock of many numbers." Within this abusive social order, the workers' worth lies only in the value of their labor power as a commodity, which depends only on their ability to nourish the unyielding appetite of their capitalist exploiters. The latter "vultures" and "hunters" reduce the workers to "raw meat" to be "butchered" and "sucked dry."

While such a formulation is rooted in a "chief is a chief through other people" and is remarkably similar to praise poetry's denunciations of Shaka, the verse also acquires its force through Marxist notions of the capitalist extraction of 'surplus value,' or the value in labor time that is created not for the worker but solely for the capitalist to appropriate as profit. The verse suggests that the "unnecessary labour" carried out by the workers is proportionally so large that the workers are being "sucked dry" and that the solution to overthrowing these chiefs/governments lies in the Marxist epiphany that the ruling class is in fact a product of working-class labor. As a corrective to a state of affairs within which workers are ironically "butchered by the products of [their] labor" or the corporate state, which uses "kwela kwelas" or police vans to enforce exploitative regimes,[82] Qabula and Hlatshwayo highlight the workers' actual worth as sustainers of their people. They deserve the right to rule themselves, be sovereign, and to serve as their own chief because they nourish others with their labor. In a morale-rousing maneuver, the poets call out to the workers:

> Are you not the backbone
> Of trade?
>
> Maker of all things
>
> Worker
> Are you not the economy's foundation?
> Are you not the engine of development and progress?
> Worker
> Remember
> Who you are;
> You are the country's foundation base and block
>
> What is then
> The nature of your sin?

---

82. Qabula and Hlatshwayo, "Tears of the Creator," 288.

> Your sin
> Can it be your power?
> Can it be your blood?
> Can it be your sweat?[83]

The verse highlights the peoples' worth in terms of their ability to sustain themselves materially; they are the "maker of all things." Rather than being helpless, workers are powerful because the worth of their "sweat" creates all forms of value—whether use, exchange, or surplus. Workers are therefore the rightful custodians of state power, for the authority to rule comes from the working people themselves. As Qabula and Hlatshwayo put it in an interview: "we don't criticize in order to divide workers but rather to do the opposite: to strengthen the unity of workers, and make the leadership accountable to us. The *imbongi*'s role, remember, was always to praise and criticize."[84]

Qabula and Hlatshwayo's poems conclude by passing the mantle on to a more worthy form of government, the trade union, characterizing the entity responsible for looking after workers' economic interests as a deserving political leader or substitute chief. Qabula's "Praise to FOSATU" for instance, proclaims:

> Kneeled we did, and prayed to our ancestors and said:
> We pray to you for a leader,
> We pray to you for a leader.
> Mvelinqangi and the ancestors have answered us
> And sent to us FOSATU.[85]

Yet, even when instating the trade union as a leader, Qabula and Hlatshwayo assert that the chief/government, here the trade union, derives its authority from the workers. Thus, just as the political power of chiefs was regarded as sanctioned by the ancestors as long as the chief lived up to his responsibilities, so, too, Qabula informs FOSATU of its duties toward workers, warning the federation not to fail them.

> Don't disappoint us FOSATU
> Don't sacrifice us to our adversaries
> To date your policies and your sons are commendable
> We don't know what's to happen tomorrow.[86]

---

83. Ibid., 286–88.
84. Qabula and Hlatshwayo in South African Labour Bulletin Staff, "Interview with FOSATU Cultural Group," disa.ukzn.ac.za/sites/default/files/pdf…/LaJul85.0377.5429.010.008.Jul1985.25.pdf.
85. Qabula, "Praise Poem to FOSATU," 12.
86. Ibid.

This is a barely disguised threat to FOSATU that its authority will be deposed of if it does not fulfill its function of serving workers' interests. Similarly, in "The Tears of a Creator," Qabula and Hlatshwayo emphasize 'rule by the people' by hailing the workers as political authority. They end the poem with a proclamation: "Woza 'msebenzi, woza COSATU, woza freedom," a declaration and call to action that translates as: "Awake workers, awake COSATU, awake freedom." The line presents the workers, COSATU, and political freedom as coextensive with one another. Once again, the people themselves are the trade union, the chief, and the embodiments of freedom.

If Qabula and Hlatshwayo describe despotic apartheid capitalism in terms of Shakan metaphors of voracious greed, their description of protective trade unions inverts the metaphor through contextual universalisms to do with the chief's economic sustenance of his tribe. In Hlatshwayo's "Black Mamba Rising," the trade union/chief provides both political and also material sustenance and is, therefore, a "black buffalo" with "tasty meat."[87] Such an equation of a just chief with the provision of nourishment echoes the nineteenth-century praises analyzed earlier, which were addressed to generous, democratic chiefs such as Khondlo.

Collectively, Hlatshwayo's and Qabula's verses conceptualize the political fight against apartheid as a struggle for economic sustenance by defining all workers as emancipated citizens with equal rights regardless of their class position or labor market status. Such universalizing principles were expressed through both institutionalized content and literary form. In terms of content, the poets glorified the democratic policies of trade unions, including nondiscrimination, nonhierarchical organization, and national and international linkages between bodies of workers and different trade unions, regardless of the industry to which they belonged. Formally, they transmitted these universalizing principles by drawing on the *izibongo*'s tradition of consensus-based multivocality.

Unlike many other resistance movements of the time, FOSATU and then COSATU were universalizing because they were nondiscriminatory, positing transcendent concepts of the human that sought to include rather than exclude difference within the category of "humanity." The Trade Union Advisory Coordinating Council (TUACC) that emerged in 1973 and founded FOSATU in 1979 insisted that only "open" trade unions could become members and defined "open" trade unions as those that accepted all workers, "regardless of race, religion or sex," challenging the widespread practice of organizing black and white workers into separate "parallel" trade unions. In his "Praise Poem to FOSATU," Qabula writes:

---

87. Hlatshwayo, "Black Mamba Rising," 298.

Is FOSATU also going to hug you with those warm Hands?
His hands that know no racism?

Protect us too with those Sacred wings of yours
That knoweth no discrimination[88]

FOSATU asserted, and Qabula celebrated, the fact that shade of skin did not matter as long as you were a worker, an unusual and contentious claim in a struggle against a system for which racial differentiation was everything. Just as chiefs were regarded as having to uphold a sacred link to the ancestors through good behavior and fulfillment of duty toward all of their subjects, FOSATU, too, has a "sacred" function in the lives of the workers it protects, that of embracing them all regardless of their racial, sexual, or social status.

FOSATU, and then COSATU, were universalizing also because they were nonhierarchical, built on the democratic principal of workers' control. The trade unions were built up from the factory floor, with workers sharing leadership roles. As Foster put it: "we must be immediately clear that we are not talking about leadership in the sense that it is usually discussed which is in terms of individuals and 'great men.' What we are interested in is the elected representatives of workers and the officials they appoint to work within the organization."[89] These representatives were shop stewards elected by shop floor workers to negotiate all changes, grievances, and dismissals with the management. They were directly accountable to their constituents, with unresponsive stewards being regularly removed.[90] This meant that workers, not union officials, led their union as part of COSATU.

Moreover, the unions themselves were extraordinarily comprehensive in their scope. Qabula's poem to FOSATU thus writes that the union body encompasses all "the Industries they work for in Africa." FOSATU has "union offices everywhere," resulting in a reach so far that its "'lion's roar' is even heard at 'Pretoria North.'" Moreover, FOSATU also universalized its activities to an international level, thus enabling it to act as a counter to the divisive power of multinational corporations in South Africa. Qabula writes:

FOSATU has given birth
Its sons are spread all over Africa
Even overseas you find its sons.[91]

---

88. Qabula, "Praise Poem to FOSATU," 12.
89. Foster, "The Workers' Struggle," 109.
90. Wood, "Solidarity, Representativity and Accountability," 326–43.
91. Qabula, "Praise Poem to FOSATU," 12.

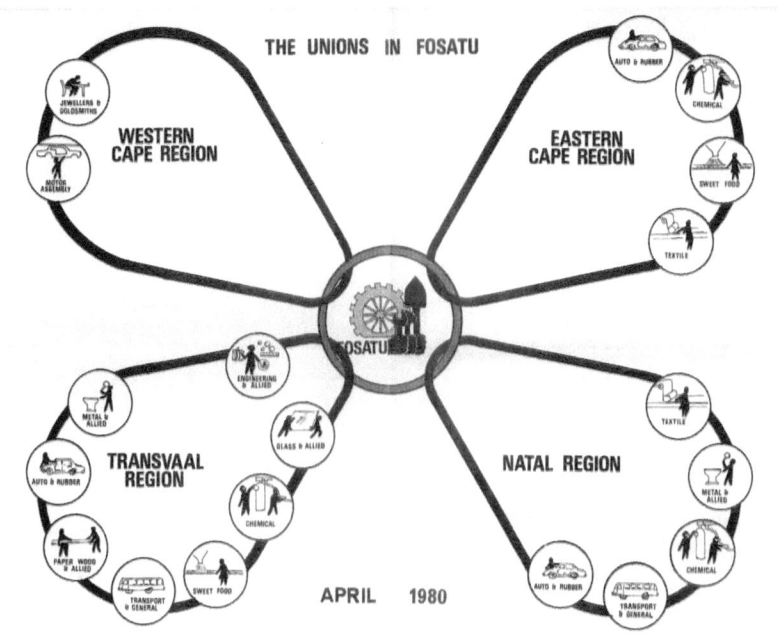

FIGURE 11. The structure of FOSATU. Source: Historical Papers Research Archive, University of the Witwatersrand, Johannesburg.

Qabula's verse suggests a common tribe of people, all united, regardless of their color, nationality, or economic status, against a common oppressor with a national as well as international face. The trade unions relate black 'selves' to black 'others' to a degree that parallels and challenges the globalizing universalizing force of the market.

The verse elaborates that this unity is achieved through multiplicity, diversity, and inclusiveness. Thus, both Qabula and Hlatshwayo celebrated FOSATU's linking of different, individual unions that shared common goals, policies, and resources, mobilizing across unions in different companies. Qabula explains this universalizing reach, or "a trade union is a trade union through other trade unions," by drawing out its historical genealogy in which all strikes and worker actions against their factory employers were connected to FOSATU's efforts. The praise poet sings:

> Whilst walking,
> Thinking about the workers' problems,
> I saw a fist flying across Dunlop's cheek
> Whilst Dunlop was still shivering,

Perhaps Bakers was asking
"What did my neighbor do
That he is being hurt like that?"
I saw a combination of fists
Bombarding Bakers on his ribs,
Until Dunlop was concerned,
He called the shop stewards and asked:
"Madoda, please tell us,
"Is MAWU now going to cause trouble at Bakers?"
"No, Banumzane."
"Who is organizing at Bakers?"
"Of course Sweet Food and Allied Workers Union."
"But where does it come from?"
"From FOSATU."
"This MAWU where does it spring from?"
"Also from FOSATU."
"Same constitution?"
"Yebo.
Same policy, same constitution,
don't worry Jim,
It's still another MAWU."
Chakijana! Wake up and wear your clothes
Of power and wisdom[92]

The poem states that all workers, regardless of which trade union they are part of, are part of the same group. Qabula therefore encourages workers to act as a united body so that an attack on one corporation becomes an attack on the others. The attacker of Bakers Biscuits is also the attacker of Dunlop; both attacks can be traced back to one source: workers with the power of FOSATU behind them: "same policy, same constitution." The poem enacts the power of such a union through the defeated shock of Dunlop and Bakers Biscuits. The verse ends with the sarcastic voice of the *imbongi* addressed to the factory owners: "don't worry Jim, It's still another MAWU." In other words, it does not matter, the *imbongi* tells the factory owner, if the attack was carried out by the Metal and Allied Workers Union, because all of the other trade unions represent MAWU, as MAWU represents them; all spring "from FOSATU, also from FOSATU."

---

92. Ibid.

FIGURE 12. Sweet Food and Allied Workers Union strike at Bakers Biscuits, February 1985. Source: Historical Papers Research Archive, University of the Witwatersrand, Johannesburg.

The *imbongi* celebrates this universalizing linking of individual trade unions by explaining the strategy through which they work. They strike through one body but with different arms on different fronts using different names so that they are everywhere at once. This is Chakijana-like because it involves the trickster's ability to encompass multiple identities. Chakijana, of course, is an allusion that links the worker struggle to the antiapartheid struggle—a legacy of the Anglo Boer presence on Zulu land—and also stresses the importance of being everywhere at once as Chakijana was. Describing the same strategy, Hlatshwayo writes that the body of workers, or "black mamba," was

> stabbed good and proper during the day
> at Sydney Road right on the premises
> to the delight of the police
> There were echoes of approval on the
> TV at Aukland [sic] Park saying:
> Never again shall it move,

Never again shall it revive,
Never again shall it return,
Yet it was beginning to tower with rage.
on rising
it was multi headed[93]

The verse describes a strike that was supposed to have been suppressed on Sydney Road, the site of the Dunlop factory, but that was then picked up by other trade unions that were part of FOSATU and continued in various other neighborhoods. The federation of trade unions, then, is a powerful, many-headed entity with multiple identities that are only seemingly paradoxical. For its paradoxes are elusive only to its oppressors/hunters; its multi-headed nature is actually coherent as an oppositional and practical political strategy.

This emphasis on multiple identities unified into a coherent whole was particularly important because it was a deliberate refusal of the apartheid regime's racist predetermination of rights according to its own imposed identity categorizations. In their effort to confine blacks to the periphery of economic activity, successive apartheid governments fragmented the country into linguistic and tribal enclaves called homelands. Consequently, black South Africans were disenfranchised, alienated from and deprived of their South African citizenship in favor of a dubious homeland citizenship. From these satellite homelands, the white captains of South African industry could tap cheap labor. Among the many laws enacted to enable whites to procure low-cost black labor was a law acknowledging the existence of Permanent Urban Residents (PURS), a term for those limited number of blacks who had permission to live and work in the cities under the apartheid regime. In response, Hlatshwayo wrote:

You black buffalo
Black yet with tasty meat
The buffalo that turns the
Foreigners' language into
Confusion.
Today you're called a Bantu,
Tomorrow you're called a
Communist
Sometimes you're called a

---

93. Hlatshwayo, "Black Mamba Rising," 297.

Native.
Today again you're called a
Foreigner,
Today again you're called a
Terrorist,
Sometimes you're called a
Plural,
Sometimes you're called an Urban
PURS.[94]

The image of the shape-shifting black buffalo undoes apartheid's racist and rigid assignations of identity, whether "PURS," "Communists," or "Terrorists." The black buffalo's ability to be everywhere at once creates a frantic confusion in the minds of the oppressors who do not know who their enemy is and what face their enemy will fight behind next. He or she may be a Bantu, communist, native, foreigner, terrorist, Plural, or Urban PURS. Hlatshwayo stresses that it is this trickster quality that enables workers to disrupt the workings of the oppressor's organizations. Other aspects of Hlatshwayo's poem also aim to upset the fixing of identity and meaning by apartheid categorizations of black workers. The central image, that of a black mamba, is characterized as elusive, with many faces, just like the trade unions and the workers they represent. The trade union/chief that represents all workers is a black mamba that knows no color, an anteater but also a black buffalo and a flock of locusts.

These poems' universalizing message is enacted through a multivocalist literary form. Hlatshwayo's "Black Mamba Rising" harnesses parallelism to emphasize a nondiscriminatory message wherein the signifier "black" refers not only to skin color but to a body of people united in their oppression and struggles:

Tell them—the borrowed
Must be given back
Tell them—the chained
Must be chained no more
Tell them—these are the
Dictates of the black mamba,
The mamba that knows no
Color,

---

94. Ibid., 299.

> Tell them—these are the
> Workers' demands,
> By virtue of their birthright
> Dunlop workers
> I'm taking
> My hat off,
> I'm bowing to you with
> Respect.[95]

Even though the mamba is black it "knows no color." The verse's parallelism enacts multiple voices repeating the same point, that "these are the worker's rights," "the black mamba's dictates," and "the worker's demands." As in tribal praises, parallelism marks a departure from the idea of poetry being private property, for it is composed by multiple people and communally shared. This can be seen as a form of cultural democratization, the aim of which is to spread knowledge beyond an elite few to enable workers to participate, on their own terms, in the production of a culture. Each statement begins with "Tell them" and means essentially the same thing but with different nuances, thereby suggesting multiple voices. Each gives a strong command to give workers their due. The *imbongi* chimes in at the end as himself to stress the universalizing message behind this multivocality; the workers must be given their rights because they are human "by virtue of their birthright" and it is this birthright that promises them "Respect" with a capital "R," a respect that is prior to color and social status and that is so powerful that it prompts even the *imbongi*, the sacred medium between man and his ancestral spirits, to "[take] My hat off" and "bow to you."

This chapter has documented how worker-poets were central to the call for collective action that was crucial to overthrowing apartheid:

> Praise poets, messengers, observers,
> Run in all directions,
> Stand on top of the mountains,
> Report to Botha at Pretoria
> Report to our heroes on the
> Island,
> Report to the angels in your
> Prayers,
> Say unto them—here is a
> Flood of workers,

---

95. Ibid., 300.

The employers have done what
Ought not to be[96]

In rallying their compatriots, these worker-academics, actors, playwrights, composers, singers, painters, and poets unified various agendas toward the same universalizing goals. They advocated the complete reorganization of their society, the eradication of racism, the release of political prisoners, the redistribution of the nation's wealth, and the triumph and ascendance of the proletariat within a democratic nation-state. Through their verse, *imbongi* such as Qabula and Hlatshwayo were fighting for the unification of the entire black community as citizens and emancipated workers. In doing so, these worker-poets were not simply harnessing symbolic but dead cultural capital. Rather, as Liz Gunner puts it, they were "collapsing the heroic past into an heroic present, making memory work for it."[97] The aspirational and localized 'past' they drew on was fragmented yet alive in the present. The nineteenth-century Zulu texts that composed this past through ideals such as "a chief is a chief through other people" served as self-regulating mechanisms that amplified certain modes of cognitive processing and transmitted democratic conceptual networks through literary devices that were contiguous with their universalizing messages. Worker-poets in the apartheid era adapted these contextual universalisms in their own struggle, serving as a catalyst for a national fight. Democratic behavior emerges as a contextual universalism, a universalizing, local idea that is ontologically prior to colonial modernity and that responds to homegrown and colonial legacies of capitalist domination. In providing evidence of a fragmented cultural lineage in which past institutions such as communal agricultural systems live on in the present in the form of dynamic contextual universalisms, these praise poems ask us to reconsider how we trace the path toward democratic change. In the African context, we are asked to revise predominant accounts of how majoritarian systems of democracy were appropriated, then repeatedly failed, in parts of Africa. This rethinking also challenges views of African indigenous cultures as always developing toward representative processes, instead showing how categories of progressive change themselves need to be recontextualized.

---

96. Ibid., 299.
97. Gunner, "Remaking the Warrior?" 52.

CODA

Contextual Universalisms and the Path to a New Postcolonialism

A FINAL STORY, not to end but to begin anew: In 1955, the African National Congress dispatched fifty thousand volunteers into townships and the countryside to collect 'freedom demands' from the South African people. This was a remarkable move, for it was truly universalizing in its bid to gather as many of the people's voices as it could to work out what a democratic future should look like. Demands included "land to be given to all landless people," "living wages and shorter hours of work," and "free and compulsory education, irrespective of colour, race or nationality." These and other 'freedom demands' were synthesized into the Freedom Charter, a statement of core principles by the ANC and its allies that began with the opening demand that "The People Shall Govern!" The charter was officially adopted on 26 June 1955 at a Congress of the People in Kliptown, with more than three thousand delegates and a massive crowd shouting approval of each section with cries of "Mayibuye Afrika!" or "Bring Back Africa!" The meeting was broken up by police on the second day, although by then the charter had been read in full. Nelson Mandela escaped the police by disguising himself as a milkman.

Significantly, the Freedom Charter was unambivalent about the interlinked nature of political and economic justice in South Africa:

> We, the People of South Africa, declare for all our country and the world to know: that South Africa belongs to all who live in it, black and white, and that no government can justly claim authority unless it is based on the will of all the people; that our people have been robbed of their birthright to land, liberty and peace by a form of government founded on injustice and inequality.[1]

The phrase "South Africa belongs to all who live in it" had both a metaphorical and a metonymic meaning. Metaphorically, South Africa 'belonged' to all the people because it was to be a rainbow nation, with a government "based on the will of all the people," no matter what race they were. South Africa, however, was also to literally 'belong' to all the people by way of a restoration of their "birthright to land." The "land of South Africa" in this case was a metonym for the physical ground on which people lived. The charter thus proclaims: "Restrictions of land ownership on a racial basis shall be ended, and all the land re-divided amongst those who work it to banish famine and land hunger."[2]

In practice, however, what remains of the democratic nation-state of the Freedom Charter is only metaphorical belonging. On 11 February 1990, Mandela was finally freed, and in May 1994 the ANC came to power. Mandela noted the direction the world was heading, away from communism and toward globalized finance, businesses, and markets: "As I moved around the world and heard the opinions of leading business people and economists about how to grow an economy, I was persuaded and convinced about the free market."[3] This was a direct reversal of his earlier plan to nationalize South Africa's main businesses: "The nationalization of the mines, banks and monopoly industries is the policy of the A. N. C., and a change or modification of our views in this regard is inconceivable," he had said.[4] By some accounts, such a fundamental change in Mandela's viewpoints came after he visited the annual meeting of the World Economic Forum, where the communist leaders of China and Vietnam told him, "We are currently striving to privatize state enterprises and invite private enterprise into our economies. We are Communist Party governments, and you are a leader of a national liberation movement. Why are you talking about nationalization?"[5] In the end, the new Constitution of South Africa addressed directly nearly all demands for equality of race and

---

1. ANC, "The Freedom Charter," accessed January 2015, http://www.anc.org.za/show.php?id=72.
2. Ibid.
3. Mandela, quoted in Bright and Hruby, *The Next Africa*, 44.
4. Mandela, quoted in Sorkin, "How Mandela Shifted Views."
5. Mboweni in Sorkin, "How Mandela Shifted Views."

language but made no reference to the nationalization of industry or redistribution of land so as not to deter foreign investment. Subsequent turns in the late 1990s to more overtly neoliberal policies favored private investors over state-led development. The government's own statistics agency concludes that the average black 'African' household income declined 19 percent from 1995 to 2000, while white income was up 15 percent.[6]

The story of 'freedom' and 'equality' after colonial rule follows a similarly neoliberal path in India, with increasing class divides and a government run by crony capitalism. The Indian economy was liberalized in July 1991 under heavy pressure from international lending agencies such as the International Monetary Fund. Economists colluded with elite bourgeois groups and large transnational corporations to offer liberalization as a panacea for all of India's ills. However, as subsequent critics have pointed out, liberalization has not reduced poverty. Rather, as the economist Amiya Bagchi notes in his description of "corporate feudalism," internal collaborators of neoliberalism often pressurized their own governments to hand out outrageously high profits to transnational corporations on the false argument that only these had the resources and the technology to build up the needed infrastructure such as power, water supply, or highways.[7] Pranab Bardhan in turn highlights the devastation caused to fragile economies by billions of dollars of volatile short-term capital stampeding around the globe in herd-like movements.[8] Both economists have stressed the damage caused to jobs, wages, and incomes of the poor by the dislocations and competition of international trade and foreign investment. Both have also noted the state's unwillingness and inability to compensate for this damage and to invest in the public sector so as to alleviate poverty and inequality.

In other words, the populations of South Africa and India have emerged into the light of postcoloniality only to be blinded by it. This book has asserted that such a state of neocolonialism, in which native elites and foreign investors conquer, subjugate, and appropriate the surplus value of a growing number of subaltern groups, is aided by a rhetorical sleight of hand that conflates the freedom and equality of democratic systems with the 'free market' and 'equality of opportunity' of a neoliberal global capitalism. Capitalism passes off the freedom of humans within the 'free market' as the freedom of the human in toto. The continual connection of capitalism's universalizing force with democratic universalisms is apparent both in popular culture and cultural criticism.

---

6. Desai and Pithouse, "What Stank in the Past," 843.

7. Bagchi, "Neoliberal Imperialism," www.networkideas.org/feathm/may2006/Amiya_Bagchi.pdf.

8. Bardhan, "Globalization, Inequality, and Poverty," https://publications.iadb.org/.../Globalization,%20Inequality,%20and%20Poverty.pdf.

For instance, Roget's New Millennium Thesaurus has the following entry for the word 'democracy':

Definition: Representation

Synonyms: capitalism, commonwealth, egalitarianism, emancipation, equalitarianism, equality, free enterprise, freedom, justice, laissez faire, liberal government, private ownership, representative government, republic, suffrage.[9]

Within this thesaurus, the conceptual network for democracy includes concepts such as 'egalitarianism,' 'emancipation,' 'equalitarianism,' 'equality,' 'freedom,' 'justice,' 'suffrage,' and 'representative government,' which are equated with capitalism itself and with terms tied to its workings such as 'free enterprise,' 'laissez faire,' and 'private ownership.' A number of economists and cultural critics have supported this supposedly synonymous relationship between capitalism and democracy.[10]

This book has challenged such conflations by differentiating colonial and postcolonial capitalism's modes of relating the self to the other from Enlightenment and contextual universalisms. In the process, I have attempted to revise the idea that Enlightenment universalisms syncretized with nondisruptive forms of indigenous 'tradition' and coupled with capitalism are the sole drivers of democratic self-understandings. Rather, Enlightenment universalisms form a small part of much larger conceptual networks pertaining to 'rationality,' 'freedom,' 'ethical exchange,' and 'rule by the people' that include contextual universalisms. By unearthing the neglected routes of anticolonial and noncapitalist change, the contextual universalisms approach complicates colonial modernity's ideal of what constituted 'humanity,' nuances accounts of the historical spread of representative public spheres, and counters the Eurocentric myopia of collapsing all universalisms into Enlightenment constructs that work in the same way and toward similar ends.

I. THE DEMOCRATIC POWER OF VERNACULAR LITERATURES OF THE WORLD

In literary terms, the conflation of capitalist freedom with the most abstract freedom of universalisms is reflected in a shift away from metonymic associa-

---

9. *Roget's New Millennium Thesaurus*, s.v. "democracy," http://www.thesaurus.com/browse/democracy?s=t.
10. The most famous example is Friedman, *Capitalism and Freedom*.

tion in the figurative language of the commodified 'world literatures' of these regions. By contrast, metonymic associations—for instance the link between milk and power—survive in the noncapitalist local 'literatures of the world' I have explored in the previous chapters. Both metaphor and metonymy are usually defined as the use of a figurative expression to describe a literal entity. In metaphor, the use is based on resemblance or analogy; in metonymy, it is based on a more concrete relation than that of similarity. In metonymy, the literal term for one thing is applied to another with which it is closely associated because of a recurrent relationship in common experience. Thus 'the crown' can be used to stand in for the figure of the king. In a mirroring of the state of postcolonial societies, within many postcolonial world literatures, metonymic notions of South Africa as the 'land of South Africa,' which represents actual material possessions such as 'the ground on which people live' are replaced with purely metaphorical notions of 'the land of South Africa' as a democratic nation-state of multicultural and multiracial citizenship. Even many well-meaning world literatures circulating in the global literary marketplace often participate in this rhetorical sleight of hand. The literary runs the risk of becoming the space where metaphoric democratic belonging rather than actual material belongings are enough. Perhaps this is because many postcolonial world literatures cannot imagine a way out of a neoliberal capitalism so entrenched that it seems to be a universal essence in itself.

A first step toward substantiating these admittedly generalizing claims regarding the enormous body of diverse texts that fall into the category of 'world literature' can be made by examining examples from two rather different postcolonial texts, one from South Africa and the other from India. The first, Phaswane Mpe's 2001 South African novel in English, *Welcome to Our Hillbrow*, registers and critiques the slippage between metaphoric democratic 'rainbow nation belonging' and metonymic material 'belongings.' Mpe describes the downtown Johannesburg area of Hillbrow, a formerly white space now being taken over by blacks, crime, drugs, "illegal aliens," and urban decay:

> Mail & Guardian and David Philip Publishers and others changing offices moving out of this increasingly dilapidated and menacing Braamfontein while others found it to be quite an investment and so coming in to build and occupy their lush offices . . . the streets of Hillbrow and Berea and Braamfontein overflowing with Makwerekwere come to pursue green pastures after hearing that the new president Rolihlahla Mandela welcomes guests and visitors unlike his predecessors who erected deadly electric wires around the boundaries of South Africa trying to keep out the barbarians from Mozambique Zaire Nigeria Congo Ivory Coast Zimbabwe . . . from

all over Africa ... Makwerekwere ... spreading like pumpkin plants filling every corner of our city and turning each patch into a Hillbrow coming to take our jobs in the new democratic rainbowism of African Renaissance that threatened the future of the locals.[11]

This quote suggests that in "our Hillbrow" everything is not in fact literally "ours." Although the "deadly electric wires across the boundaries of South Africa trying to keep out the barbarians" are gone, this spatial opening up only enables the metaphorical belonging of 'others' within a rainbow nation, for Hillbrow does not materially belong either to the "Makwarekwere" (immigrants) or to the previous residents. It belongs only to capital and to the "lush" quarters of businesses whose wealth does not seem to be trickling down. The style of the passage, with phrases collapsing and running into each other, evokes the rampant encroachment of capital and the chaos that results.

The simile of the immigrant "barbarians" as encroaching pumpkin plants is especially notable as a metaphoric invocation of the intrusion of capital because, as the origin story in chapter three on *ubuntu* recalled, the spreading vines of the pumpkin plant were a precolonial metonym for a plentiful communal economy of reciprocal exchange made up of linked homesteads. But in the new South Africa, the pumpkin plant has been reduced merely to a figurative device—a simile—rather than a metonymic retainer of concrete associations to do with the pumpkin's use as a staple item of widespread reciprocal exchange within rural areas. Moreover, this simile has morphed into representing something quite lethal: "the barbarians from Mozambique Zaire Nigeria Congo Ivory Coast Zimbabwe ... from all over Africa ... Makwerekwere ... spreading like pumpkin plants filling every corner of our city and turning each patch into a Hillbrow coming to take our jobs in the new democratic rainbowism of African Renaissance that threatened the future of the locals." Without the accompanying material "belongings," metaphoric belonging is itself turned into something nefarious, with the different colors of the rainbow nation turning against each other into a fight for "our jobs." The word "our" is in turn reduced to a negative and proprietary pronoun rather than a term tied to a shared resource. The pumpkin plant, stripped of its metonymic associations, represents nothing more than competition for limited resources and the survival of the fittest—a state of affairs that breeds xenophobia and judges the influx of the Makwerekwere as "barbarians." The demos shrinks rather than expands. "Hillbrow" and Heathrow and the multiple other locations that are "ours" are "ours" only metaphorically in terms of the medley of different races,

---

11. Mpe, *Welcome to Our Hillbrow*, 26–27.

colors, ethnicities, and nationalities that unhappily occupy it. Mpe's novel suggests that true democratic belonging cannot be achieved by way of "free trade" and a parasitic expanding capitalism. But the novel is restricted to diagnosis, not cure, for it cannot imagine a way out of such a globalized capitalism.

The representation of metaphorical belonging alone is also the case in some of the most well regarded texts about postcolonial freedom in South Asia. Take, for instance, the paradigmatic postcolonial Indian novel in English, Salman Rushdie's *Midnight's Children,* in which the life of the upper-class protagonist Saleem Sinai, one of the offspring of India's independence, is merely an extended metaphor for the constitution of the new postcolonial nation-state. Saleem stands for the collective dream of all Indians to inhabit a democratic India. At the end of the text, on his birthday, also the anniversary of India's independence, this dream is metaphorically realized when Saleem falls apart. Having given everything he has through the telling of his story, Saleem dissolves into a metaphor for his nation, as he crumbles into as many pieces of dust as there are people in India. This symbolic composition through disintegration suggests that the text can only celebrate and realize the metaphorical belonging of India's diverse population, not the metonymic belonging/s of its many citizens.

In fact, the democratic composition of the nation-state, in being made up of Saleem's body dust, is symbolic of the reimagining of India on liberal capitalist terms. The idea of the midnight's children can be viewed as the extension of Saleem's privileged upbringing over the entire nation."[12] In other words, *Midnight's Children* does not posit an alternative vision of material relations because the democratic public sphere that Saleem metaphorically represents is itself theorized as an outgrowth of capitalism. Eric Strand notes that Saleem's narrative is marked by hostility to state intervention in the economy. The freezing of his father's assets on the stock market leads to a literal emasculation, the icing over of his loins, while conversely baby Saleem is motivated to walk for the first time when the ensuing legal case is decided in the family's favor. The result of these ideological free market underpinnings in the novel means that 'national belonging/s' is once again an abstract metaphor and not a concrete metonym. Fittingly, when Saleem realizes his telepathic powers to conduct a mapping and census of the new nation, itself a resonantly colonial act—the people he observes are abstracted from their embeddedness in material relations and landscapes: he "nestled among the woolly, mystical perceptions of a chanting priest," "toured Connaught Place in New Delhi in the guise of an auto-rickshaw driver," flew "up into the Himalayas, into the neanderthal

---

12. Strand, "Gandhian Communalism," 991.

moss-covered hut of a Goojar tribal."[13] This quote is notable not only for its almost commercial advertisement of the democratic diversity of the population of 'Incredible India' but for its remarkably patronizing othering of subaltern groups and cultures; the priest's perceptions are "woolly," the Goojar tribal is so backward as to be a "neanderthal" and the autorickshaw driver's menial labor becomes nothing more than a vehicle for Saleem's elite voyeurism. *Midnight's Children* remains a text that reduces national belonging/s to metaphor because of its investment in bourgeois cultures, not those of the subaltern dispossessed.

On the other hand, the literatures of the world I have charted in this book are very different from both these texts of world literature, for they do not only diagnose or critique the conflation of democracy with capitalism as *Welcome to Our Hillbrow* does. And nor do they uphold these conflations in an attempt to participate within a global literary marketplace for an exclusively bourgeois readership as *Midnight's Children* does. The postcolonial poems, proverbs, and novels that I have read function as aspirational cognitive blueprints for realizing truly universalizing material arrangements through metonymic associations. My chapters have documented how food or agricultural products, including the pumpkin plant, survive as metonyms for a communal economy of reciprocal exchange so as to highlight the contextual universalism of "a person is a person through other people." Similarly, "a chief is a chief through other people" is propagated through the metonym of milk, which ties the flowing of power between a people and their government/chief to the material nourishment of subjects by their chief. It is significant that Mandela disguised himself as a milkman on the eve of the celebration of the Freedom Charter, for such a disguise was symbolic of a leader then intent on distributing milk/power to all the people. In my Indian chapters, the food the guru and the disciple partake of together, as well as their "piss, shit, skin, and bones," become metonyms for the common and equal substance of the divinity that lives in every human being.

I am suggesting that these contextual universalisms 'work' precisely because they are expressed through a whole host of figurative devices such as metonyms that carry concrete associations with the lived realities of marginalized groups. Moreover, such metonymy is propagated through modes of expression that encourage and engender popular involvement. When these contextual universalisms are recuperated through communal chantings within mass gatherings, or even when they exist as multivocal oralities in textual form, they are acknowledging and awakening alternative ways of being and thinking.

---

13. Rushdie, *Midnight's Children*, 207

These universalisms show that human beings share the cognitive capacity to move beyond problematic social norms dictated by structures of power, such as colonialism, caste, and patriarchy. And, as many theorists of cognitive approaches to literature have stressed, contextual universalisms also suggest that human beings are not limited to any one set of collective values.[14] We are capable of changing the way we think by participating in the emotions and ways of thinking of others and by having our own informed by collectives, thereby increasing knowledge and empathy and expanding the demos.

II. CALLING FOR A NEW POSTCOLONIALISM

The surviving yet fragmented lineages of contextual universalisms charted by this book encourage us to recast democratic change in the *longue durée,* as well as in terms of geographical expansiveness. Recognizing the diverse roots/routes of representative social change is all the more necessary given that lineages of contextual universalisms precede the hegemony of global capital, which is a relatively recent phenomenon, and thereby highlight resistance to it. In exceeding and resisting capital, the literatures of the world that articulate contextual universalisms extend the category of the postcolonial beyond the emancipatory aims of national anticolonial struggles between the colonizer and native. Instead, they are registering a shift from the exploitation of national resources by colonial capitalism to a very different global state of inequality in which the working class majority is reduced to nothing more than commodified producers of surplus. In recognition of these realities, a new postcolonialism is needed that is both deconstructive and recuperative; it must not only provide tools for dismantling the powerful hierarchies and modes of thinking on which colonial capitalism and neoliberal capitalism rests, it should also highlight, recuperate, and propagate alternative ontologies and institutional arrangements in their place.

In the spirit of a Saidian expanded critical humanism, such a new postcolonialism would need to address relevant universalisms that are being harnessed by the marginalized in various literatures not only in the Global South but also other previously colonized areas of the world such as, for instance, the Middle East. Various commentators, for instance, have noted the role of Arabic poetry in fuelling the mass working class and youth protests for democratic government in Egypt's Tahrir Square. These protest poems transcend nationalist divi-

---

14. See Kim, "Anger, Cognition, Ideology"; Hogan, *The Mind and Its Stories*; and Zunshine, *Why We Read Fiction.*

sions (some of the most prominent poems harnessed by the revolutionaries were by an anticolonial Tunisian poet, Abul Qassem Al-Shabbi, from the early twentieth century) and harness universalizing notions of 'rule by the people.' Take, for instance, the repeated references to the *al-sha'b*, or "the people," in a famous verse of the Tunisian poet Abul Qassem Al-Shabbi:

> If, one day, a people desires to live, then fate will answer their call.
> And their night will then begin to fade, and their chains break and fall.[15]

Other poems made similar references to rule by the *al-sha'b*, or 'the people.' On 18 November 2011, after months of chanting "al sha'b yurid," or the 'people demand,' a slogan that placed the people in a position of supplication, the chant transformed itself and repositioned the people as the sole authority and power: "IHna al sha'b, la gish wala shurta, wala ahzab bit'assim turta," or, "We are the people; no army, no police; no parties dividing the cake, each a piece."[16] Significantly, this formulation recognizes the twinned nature of democratic belonging as an entitlement to symbolic as well as material belonging, for the cake, as a symbol of power, ties the notion of the rule of the people to the direct access to material resources.

These revolutionary poems highlight principles of 'rule by the people' within a long lineage of the political poet in the Middle East and Northern Africa.[17] A contextual universalisms approach to this body of protest poems would need to investigate which literary features and unique cultural formulations characterize these contextual universalisms. What, for instance, are the semantic connotations of the Arabic *al-sha'b* within this lineage? What layers of syncretic *longue durée* associations do these universalizing notions draw on? What material infrastructures, if any, have they been tied to, and how have these contextual universalisms been transferred to the political struggles of the postcolonial present? How do these nascent contextual universalisms come to fruition within struggles for representative cultures and government?

A contextual universalisms approach would also lead to an exploration of continuing and relevant European universalisms, both Enlightenment and non-Enlightenment, within postcolonial struggles. For European humanism was itself by no means a singular discourse. Rather, it was made up of various

---

15. Al-Shabbi, Abul Qassem, "If the People Wanted Life One Day," trans. Elliott Colla, https://arablit.org/2011/01/16/two-translations-of-abu-al-qasim-al-shabis-if-the-people-wanted-life-one-day/.

16. See Mehrez, *Translating Egypt's Revolution*, 13.

17. See Colla, Elliott, "The Poetry of Revolt," http://www.jadaliyya.com/pages/index/506/the-poetry-of-revolt.

diverse contextual universalisms that rarely get read as such within postcolonial studies because, as Dipesh Chakrabarty has noted, particular European universalisms were imposed onto colonized contexts as the singular and hegemonic example of the 'universal.'

One such overlooked European universalism is that of the Diggers Movement begun by Gerrard Winstanley during the English Revolution (1640–60). At a time when the enclosure of common lands threw vast numbers of peasants into wage labor and grinding poverty, Winstanley equated the private ownership of land and wage labor with the exploitation and degradation of people and the earth. Though never fully systematized due to severe repression, the Diggers' philosophy was consistently antiauthoritarian and egalitarian. Winstanley saw God—or Reason, Winstanley's substitute for God—as an entity that dwelled within all human beings and throughout the natural world. This divinity within the self, moreover, was to be realized through an ecological reclaiming of the commons for the poor and dispossessed.

The new postcolonialism would, then, need to consider what modes of democratic inclusiveness have looked like across geographies and histories—not just in Europe or India or South Africa but also in the Middle East or the Caribbean. We would need to explore how forms of demos expansion have been organized in relation to residual indigenous systems of social, political, and economic organization as well as in relation to forms of colonialism. We would also need to expand our analysis to places like Japan, where colonialism never happened but industrialization did. What do the mixed conceptual networks of universalizing concepts look like in these places? What cognitive modes do they harness? What literary and cultural forms do they appear in, and what embedded material arrangements are they related to? How do these alternative conceptual networks and associated material arrangements disrupt the workings of neocolonialism and neoliberalism? Which colorful pathways of demos expansion can a shifting kaleidoscope of universalisms reveal next, and which other hermeneutics are needed to bring these narrative strands into focus?

BIBLIOGRAPHY

Abhinavagupta. *The Aesthetic Experience According to Abhinavagupta*. Edited and translated by Raniero Gnoli. Varanasi, India: Chowkhamba Sanskrit Series, 1968.

———. *The Dhvanyaloka of Anandavardhana with the Locana of Abhinavagupta*. Translated by Daniel Ingalls, Jeffrey Masson, and M. V. Patwardhan. Cambridge, MA: Harvard University Press, 1990.

Adler, Glenn, Judy Maller, and Eddie Webster. "Unions, Direct Action, and Transition in South Africa." In *Peace, Politics, and Violence in the New South Africa*, edited by Norman Etherington, 306–34. London: Hans Zell, 1992.

Adler, Glenn, and Eddie Webster. "Challenging Transition Theory: The Labor Movement, Radical Reform, and Transition to Democracy in South Africa." *Politics & Society* 23 (March 1995): 75–106.

Agamben, Giorgio. *Means Without End: Notes on Politics*. Minneapolis: University of Minnesota Press, 2000.

Agrawal, Purushottam. *Akath Kahani Prem Ki: Kabir Ki Kavita Aur Unka Samay* (*Love is an Unspeakable Tale: Kabir's Poetry and his Times*). New Delhi: Rajkamal Prakashan, 2009.

Anker, Elizabeth. *Fictions of Dignity: Embodying Human Rights in World Literature*. Ithaca, NY: Cornell University Press, 2012.

Appiah, Kwame Antony. *In My Father's House: Africa in the Philosophy of Culture*. New York: Oxford University Press, 1992.

Aravamudan, Srinivas. *Guru English: South Asian Religion in a Cosmopolitan Language*. Princeton, NJ: Princeton University Press, 2005.

Banerjee-Dube, Ishita. "Issues of Faith, Enactment of Contest: The Founding of Mahima Dharma in Nineteenth Century Orissa." In *Jagannath Revisited*, edited by H. Kulke and B. Schepnel, 149–77. New Delhi: Manohar, 2001.

———. *Religion, Law and Power*. London: Anthem Press, 2007.

Banerjee, Nirmala. "Working Women in Colonial Bengal: Modernization and Marginalization." In *Recasting Women*, edited by Kumkum Sangari and Sudesh Vaid, 269–301. New Delhi: Kali for Women, 1989.

Barayi, Elijah. Quoted in Martin Plaut, "The Political Significance of COSATU." *Transformation* 2 (1986).

Barnard, Rita. "On Laughter, the Grotesque, and the South African Transition: Zakes Mda's *Ways of Dying.*" *Novel* 37, no. 3 (Summer 2004): 277–302.

Baskin, Jeremy. *Striking Back: A History of COSATU.* Johannesburg: Ravan, 1991.

Bayart, Jean Francis. *The State in Africa: The Politics of the Belly.* London: Longman Group, 1993.

Beinart, W. *The Political Economy of Pondoland, 1869–1930.* Cambridge: Cambridge University Press, 1982.

Beltz, Johannes, and Bettina Baumer. *Bhīma Bhoi: Verses from the Void.* New Delhi: Manohar, 2010.

Bendix, S. *Industrial Relations in South Africa.* Cape Town: Juta, 1989.

Bharata Muni. *The Natya Shastra.* Vol. 1, translated by Manmohan Ghosh. Calcutta: Manisha Granthalaya, 1967.

Bhatia, Nandi. *Acts of Authority/Acts of Resistance: Theater and Politics in Colonial and Postcolonial India.* Ann Arbor: University of Michigan, 2004.

———. *Modern Indian Theatre: A Reader.* New Delhi: Oxford University Press, 2009.

Bhattacharya, Rimli. "The Nautee in 'the Second City of the Empire.'" *Indian Economic Social History Review* 40 (2003): 191–235.

Binodini Dasi. *My Story and My Life as an Actress.* New Delhi: Kali for Women, 1998.

Bjerk, Paul J. "They Poured Themselves into the Milk: Zulu Political Philosophy Under Shaka." *Journal of African History* 47 (2006): 1–19.

Braidotti, Rosi, and Paul Gilroy. *Conflicting Humanities.* New York: Bloomsbury, 2016.

Bright, Jake, and Aubrey Hruby. *The Next Africa: An Emerging Continent Becomes a Global Powerhouse.* London: Macmillan, 2015.

Brown, Duncan. *Voicing the Text: South African Oral Poetry and Performance.* Oxford, UK: Oxford University Press, 1998.

Buchta, David, and Graham Schweig. "Rasa Theory." In *Brill's Encyclopedia of Hinduism.* Vol. 2, *Sacred Texts, Ritual Traditions, Arts, Concepts,* edited by Knut A. Jacobsen, Helene Basu, Angelika Malinar, and Vasudha Narayanan. Leiden, Neth.: Brill, 2010.

Byerly, Ingrid Bianca. "Mirror, Mediator, and Prophet: The Music Indaba of Late-Apartheid South Africa." *Ethnomusicology* 42, no. 1 (Winter 1998): 1–44.

Callaway, Reverend Henry. *Nursery Tales, Traditions, and Histories of the Zulus.* Westport, CN: Greenwood Press, 1868.

Carey, Daniel, and Lynn Festa, eds. *Postcolonial Enlightenment: Eighteenth Century Colonialism and Postcolonial Theory.* Oxford, UK: Oxford University Press, 2009.

Carr, Philip. "The Philosophy of Phonology." In *Philosophy of Linguistics.* Philadelphia: Elsevier, 2012.

Chakrabarty, Dipesh. *Provincializing Europe: Postcolonial Thought and Historical Difference.* Princeton, NJ: Princeton University Press, 2000.

Chakrabarty, Dipesh and Amitav Ghosh. "A Correspondence on Provincializing Europe," *Radical History Review* 83 (2002): 146–72.

Chapman, Michael. "From Shaka's Court to the Trade Union Rally: Praises in a Usable Past." *Research in African Literatures* 30, no.1 (1999): 34–43.

———. *Southern African Literatures*. KwaZulu-Natal, South Africa: University of KwaZulu-Natal Press, 2003.

———. *Soweto Poetry: Literary Perspectives*. Ann Arbor: University of Michigan Press, 1982.

Chatterjee, Partha. *The Nation and Its Fragments: Colonial and Post-Colonial Histories*. Princeton, NJ: Princeton University Press, 1993.

———. "Nationalist Resolution of the Woman Question." In *Recasting Women: Essays in Indian Colonial History*, edited by Kumkum Sangari and Sudhesh Vaid. New Brunswick, NJ: Rutgers University Press, 1990.

Chaudhuri, Amit. "The Construction of the Indian Novel in English." In *The Picador Book of Modern Indian Literature*, edited by Amit Chaudhuri. London: Picador, 2001.

Cheah, Pheng. *Inhuman Conditions: On Cosmopolitanism and Human Rights*. Cambridge, MA: Harvard University Press, 2007.

———. *What Is a World? On Postcolonial Literature as World Literature*. Durham, NC: Duke University Press, 2016.

Chomsky, Noam, and Michel Foucault. "Human Nature: Justice vs. Power." In *The Chomsky-Foucault Debate*. New York: The New Press, 2006.

Clark, Nancy L., and William H. Worger. *South Africa—The Rise and Fall of Apartheid*. New York: Pearson Education Limited, 2004.

Comaroff, Jean. "Beyond Bare Life: AIDS, (Bio)Politics, and the Neoliberal Order." *Public Culture* 19, no. 1 (2007): 197–219.

Comaroff, John, and Jean Comaroff. *Ethnography and the Historical Imagination*. Oxford, UK: Oxford University Press, 1992.

Cornell, Drucilla. *Law and Revolution in South Africa: Ubuntu, Dignity and the Struggle for Constitutional Transformation*. New York: Fordham University Press, 2014.

Cronin, J. "'Even Under the Rine of Terror . . .': Insurgent South African Poetry." *Staffrider* 8, no. 2 (1988): 12–23.

Dalmia, Vasudha. *Poetics, Plays and Performances*. Oxford, UK: Oxford University Press, 2006.

Dasi, Binodini. "Amar Abhinetri Jibon." In *Binodini Dasi: My Story and My Life as an Actress*, edited and translated by Rimli Bhattacharya, 127–58. New Delhi: Kali for Women, 1998.

———. "Amar Katha." In *Binodini Dasi: My Story and My Life as an Actress*, edited and translated by Rimli Bhattacharya, 47–126. New Delhi: Kali for Women, 1998.

———. Quoted in *Binodini Dasi: My Story and My Life as an Actress*, edited and translated by Rimli Bhattacharya, viii. New Delhi: Kali for Women, 1998.

de Bolla, Peter. *The Architecture of Concepts: The Historical Formation of Human Rights*. New York: Fordham University Press, 2013.

Decety, Jean, and Thierry Chaminade. "When the Self Represents the Other: A New Cognitive Neuroscience View on Psychological Identification." *Consciousness and Cognition* 12 (2003): 577–96.

Decety, Jean and Sommerville, J. A. "Shared Representations." *Trends in Cognitive Sciences* 7, no. 12 (2003): 527–33.

Derrida, Jacques. *Given Time: I. Counterfeit Money*. Translated by Peggy Kamuf. Chicago: University of Chicago Press, 1992.

Desai, Ashwin and Richard Pithouse. "'What stank in the past is the present's perfume': Dispossession, Resistance, and Repression in Mandela Park" *South Atlantic Quarterly* 103, no. 4 (Fall 2004): 841–87.

Diderot, Denis. "Article on Political Authority." In *Diderot's Selected Writings*, edited by Lester G. Crocker. London: Macmillan, 1966.

Dimberg U, Thunberg M, Elmehed K. "Unconscious Facial Reactions to Emotional Facial Expressions." *Psychological Science* 11 (2000): 86–89.

Dirks, Nicholas. *Castes of Mind: Colonialism and the Making of Modern India*. Princeton, NJ: Princeton University Press, 2001.

Draper, Hal. "Marx on Democratic Forms of Government." *Socialist Register* 11. (1974): 101–24.

Emery, Alan. "Privatization, Neoliberal Development, and the Struggle for Workers' Rights in Post-Apartheid South Africa." In "Privatization and Resistance: Contesting Neoliberal Globalization." Special issue, *Social Justice* 33, no. 3 (2006): 6–19.

Eschmann, Anncharlott. "Mahima Dharma: An Autochtonous Hindu Reform Movement." In *The Cult of Jagannath and the Regional Tradition of Orissa*, edited by Anncharlott Eschmann, Herman Kulke, and Gaya Charan Tripathi. New Delhi: Manohar, 1978.

Fahnestock, Jeanne. "Verbal and Visual Parallelism." *SAGE* 20, no. 2 (1 April 2003): 123–52.

Farred, Grant. "Mourning the Postapartheid State Already? The Poetics of Loss in Zakes Mda's *Ways of Dying*." *Modern Fiction Studies* 46 (2000):183–206.

Fine, Bob. "The Workers' Struggle in South Africa." *Review of African Political Economy* 24 (May–August 1982): 95–99.

Finnegan, Ruth. *Oral Poetry: Its Nature, Significance and Social Context*. Bloomington: Indiana University Press, 1992.

Finnemore, M., and R. Van Rensburg. *Contemporary Labour Relations*. Durban, South Africa: LexisNexis Butterworths, 2002.

Ford, Henry. *My Life and Work*. Lockport, NY: Snowball Publishing, 2012.

Foster, Joe. "The Workers' Struggle: Where does FOSATU Stand?" *Review of African Political Economy* 9, no. 24 (May–August 1982): 99–114.

Foucault, Michel. *Power/Knowledge: Selected Interviews and Other Writings 1972–1977*. Edited by Colin Gordon. London: Harvester, 1980.

———. "Sex, Power, and the Politics of Identity." In *Ethics, Subjectivity and Truth: The Essential Works of Michel Foucault, 1954–1984*. Vol. 1, edited by P. Rabinow and translated by R. Hurley and others. London: Penguin, 1997.

———. "What Is an Author?" In *Language, Counter-Memory, Practice*. Edited and translated by Donald F. Bouchard and Sherry Simon. Ithaca, NY: Cornell University Press, 1977.

Frazier, Lyn, Lori Taft, Tom Roeper, Charles Clifton, and Kate Ehrlich. "Parallel structure: A source of facilitation in sentence comprehension." *Memory & Cognition* 12, no. 5 (September 1984): 421–30.

Friedman, Milton. *Capitalism and Freedom*. Chicago: University of Chicago Press, 1962.

Fuller, C. J. *The Camphor Flame: Popular Hinduism and Society in India*. Princeton, NJ: Princeton University Press, 2004.

Gade, Christine B. N. "What Is Ubuntu? Different Interpretations among South Africans of African Descent." *South African Journal of Philosophy* 31, no. 3 (2013): 484–503.

Gallese V., C. Keysers, and G. Rizzolatti. "A Unifying View of the Basis of Social Cognition." *Trends in Cognitive Sciences* 8 (2004): 396–403.

Gaonkar, Dilip. *Alternative Modernities*. Durham, NC: Duke University Press, 2001.

Gerow, Edwin. "Sanskrit Dramatic Theory and Kalidasa's Plays." In *Theater of Memory: The Plays of Kalidasa*, edited by Barbara Stoler Miller. New York: Columbia University Press, 1984.

Gold, Daniel. "The Dadu-panth: A Religious Order in Its Rajasthan Context." In *The Idea of Rajasthan: Explorations in Regional Identity*. Vol. 2, edited by Karine Schomer, Joan L. Erdman, Deryck O. Lodrick, and Lloyd I. Rudolph. New Delhi: Manohar, 2001.

Groenewald, H. M. "The Praises of Prince James Senzangakhona Mahlangu—Text in Context." *South African Journal of African Languages* 16, no. 3 (1996): 73–79.

Guha, Ranajit. *Dominance without Hegemony: History and Power in Colonial India*. Cambridge, MA: Harvard University Press, 1997.

———. "The Prose of Counter-Insurgency." In *Selected Subaltern Studies*, edited by Ranajit Guha and Gayatri Spivak. Delhi, India: Oxford University Press, 1988.

Gunner, Elizabeth. "Africa and Orality." In *The Cambridge History of African and Caribbean Literature*. Vol. 1, edited by Abiola Irele and Simon Gikandi. Cambridge: Cambridge University Press, 2004.

———. "A Dying Tradition? African Oral Literature in Contemporary Context." *Social Dynamics* 12, no. 2 (1986): 31–38.

———. "Remaking the Warrior?" *Current Writing: Text and Reception in Southern Africa* 7, no. 2 (1995): 19–30.

Gunner, Elizabeth, and Mafika Pascal Gwala. *Musho! Zulu Popular Praises*. East Lansing: Michigan State University Press, 1991.

Hamilton, Caroline. *Terrific Majesty: The Power of Shaka Zulu and the Limits of Historical Invention*. Cambridge, MA: Harvard University Press, 1998.

Hatfield, E., J. L. Cacioppo, and R. L. Rapson. "Emotional Contagion." *Current Directions in Psychological Sciences* 2 (1993): 96–99.

Hess, Linda. *Bodies of Song: Kabir Oral Traditions and Performative Worlds in North India*. New York: Oxford University Press, 2015.

———. "Kabir's Rough Rhetoric." In *The Sants: Studies in a Devotional Tradition of India*, edited by Karine Schomer and W. H. McLeod. New Delhi: Motilal Banarsidass Publication, 1987.

Hlatshwayo, Mi S'dumo. "Black Mamba Rising." In *Black Mamba Rising: South African Worker Poets in Struggle*, edited by Ari Sitas, 25–28. Durban, South Africa: Culture and Working Life Publication, 1986.

Hlatshwayo, "We Workers Are a Worried Lot!" In *Fosatu Worker News* 38 (1985): 8.

Hogan, Patrick Colm. *The Mind and Its Stories: Narrative Universals and Human Emotion*. Cambridge: Cambridge University Press, 2009.

———. "Toward a Cognitive Science of Poetics: Ānandavardhana, Abhinavagupta, and the Theory of Literature." In "Comparative Poetics: Non-Western Traditions of Literary Theory." Special issue, *College Literature* 23, no. 1 (February 1996): 164–78.

Hogan, Patrick Colm. *Understanding Indian Movies: Culture, Cognition, and Cinematic Imagination*. Austin: University of Texas Press, 2008.

Huggan, Graham, and Helen Tiffin. *Postcolonial Ecocrticism: Literature, Animals, Environment*. New York: Routledge, 2015.

Hunt, Lynn. *Inventing Human Rights: A History.* New York: Norton, 2008.

Hunter, W. W. *A Statistical Account of Bengal.* Delhi: D.K. Pub. House, 1876.

Johar, Karan. *Kabhi Khushi Kabhi Gham (K3G).* 2001.

Jones, Matthew. "Bollywood, Rasa and Indian Cinema: Misconceptions, Meanings and Millionaire." *Visual Anthropology* 23, no. 1 (2010): 33–43.

———. *Kabir: The Weaver's Songs.* Edited and translated by Vinay Dharwadker. New Delhi: Penguin Classics, 2003.

———. *Songs of Kabir.* Edited and translated by Rabindranath Tagore and Evelyn Underhill. London: Dover Publications, 2004.

Kalidasa. *Abhijnanasakuntalam of Kalidasa.* 10th ed. Translated by M. R. Kale. Delhi: Motilal Banarasidass Publishers, 1980.

———. *The Recognition of Sakuntala: A Play In Seven Acts.* Translated by W. J. Johnson. Oxford, UK: Oxford University Press, 2001.

Kant, Immanuel. *The Critique of Pure Reason.* Edited by H. Caygill, G. Banham, and N. Kemp Smith. New York: Springer, 2016.

Kaschula, Russell H. "Imbongi in Profile." *English in Africa.* 20, no. 1 (May 1993): 65–76.

Kaviraj, Sudipta. "Ideas of Freedom in Modern India." In *The Idea of Freedom in Asia and Africa,* edited by Robert H. Taylor. Redwood, CA: Stanford University Press, 2002.

Kim, Sue J. "Anger, Cognition, Ideology: What Crash Can Show Us About Emotion." *Image & Narrative* 11, no. 2 (2010): 4–17.

King, Richard. *Orientalism and Religion.* London: Routledge, 1999.

Krige, E. J. *The Social System of the Zulus.* Pietermaritzburg, South Africa: Shuter and Shooter, 1950.

Krishnamoorthy, K. *Kalidasa.* New York: Twayne, 1972.

Kroeze, Irma J. "Doing Things with Values: The Case of Ubuntu." *Stellenbosch Law Review* 13 (2002): 252–64.

Krog, Antjie. *Country of My Skull.* New York: Three Rivers Press, 2000.

Kromberg, S. "Worker Izibongo and Ethnic Identities in Durban." *Journal of Literary Studies* 10, no. 1 (1994): 57–74.

Kumar, Sanjay. *Medieval Indian History Part 2.* Vol. 3. New Delhi: Jawahar Publishers, 2006.

Kunene, Daniel P. *The Zulu Novels of C. L. S. Nyembezi: A Critical Appraisal.* Lewiston, NY: Edwin Mellen Press, 2007.

Kuritz, Paul. *The Making of Theatre History.* London: Prentice Hall, 1988.

Labar, Kevin S., and Roberto Cabeza. "Cognitive Neuroscience of Emotional Memory." *Nature Reviews Neuroscience* 7 (January 2006): 54–64.

Lakoff G., and M. Johnson. *Metaphors We Live By.* Chicago: University of Chicago Press, 1980.

Laurence, Stephen, and Eric Margolis. "Concepts and Cognitive Science." In *Concepts: Core Readings,* edited by Eric Margolis and Stephen Laurence, 3–77. Cambridge, MA: MIT Press, 1999.

Lazarus, Neil. *Nationalism and Cultural Practice in the Postcolonial World.* Cambridge: Cambridge University Press, 1999.

LeDoux, Joseph. *The Emotional Brain: The Mysterious Underpinnings of Emotional Life.* New York: Simon Schuster, 2015.

Loomba, Ania. *Colonialism/Postcolonialism.* New York: Routledge, 2005.

Lorenzen, David. "*The Kabir-panth* and Social Protest." In *The Sants: Studies in a Devotional Tradition of India,* edited by Karine Schomer and W. H. McLeod. New Delhi: Motilal Banarsidass Publishers, 1987.

———. "The Kabir Panth: Heretics to Hindus." In *Religious Change and Cultural Domination.* Mexico City: Colegia de Mexico, 1981.

Lowe, Lisa. *The Intimacies of Four Continents.* Durham, NC: Duke University Press, 2015.

Macaulay, Thomas. "Minute on Indian Education." In *Archives of Empire.* Vol. 1, *From The East India Company to the Suez Canal,* edited by Mia Carter and Barbara Harlow. Durham, NC: Duke University Press, 2003: 227–38.

MacKinnon, Aran S. "The Persistence of the Cattle Economy in Zululand, South Africa, 1900–1950." *Canadian Journal of African Studies* 33, no. 1 (1999): 98–135.

Mahapatra, Sitakant. *Bhima Bhoi.* Delhi: Sahitya Akademi, 1983.

Mahmood, Saba. *Politics of Piety: The Islamic Revival and the Feminist Subject.* Princeton, NJ: Princeton University Press, 2005.

Maluleke, T. "The Misuse of 'Ubuntu.'" *Challenge* 53 (1999): 12–13.

Metz, Thaddeus. "Toward an African Moral Theory." *Journal of Political Philosophy* 15, no. 3 (2007): 321–41.

Niedenthal, Paula M. "Embodying Emotion." *Science* 316, no. 5827 (2007): 1002–5.

Marr, David. *Vision: A Computational Investigation into the Human Representation and Processing of Visual Information.* Cambridge, MA: The MIT Press, 2010.

Marx, Karl. *Capital: A Critique of Political Economy.* Vol. 1, translated by Ben Fowkes. London: Penguin Classics, 1992.

Marx, Karl, and Frederick Engels. *The German Ideology Part One, with Selections from Parts Two and Three, together with Marx's "Introduction to a Critique of Political Economy."* New York: International Publishers, 2001.

Mauss, Marcel. *The Gift: Forms and Functions of Exchange in Archaic Societies.* London: Routledge, 1990.

Mayr, Franz. "Zulu Proverbs." *Anthropos* 7, no. 4 (1912): 957–63.

Mbembe, Achille. *On the Postcolony.* Berkeley: University of California Press, 2001.

McGetchin, Douglas T. *Indology, Indomania, and Orientalism: Ancient India's Rebirth in Modern Germany.* Hackensack, NJ: Fairleigh Dickinson, 2009.

Mda, Zakes. *Ways of Dying.* London: Picador, 2002.

Medin, D. L., E. B. Lynch, J. D. Coley, and S. Atran. "Categorization and Reasoning among Tree Experts." *Cognitive Psychology* 32 (1997): 49–96.

Mehrez, Samia. *Translating Egypt's Revolution: The Language of Tahrir.* Cairo: American University of Cairo Press, 2012.

Mill, James. *The History of British India.* Vol. 1. London: H. H. Wilson, 1840.

Mill, J. S. *Autobiography of John Stuart Mill.* Auckland, NZ: The Floating Press, 2009.

Mohanty, Satya. "Introduction." In *Six Acres and a Third: The Classic Nineteenth-Century Novel about Colonial India,* by Fakir Mohan Senapati. Edited by Satya Mohanty and translated by Rabi Shankar Mishra, Satya P. Mohanty, Jatindra K. Nayak, and Paul St.-Pierre, 1–32. Berkeley: University of California Press, 2005.

Moyn, Samuel. *The Last Utopia: Human Rights in History.* New York: Belknap Press, 2012.

Mpe, Phaswane. *Welcome to Our Hillbrow.* Pietermaritzburg, South Africa: University of Natal Press, 2001.

Mukherjee, Prabhat. "The Siddhacharyas in Orissa." In *The History of Medieval Vaishnavism in Orissa.* New Delhi: Asian Educational Services, 1981.

Mukherjee, Tutun. *Staging Resistance: Plays by Women in Translation.* Oxford, UK: Oxford University Press, 2005.

Muthu, Sankar. *Enlightenment Against Empire.* Princeton, NJ: Princeton University Press, 2003.

Nair, Janaki. *Women and Law in Colonial India: A Social History.* New Delhi: Kali for Women, 1996.

Nandy, Ashis. *The Intimate Enemy: Loss and Recovery of Self Under Colonialism.* Oxford, UK: Oxford University Press, 1988.

Ndebele, Njabulo S. *South African Literature and Culture: The Rediscovery of the Ordinary.* Manchester, UK: Manchester University Press, 1994.

Nyembezi, C. S. *Zulu Proverbs.* Johannesburg: Witwatersrand University Press, 1963.

Nyembezi, Sibusiso. *The Rich Man of Pietermaritzburg.* Translated by Sansile Ngidi. Wiltshire, UK: Aflame Books, 2008.

Obiechina, Emmanuel. "Narrative Proverbs in the African Novel." *Research in African Literatures* 24, no. 4 (1993): 123–40.

Olckers, Martha. Quoted in Garth Verdal, "Praise Singers in Parliament a 'Culture Shock' to New Minister," *Cape Argus*, May 26, 1994.

Opland, Jeff. *Xhosa Oral Poetry: Aspects of a Black South African Tradition.* Cambridge: Cambridge University Press, 1983.

Pandey, Janak, and Arvind K. Sinha. *Dialogue for Development: Festschrift Dedicated to Professor Jai B. P. Sinha.* New Delhi: Concept Publishing Company, 2011.

Pandian, M. S. S. "One Step outside Modernity: Caste, Identity Politics and Public Sphere." *Economic and Political Weekly* 37, no. 18 (May 4, 2002): 1735–41.

Pandit, Lalita. "Caste, Race and Nation: History and Dialectic in Rabindranath Tagore's Gora." In *Literary India: Comparative Studies in Aesthetics: Colonialism, and Culture,* edited by Patrick Colm Hogan and Lalita Pandit: 207–36. Albany: State University of New York Press, 1995.

Patwardhan, Anand. *Jai Bhim Comrade.* Documentary. 2011.

Plaut, Martin. "Debates in a Shark Tank—The Politics of South Africa's Non-Racial Trade Unions." *African Affairs* 91, no. 364 (July 1992): 389–403.

———. "The Political Significance of COSATU." *Transformation* 2 (1986): 62–72.

Qabula, Alfred Temba. "Praise Poem to FOSATU." *Fosatu Worker News* 30 (August 1984).

Qabula and Hlatshwayo. "Tears of the Creator." In *Black Mamba Rising,* by Ari Sitas, 49–51. Durban: Workers' Resistance and Culture Publications, 1986.

Raghavabhatta. "Arthadyotanika." In *The Abhijnana-S'akuntala: With the Commentary (Arthadyotanika) of Raghavabhatta.* Mumbai: Nirnaya-Sagara Press, 1886.

Rancière, Jacques. "Ten Thesis on Politics." *Theory & Event* 5, no. 3 (2001).

———. "Who is the Subject of the Rights of Man?" In *Dissensus: On Politics and Aesthetics,* 62–75. New York: Bloomsbury, 2015.

———. "The Thinking of Dissensus: Politics and Aesthetics." In *Reading Rancière*, edited by Paul Bowman and Richard Stamp, 1–17. London: Continuum, 2011.

Rao, Anupama. *The Caste Question: Dalits and the Politics of Modern India*. Berkeley: University of California Press, 2009.

Ritchken, Edwin. "Trade Unions and Community Organizations: Towards a Working Alliance?" *Transformation* 10 (1989): 40–53.

Rizzolatti, G., and L. Craighero. "The Mirror-Neuron System." *Annual Review of Neuroscience* 27 (2004): 169–92.

Robins, Steven. "City Sites." In *Senses of Culture: South African Culture Studies*, edited by Sarah Nuttall and Cheryl-Ann Michael. Oxford, UK: Oxford University Press, 2000.

Rushdie, Salman. *Midnight's Children*. London: Random House, 2010.

Said, Edward. *Humanism and Democratic Criticism*. New York: Columbia University Press, 2004.

Said, Edward. "The Politics of Knowledge." In *Contemporary Critical Theorists: Lacan to Said*, edited by J. Simons. Edinburgh: Edinburgh University Press: 269–85.

Sampson, Anthony. *Black and Gold: Tycoons, Revolutionaries, and Apartheid*. New York: Pantheon Books, 1987.

Sanders, Mark. "Undone by Laughter." *Safundi: The Journal of South African and American Studies* 10, no. 3 (2009): 351–57.

Sarkar, Tanika. *Hindu Wife, Hindu Nation: Community, Religion, and Cultural Nationalism*. Bloomington: Indiana University Press, 2010.

Sarkar, Sumit and Tanika Sarkar. *Women and Social Reform in Modern India: A Reader*. Bloomington: Indiana University Press, 2007.

Satpathy, Siddharth. *Bhīma Bhoi, Prayers and Reflections, Selections from Stuti Chintamoni*. Bhubaneswar, India: Rupantar, 2006.

Sawhney, Simona. "Who is Kalidasa? Sanskrit Poetry in Modern India." *Postcolonial Studies* 7, no. 3 (2004): 295–312.

Schelling, Andrew. *Dropping the Bow: Poems from Ancient India*. Buffalo, NY: White Pine Press, 2008.

Schwarz, Henry. *Constructing the Criminal Tribe in Colonial India: Acting Like a Thief*. Oxford, UK: John Wiley and Sons, 2010.

Seidman, Gay. "Monitoring Multinationals: Lessons from the Anti-Apartheid Era." *Politics & Society* 31, no. 3 (2003): 381–406.

Sel, Alejandra, Beatriz Calvo-Merino, Simone Tuettenberg, and Bettina Forster. "When You Smile, the World Smiles at You." *Social Cognitive and Affective Neuroscience* 10, no. 10 (2015): 1316–22.

Sen, Amiya P. *The Indispensable Vivekananda: An Anthology of Our Times*. Hyderabad, India: Orient Blackswan, 2006.

Sen, Meheli. "'It's All About Loving Your Parents': Liberalization, Hindutva and Bollywood's New Fathers." In *Bollywood and Globalization: Indian Popular Cinema, Nation, and Diaspora*, edited by Rini Bhattacharya Mehta and Rajeshwari V. Pandharipande. London: Anthem Press, 2010.

Shankar, Subramanian. *Flesh and Fish Blood: Postcolonialism, Translation, and the Vernacular*. Berkeley: University of California Press, 2012.

Shapiro, Lawrence E. *Embodied Cognition*. New York: Routledge, 2010.

Sharma, R. N. "Group Violence in a Neighbourhood." *Indian Journal of Social Work* 43, no. 4 (1983): 419–29.

Shutte, Augustine. *Philosophy for Africa*. Rondebosch, South Africa: University of Cape Town Press, 1993.

———. *Ubuntu: An Ethic for the New South Africa*. Cape Town: Cluster Publications, 2001.

Sindane, Jabu. *Ubuntu and Nation Building*. Pretoria: Ubuntu School of Philosophy, 1994.

Singh, Lata. "Foregrounding the Actress's Question—Bengal and Maharashtra." In *Theatre in Colonial India—Playhouse of Power*, edited by Lata Singh. New Delhi: Oxford University Press, 2009.

Singh-Sengupta, Sunita. "Reconceptualizing the Meaning of Work." In *Dialogue for Development: Festschrift Dedicated to Professor Jai B. P. Sinha*. New Delhi: Concept Publishing Company, 2011.

Sisk, Timothy D. *Democratization in South Africa: The Elusive Social Contract*. Princeton, NJ: Princeton University Press, 1995.

Sitas, Ari. *Black Mamba Rising*. Durban: Workers' Resistance and Culture Publications, 1986.

Slaughter, Joseph R. *Human Rights Inc.: The World Novel, Narrative Form, and International Law*. New York: Fordham University Press, 2007.

Sorkin, Andrew Ross. "How Mandela Shifted Views on Freedom of Markets." *New York Times Deal Book*, December 9, 2013.

Spivak, Gayatri Chakravorty. *In Other Worlds: Essays in Cultural Politics*. New York: Routledge, 1987.

———. "More on Power/Knowledge." In *The Spivak Reader*, edited by Donna Landry and Gerard Maclean, 141–74. New York: Routledge, 1996.

Stein, Burton. *A History of India*. New Delhi: Oxford University Press, 2001.

Stoler Miller, Barbara. "Kalidasa's World and His Plays." In *Theater of Memory: The Plays of Kalidasa*, edited by Barbara Stoler Miller, 3–41. New York: Columbia University Press, 1984.

Strand, Eric. "Gandhian Communalism and the Midnight's Children's Conference." *ELH* 72, no. 4 (2005): 975–1016.

Stuart, James. *Izibongo: Zulu Praise Poems*. Edited by Daniel Malcolm and Trevor Cope. Oxford, UK: Clarendon Press, 1968.

Tagore, Rabindranath. *Sakuntala: Its Inner Meaning*. Edited by K. N. Das Gupta and Laurence Binyon. Calcutta: Macmillan and Co., 1920.

———. *Home and the World*. Edited by William Radice and translated by Surendranath Tagore. New York: Penguin Classics, 2005.

Thapar, Romila. *Sakuntala: Texts, Readings, Histories*. New York: Columbia University Press, 2011.

Tutu, Desmond. *No Future Without Forgiveness*. New York: Random House, 1999.

Vale, Leroy, and Landeg White. *Power and the Praise Poem: Southern African Voices in History*. Charlottesville: University Press of Virginia, 1991.

Van Buitenen, J. A. B. *Two Plays of Ancient India*. New York: Columbia University Press, 1968.

Van der Merwe, Willie. "Philosophy and the Multi-Cultural Context of (Post)apartheid South Africa." *Ethical Perspectives* 3, no. 2 (1996): 1–15.

Van Niekerk, P. "The Trade Union Movement in the Politics of Resistance in South Africa." In *South Africa: No Turning Back,* edited by S. Johnson, 153–71. Basingstoke, UK: Macmillan, 1988.

Vaudeville, Charlotte, and Kabir. *A Weaver Named Kabir.* Translated by Charlotte Vaudeville. New Delhi: Oxford University Press, 1993.

Vilikazi, A. *Zulu Transformations.* Pietermaritzburg, South Africa: University of Natal Press, 1965.

Virmani, Shabnam. *Kabira Khada Bazaar Mein.* Bangalore: Kabir Project, Srishti School of Art Design and Technology, 2009.

———. "White Labor Aristocracy and Black Proletariat: The Origins and Deployment of South Africa's Racially Divided Working Class." *ITH Tagungsberichte* 34 (2000): 220–45.

Vivekananda, Swami. *Selections from Swami Vivekananda.* Calcutta: Advaita Ashrama 1964.

Weber, Max. *The Protestant Ethic and the Spirit of Capitalism.* New York: Routledge, 2001.

Wood, Geoffrey. "Solidarity, Representativity and Accountability: The Origins, State and Implications of Shopfloor Democracy within the Congress of South African Trade Unions." *Journal of Industrial Relations* 45, no. 3 (September 2003): 326–43.

Zunshine, Lisa. *Why We Read Fiction: Theory of Mind and the Novel.* Columbus: The Ohio State University Press, 2006.

INDEX

Abhinavagupta, 88, 91, 93, 99, 100, 118, 121
adivasis, 36, 37, 62–63, 65, 70
adla ngandoda, 13, 149
affect, 5, 11, 13, 18, 21, 86, 88, 91–99, 120, 126–28
affective agency, 86–88, 100–104, 110, 112, 115–17, 119, 122–24, 126–28, 131–32
African National Congress (ANC), 143, 179, 194, 196–99, 221–22
Afrikaans, 136, 203
agency, 4, 10–11, 19, 30, 91, 109, 129. *See also* affective agency
Amar Katha (Binodini), 102–4, 106, 108–10, 112–15, 117–22, 125, 129, 131
Ambedkar, Bhimrao, 9, 14, 35, 71, 74, 76, 77, 79–81
anubhava, 92–93, 95, 97, 120, 122, 126, 129
apartheid, 12, 32–33, 132, 136–38, 143, 163–64, 166, 174, 176–78, 187, 193–99, 204, 206, 208, 209, 211, 216–17, 219
authority, 37, 63, 65, 160, 173, 176–78, 195, 205, 210, 211, 222, 230

Banaras, 37, 41, 42
Banerjee-Dube, Ishita, 36, 63–65
Bantu Education Act, 6, 136, 144, 203
Bantu language, 6, 13, 18, 20, 136, 138, 143, 144, 203, 217
becoming, 13, 46, 56, 77, 83, 108, 197, 225
Bengal, 43, 62, 85, 107, 110, 113, 115
Bengali language, 11, 23, 87, 91, 100–102, 104, 105, 107, 112, 113

bhakti, 18–19, 28, 59, 65–67, 73–77, 79, 101–2, 104, 115, 120–21. See also *nirguna bhakti*
Bharata, Muni, 88, 89, 91, 93, 95, 98, 118
bhava, 45, 91–92, 96, 102, 112, 116–18, 122, 125; *dasya*, 46; *vatsalya*, 129–30. See also *anubhava*
Bhoi, Bhīma, 36, 38–39, 62, 64–67, 71, 83
Bjerk, Paul J., 180–81, 188
bodily action, 22, 38, 52, 54, 68–69, 71, 74–75
bodily practice, 51–52, 56, 57, 68

Callaway, Henry, 136, 143, 145–46, 181
capitalism, 1–3, 7, 12, 15, 16, 19, 23–28, 30–31, 45, 47, 52, 55, 61, 69–71, 77, 79, 82–83, 107–9, 114, 123–25, 127–28, 136, 139, 148, 151–52, 156–57, 166, 174, 178, 196, 198, 211, 223–25, 227–29; colonial, 31–32, 51, 61, 87, 107, 112, 122, 131, 136–37, 157–58, 162, 229; logic of, 153, 158; postcolonial, 52, 224; structures of, 101, 153
caste, 2, 3, 7, 9, 13, 15, 19, 22, 28, 30, 36–41, 49, 51, 55–59, 61–65, 67, 71–75, 77, 79–80, 82, 87, 123, 129, 132, 136, 229
cattle, 58, 145, 147–48, 152–54, 157–61, 167, 178–80, 186, 188, 190, 192, 209; exchange of, 31, 135, 151; sharing of, 22, 134, 136, 147, 180–81, 194–95
Chakijana, 151, 153–55, 205, 215–16
Chakrabarty, Dipesh, 2–3, 26–29, 231
Chapman, Michael, 147, 170, 178, 180, 183, 187, 204–5
Chatterjee, Partha, 105, 112
Cheah, Pheng, 15, 19, 24

243

colonial encounter, 3, 4, 13, 78, 104, 146
colonialism, 2–4, 6, 28, 32, 62, 65, 86, 105, 123, 132, 136, 184, 204, 229, 231
commodification, 24, 46–48, 55, 83, 114, 115, 118, 142, 164, 174
conceptual networks, 10, 16, 19–22, 39, 66, 73, 164, 179, 191, 219, 224, 231; postcolonial, 17–18; syncretic, 6, 17, 19–20, 79–80, 101, 115, 124, 131, 168–69, 194
Congress of South African Trade Unions (COSATU), 176–77, 196–98, 200, 207, 211–13, 215
contextual universalisms, 4–7, 9–10, 12, 14–26, 30–33, 38–39, 45, 51, 61–62, 73–75, 77–78, 83, 86–87, 100, 101, 112, 115, 124, 131–32, 136, 142, 144–45, 147, 158, 163, 165, 167, 169, 174, 178–79, 194–95, 219–21, 228–31
contingency, 5, 12, 13
corporations, 31, 178, 197, 206, 213, 223

Dalit Buddhism, 77–78
Dalit politics, 36, 73
Dalits, 8, 30, 35, 43, 58, 71–77, 80–83
Dasi, Binodini, 11–14, 23, 85, 87, 101–22
de Bolla, Peter, 17, 19–20
decolonization, 3–4
democracy, 3, 10, 17, 18, 71, 80, 132, 176, 179, 193–99, 207, 220, 224, 228
democratic change, 2, 6, 16, 18, 24–26, 28, 136, 195, 220, 229
democratic government, 22, 177, 179, 193, 207, 229
demos, 2, 10, 11, 22, 25, 77, 82, 83, 87, 170, 206, 226, 229; expansion of, 12, 16, 24–25, 28, 32, 34, 56, 71, 83, 117, 122, 132, 142, 179, 231
Dialogue for Development, 45–47, 58

embodied cognition, 22, 39, 45, 47, 71, 82, 124
Enlightenment, 1–4, 6, 9, 14, 16–18, 20, 25–26, 28–29, 76, 83, 115, 143, 224

fallen woman, 102–3, 108–10, 112, 114–15, 119–21
Federation of South African Trade Unions (FOSATU), 12, 196, 198–201, 208, 210–16
FIFA, 31, 137, 140–41
food, 38, 67–70, 82, 133, 182, 228; sharing of, 13, 64, 134–37, 146–48, 150, 156–57,

164–66, 177–81, 185, 188–90, 193–95. *See also* cattle

gift, 146–50, 161, 165–66, 239

Hamilton, Caroline, 146, 183, 187
hegemony, 3, 15, 24, 50, 77, 86, 229
Hindu culture, 105–6
Hindu identity, 64, 123
Hinduism, 40, 43, 47–49, 53, 63, 65–66, 71–72, 74, 77, 106
Hindu patriarchies, 23, 123, 129
Hindu tradition, 47, 66, 90, 106
Hindu womanhood, 11, 32, 102–4, 123, 136; upper-caste, 86, 103, 105, 108, 131
Hlatshwayo, Mi S'dumo, 176, 194–95, 200, 202–4, 207–11, 213, 216–17, 219
humanism, 2, 6, 15, 16, 33, 144, 174, 229, 230
human rights, 2, 23, 171, 174

imbongi (Zulu praise poets), 12, 170, 172, 177, 179, 184, 185, 187–90, 192–94, 201–6, 213, 215, 218–19
indaba (Zulu folk storytelling), 169, 173, 234
India, 4–6, 8, 18, 20, 28–32, 36, 38, 41, 45, 48–49, 58, 66, 71, 73–74, 77–79, 86, 89, 101, 105–6, 109, 113, 123–24, 127, 223, 225, 227–28, 231
individualism, 2, 18, 123, 124, 132
Islam, 40, 43
izibongo (Zulu praise poetry), 12, 22, 172, 176–77, 179, 183, 185, 189–91, 193–95, 199–201, 203–9, 212, 220

Jagannath, 36, 63–65
Johar, Karan, 84–85, 123, 126, 128–30
Johnson, Mark, 22, 188

Kabhi Khushi Kabhie Gham (K3G; *Sometimes Happiness, Sometimes Sadness*), 18, 84, 123, 125, 129–32
Kabir, 3, 7–9, 28, 30, 35–58, 60–62, 64–66, 69, 74, 76–79, 83
Kabira Khada Bazaar Mein (Virmani), 43–44, 48, 57–58, 60
Kabir Kala Manch (KKM; Kabir's Stage of Talent), 8–9, 35–36, 39–41, 61, 71, 73–74, 77–78

Kabir Panth (Followers of the Path of Kabir), 43, 47–48, 57
Kabir poets, 52, 54, 56–57, 60, 75
Kalidasa, 85, 88–90, 93–96, 98–101, 111, 123
Kant, Immanuel, 1, 124
kavya nataka, 90–92, 102, 126
kinship, 41, 64, 87
kraal, 158, 167, 190, 192
Kromberg, S., 194, 205
Kshatriya caste, 56–57

labor, 25–26, 31, 39, 46, 47, 52, 54–58, 60, 62, 108, 114, 164, 177, 203, 216, 231
labor power, 27, 33, 51, 55, 87, 101, 174, 178, 209
Lakoff, George, 22, 188
Lazarus, Neil, 7, 16
literature, 21, 74, 89, 102, 104, 116, 138, 162, 204, 229
literatures of the world, 7, 23–24, 40, 224–25, 228–29
Lowe, Lisa, 13–14

Mahabharata, 66, 87, 90
Mahima Dharma, 36, 61–62, 64–65
Mandela, Nelson, 133, 135, 137, 164, 193, 197, 202, 221–22, 225, 228
Marx, Karl, 26–27, 77
Marxism, 3, 9, 18, 40, 73, 76–78, 81, 179, 195, 198, 209; postcolonial, 30
Mda, Zakes, 31, 135, 137, 162–70, 172–74
Metal and Allied Workers Union (MAWU), 201, 214–15
Mill, John Stuart, 14, 86, 113
modernity, 3, 7, 24–30, 88, 124, 144, 151, 163; capitalist, 16, 151, 162, 166; colonial, 11–12, 18, 32–33, 39, 132, 143, 151, 219, 224; colonialist, 33, 151; global, 23; Indian, 32, 80, 86; postcolonial, 33, 39, 123, 137, 162, 164, 179
moksha, 40, 69, 74, 91, 121
morality, 1, 63, 134–35
mukti, 19, 40–41

nationalism 7, 16, 25, 86, 90, 103, 106, 187; Hindu, 39, 73, 103, 106; Zulu, 187
nativism, 89, 143, 162, 204
Natya Shastra, 88–92, 116, 118, 121

nirguna bhakti, 36, 38–40, 41, 44–45, 49–50, 61, 73–74, 76–77, 81, 83
nirguna movements, 40, 62, 63
Nyembezi, C. S., 136, 143–46, 148–51, 154–56, 159–60, 162, 168, 174

ontology, 7, 13, 24, 39, 45, 51–52, 58, 60–61, 82–83, 88, 101, 132, 136, 139, 142, 147, 150, 152, 155, 162, 164, 166–67, 176, 178, 229
oral literatures, 4, 5, 22, 183
oral poetry, 5, 22, 171, 194, 202, 205
oral texts, 5, 180, 184
oral tradition, 162, 173, 183, 205

pativrata, 84, 86, 105, 126
pativratadharma, 84–86, 88, 95, 124, 131
postcolonial literatures, 5–7, 23, 33, 40, 174, 203, 225, 228
pouvoir, 30, 31, 166, 174
precapitalist economy, 59, 69, 71, 135
primitive accumulation, 31–32, 152
prostitution, 11, 85, 87, 101–2, 106–8, 111, 114
proverbs, 5, 20, 208, 228. See also Zulu proverbs
puissance, 30–31, 137, 166

Qabula, Alfred Temba, 12, 176, 179, 194–95, 199–204, 207–13, 215, 219

racism, 12, 32, 136, 152, 163, 178–79, 196, 198, 212, 216–17, 219
Raghavabhatta, 91, 93
Rancière, Jacques, 10, 174
rasa, 11, 18–19, 21, 89, 91–92, 94–96, 99, 101–3, 109, 112, 116–18, 120–23, 129, 132; *shanta-rasa*, 88, 91, 93, 97, 100, 122; *vatsalya*, 125–26, 131; *vira*, 93, 97
The Rich Man of Pietermaritzburg (Nyembezi), 136–37, 143, 145, 151, 153, 162, 174
Rousseau, Jean Jacques, 1, 14, 113
Roy, Ram Mohan, 49, 105

Said, Edward, 14–16
Sakuntala (Kalidasa), 85, 87–91, 93–103, 109–12, 119, 122, 125, 129, 131
Sanskrit, 13, 29, 37, 41, 48, 50, 66, 86–88, 90, 91, 101, 115–17, 120
Sanskrit dramatic theory, 13, 120

Sathe, Sheetal, 8, 71
sattvika, 92–93
Shaka, 177, 179, 186–90, 192–93, 201, 209
sharing. *See* cattle: sharing of; food: sharing of
shudras, 37, 42, 57, 74
Slaughter, Joseph, 23, 174
South Africa, 4–6, 12, 18, 20, 31–32, 132, 135–38, 142, 145, 151, 157, 163, 176–78, 182, 193, 196–97, 200, 202–3, 206–7, 213, 221–23, 225–26, 231
spiritual economy, 30, 58–60, 69, 70–71, 76
Spivak, Gayatri, 2–3
Stuti Chintamoni, 66–67, 69
subaltern: consciousness, 67, 146; groups, 5–6, 28, 32–33, 50, 62, 223, 228; poetics, 41; politics, 11, 80; subjectivity, 4, 11, 86, 132, 146; universalisms, 20, 83, 136
surplus value, 25, 60, 178, 198, 199, 206, 209, 223
syncretism, 9, 20, 26, 31, 75, 77, 81, 124–25, 200, 204, 230

Tagore, Rabindrath, 48, 49, 104–5, 110–11
tantrism, 40–41, 50, 66
trickster, 5, 151, 153–55, 159, 162, 215, 217. *See also* Chakijana

ubuntu, 3, 13, 18, 20, 30–31, 133, 135–48, 150–53, 155–57, 159, 162, 164, 166–68, 170, 174–75, 206, 226

universalism, 3, 5, 9, 18, 21, 25, 38, 44, 52, 58, 60, 65, 74, 77, 93, 123, 128, 136–37, 151, 164, 195, 231; capitalist, 45; Enlightenment, 1–5, 15, 26–28, 30, 33, 39–40, 76, 78, 83, 132, 178–79, 224; *nirguna*, 61–62, 65; post-Enlightenment, 15, 39, 73, 76, 78, 83, 132, 179; subaltern, 20, 83, 136
universalizing concepts, 17, 19, 21, 88, 137, 231
untouchables, 32, 64, 72, 75, 81–82
upper-caste Hindus, 47, 48, 50, 86, 102, 103, 106, 123. *See also* Hindu womanhood: upper-caste
upside down language (*ulti bamsi*), 22–23, 40, 41, 54, 67, 69, 81, 82

Virmani, Shabnam, 43, 44, 57, 58, 60
Vivekananda, 49, 50, 62, 65, 66

Ways of Dying (Mda), 31, 135, 137, 162–64, 171–72, 174
world literatures, 23–24, 225, 228

Zululand, 135, 136, 157, 170, 177, 183, 186, 203
Zulu novel, 136, 142, 161
Zulu oralities, 136, 147, 179
Zulu proverbs, 13, 134–35, 143, 145–50, 153, 156–57, 168–69, 181, 183
Zulu Proverbs (Nyembezi), 143, 145–46, 156–57
Zulus, 133, 145, 147, 148, 150, 157, 161, 186

COGNITIVE APPROACHES TO CULTURE
FREDERICK LUIS ALDAMA, PATRICK COLM HOGAN, LALITA PANDIT HOGAN, AND SUE KIM, SERIES EDITORS

This new series takes up cutting edge research in a broad range of cognitive sciences insofar as this research bears on and illuminates cultural phenomena such as literature, film, drama, music, dance, visual art, digital media, and comics, among others. For the purpose of the series, "cognitive science" will be construed broadly to encompass work derived from cognitive and social psychology, neuroscience, cognitive and generative linguistics, affective science, and related areas in anthropology, philosophy, computer science, and elsewhere. Though open to all forms of cognitive analysis, the series is particularly interested in works that explore the social and political consequences of cognitive cultural study.

Literatures of Liberation: Non-European Universalisms and Democratic Progress
MUKTI LAKHI MANGHARAM

Affective Ecologies: Empathy, Emotion, and Environmental Narrative
ALEXA WEIK VON MOSSNER

A Passion for Specificity: Confronting Inner Experience in Literature and Science
MARCO CARACCIOLO AND RUSSELL T. HURLBURT

www.ingramcontent.com/pod-product-compliance
Lightning Source LLC
Chambersburg PA
CBHW021848300426
44115CB00005B/58